A READERS GUIDE TO

great Twentieth-Century

Frederick R. Karl & Marvin Magalane

English novels

OCTAGON BOOKS

A Division of Hippocrene Books, Inc.

New York   1984

To Dolores, Deborah, and Brenda

ACKNOWLEDGMENTS

The authors gratefully acknowledge use of copyrighted material from the following publishers and publications:

From THE COMMON READER by Virginia Woolf, copyright, 1925, by Harcourt, Brace and Company, Inc.; renewed 1953, by Leonard Woolf. From A PASSAGE TO INDIA by E. M. Forster, copyright, 1924, by Harcourt, Brace and Company, Inc.; renewed by E. M. Forster. From MRS. DALLOWAY by Virginia Woolf, copyright, 1925, by Harcourt, Brace and Company, Inc.; renewed by Leonard Woolf. From TO THE LIGHTHOUSE by Virginia Woolf, copyright, 1927, by Harcourt, Brace and Company, Inc.; renewed by Leonard Woolf. From THE WAVES by Virginia Woolf, copyright, 1931, by Harcourt, Brace and Company, Inc. and reprinted with their permission.

From THE PAST RECAPTURED by Marcel Proust, copyright 1932, and ULYSSES by James Joyce, copyright 1934, to Random House, Inc.

From THE HEART OF DARKNESS, LORD JIM, NOSTROMO, UNDER WESTERN EYES, VICTORY, by Joseph Conrad; and JOSEPH CONRAD: LIFE AND LETTERS, to Dent & Sons, Ltd.

From A PORTRAIT OF THE ARTIST AS A YOUNG MAN by James Joyce; and SONS AND LOVERS, THE RAINBOW, WOMEN IN LOVE, THE MAN WHO DIED, PHOENIX, and LETTERS, by D. H. Lawrence, to The Viking Press.

From AXEL'S CASTLE by Edmund Wilson, to Charles Scribner's Sons.

From LETTERS TO BERTRAND RUSSELL by D. H. Lawrence, to The Gotham Book-Mart.

From ANTIC HAY, POINT COUNTER POINT, EYELESS IN GAZA, and BRAVE NEW WORLD by Aldous Huxley, to Harper and Brothers.

From "The Rise and Fall of UNDER WESTERN EYES," reprinted from NINE-TEENTH-CENTURY FICTION, XIII, No. 4, to the University of California Press.

From "Conrad's Stein: The Destructive Element," reprinted from TWENTIETH CENTURY LITERATURE, III, No. 4, to Alan Swallow.

Contents

XX

Introduction

As a social and moral document, as well as a contained art form, the novel, from Cervantes' *Don Quixote* through Joyce's *Ulysses*, has responded more quickly and fully to new ideas than any other literary genre. Accordingly, the twentieth-century novel, following the rapid introduction of new modes of thought in psychology, natural science, and sociology, has reacted boldly to absorb and transform this material into literary communication. Moreover, the novel, while ever mirroring change in the larger world, has, like every other art medium, responded also to inner developments in its own form, demonstrating that tradition together with innovation are the twin stuff of the genre. The traditional and the new determine the distinctive nature of the contemporary English novel; its difficulties are the difficulties of the age, and its ideas are those that have by now become commonplaces in our society. To appreciate the modern novel in its diversity, however, one must understand seemingly unlike materials and at the same time be congenial to the experimental. One must ask, along the way, and then try to answer: What is the experimental? What is the traditional? Why is the modern novel distinctive? Why is it important? What is a *modern* novel?

Perhaps the greatest difficulty encountered in the contemporary novel by the reader accustomed to the fiction of Jane Austen, Dickens, Thackeray, and even George Eliot, is that his point of view must adjust, perhaps change radically, before he can meet on equal terms with new forms. He soon realizes that his knowledge of Dickens, for example, will not provide in itself adequate basis for the intentions and conclusions of Lawrence, Joyce, or Virginia Woolf. Between the sprawling, lengthy novels of Dickens and his contemporaries and the neatly-formed and modulated novels of Joseph Conrad, there occurred a displacement of the traditional three-volume novel by the single-volume novel. This shift in length meant a corresponding change in the structure of post-eighties fiction. The huge, almost arbitrary, Victorian novel existed no more as a major force; in its place, the French-type novel was encouraged. The Victorian habit of what Henry James had called *remplissage* (filling up with rubbish or trash) gave way, and the novelist now had to select more carefully. Thus the French-type novel, consciously shaped as an autonomous unit, provided an unconscious assist in the shift of reading tastes from the long, expensive novel lent by circulating libraries to the shorter, more wieldy novel which could be sold at low price in railway bookstalls.

This is, of course, only one minor external force operating among many to shape the novels of Conrad, Joyce, Virginia Woolf, Forster, Lawrence, and Huxley; several personal and social forces go much deeper and are more conclusive in their impact. Of first importance is the nature of the literary revolt against the Victorian age that occurred toward the last decade of the nineteenth century. Victorian England stood for a set of values rooted in a belief in materialism and progress, and its optimism had been able to withstand the inroads of skepticism and eccentricity by making peripheral outspoken discussions of religious doubts and anything connected with the details of sex and marital relations. Although the age did allow for great diversity of literary talent, the center of society was mainly concerned with well-being; withal, its values were bourgeois, complacent, and relatively stable. Tennyson was society's spokesman, Thackeray its wit, Dickens its social conscience, George Eliot its "fast" woman, and Browning its intellectual. In the last quarter of the century, however, skepticism of the age's values had become more than peripheral, and doubt in linear or unqualified progress had crept into the work of Tennyson and several of his contemporaries. Outspoken optimism was tempered; belief in linear progress was transformed into shaky faith in cyclical progress, in which, while one allowed for setbacks, the general direction was still forward. However, the era that had begun with so much bounding energy was, like its namesake, lost in reverie for its own might.

Disillusion with seemingly commonplace Victorian intentions, with its vulgar commercialism, with its bourgeois disregard of artistic values, and with its self-satisfied complacency played a large role in the development of both verse and prose fiction toward the close of the century. With old values gone, and only doubts and skepticism to replace them, the void became partially filled by literary experimentation and by a dogmatic defense of the artist's aims calculated to outrage the middle-class. The former sense of community belief now became the chaos of the individual artist going his own way. Religious faith, once accepted by nearly every major Victorian writer, was no longer central. Writers like William Butler Yeats in his poetically formative years, the apprentice-novelist Conrad, the young D. H. Lawrence and James Joyce had to find new areas of faith either in art itself or in religions of their own construction. With the breakdown of common terms of reference, there succeeded a fierce interest in discovering new terms of artistic exploration, with the concomitant emphasis on technique, form, structure—all toward discovering original ways of presenting new subjects and new feelings.

Subject matter itself was anti-materialistic, increasingly outspoken in sex, skeptical of Victorian commercial values, and, of course, strongly influenced by new explorations in science and psychology. Traditions in the novel now were subjected to close scrutiny in the search for freshness, and while Conrad found affinities with Dickens, Lawrence with Hardy, Woolf with Sterne, and Forster with Meredith, the individual novelist seemed to reject more than he accepted. Accordingly, with much of Lawrence, Woolf, and Joyce, the break with the past seems great indeed, although close reading reveals their early indebtedness to Victorian writers. So Lawrence, in *Sons and Lovers*, writes in the tradition of the typical Victorian apprenticeship novel, allowing, of course, for his greater frankness on subjects hitherto taboo. However, by the time of *The Rainbow* and *Women in Love*, we recognize that Lawrence is now his own man, no longer reliant on the ingenuity of others. So with elements of Conrad, Joyce, and Woolf; and while all major writers appear to follow similar lines of development, the degree of rejection here forces new terms. With Forster and Huxley, though, we never feel the same break, for the former was, after all, writing in the Edwardian era that directly followed Victoria, and the latter has been more successful in formulating a "modern" philosophy than a "modern" novelistic technique.

What tends to be traditional among the contemporary novelists is often not English but a French tradition that came from poets like Baudelaire, Verlaine, and Mallarmé and from novelists like Flaubert and Maupassant. In these writers, the English novelist found the congenial artistic atmosphere and the ingenious experimentation so lacking in England. Adhering to the doctrines of the French, borrowing what they could from the English, and amassing knowledge from the new social sciences, the twentieth-century novelist made his work the most eclectic in the history of the genre. In Maupassant's now famous Preface to *Pierre et Jean* (1885), he found an admirable answer to Victorian formlessness and externality. Maupassant had written about the necessity of selection and arrangement in all forms of art:

> Life leaves everything on the same scale; it crowds facts together or drags them out indefinitely. Art, on the contrary, consists in using precautions and making preparations, in contriving artful and imperceptible transitions, in bringing the essential events into full light by simple ingenuity of composition, and giving to all others the degree of relief suited to their importance, so as to produce a profound sense of the special truth which one wishes to exhibit.

He continued:

> The novelist who professes to give us an exact representation of life ought to avoid with care any linking together of events which might appear exceptional. His aim is not to tell a story, to entertain us or touch our hearts, but to force us to think and understand the deep and hidden significance of events. . . .
>
> The artfulness of his plan is not to be found . . . in emotional effects or charm of writing, in an attractive beginning or a moving catastrophe, but in the skilful massing of little insistent details which will serve to bring out the essential meaning of his work.

Although Maupassant was writing about the realistic novel, nevertheless how appropriate his successors thought his remarks were to their own hardly realistic work. In effect, Maupassant was turning from Victorian formlessness and disdaining the practice, common in France and England, of padding with extraneous material to fulfill a required serial installment. Moreover, Maupassant was, in a way, pointing ahead to a kind of fiction that would make obsolete his own type of realism, in which the characters are seen from the outside and their external reactions catalogued. With Conrad, Joyce, Virginia Woolf, and Lawrence, the external realities are no longer paramount—the inner flux is emphasized through several psychological devices, the most effective of which is Joyce's development, following Dujardin, of the stream-of-consciousness technique. Even by Conrad's time in the mid-nineties, however, there was an approximation of this technique, despite the fact that Conrad, like his naturalist predecessors, worked essentially from the outside. Through the accumulation of concrete imagistic details from as many sides as possible, he created, as it were, a stream of consciousness (a flow of thought emanating from the character himself, not from the novelist) from the outside. With his ability to rove back and forth into memory and into different time sequences through recurring images, as Joyce was shortly to do in *A Portrait of the Artist as a Young Man* and as Proust in *A Remembrance of Things Past*, Conrad developed (without originating) a method that is almost equivalent to the stream itself. If we agree that the stream works through psychologically conceived images which relate to the outside world, then we shall see that Conrad's method was similar, although his procedure was to begin not with internal facts but with surface images. In his hands, psychological associations are conveyed through outside detail, an impersonal process in which physical images bore in toward the subject while carefully defining and categorizing their effects. Later, D. H. Lawrence was to modify Conrad's method, and then Joyce and Virginia Woolf were to turn to inward detail and work toward the exterior.

All, however, were following Conrad's famous dictum in his Preface to *The Nigger of the "Narcissus"* (1897), his third novel and an important step in his development as a mature novelist. In the Preface, Conrad, following Maupassant and especially James and Flaubert, whose influence on contemporary literature as a whole will be indicated below, was concerned with how the novelist could catch the feeling of "sensory reality"; how, in short, he could "penetrate to the colors of life's complexities." We note that Conrad had rejected the Realism that catalogues and the Romanticism that sentimentalizes and falsifies life. Art must, he says,

strenuously aspire to the plasticity of sculpture, to the colour of painting, and to the magic suggestiveness of music—which is the art of arts. And it is only through complete, unswerving devotion to the perfect blending of form and substance; it is only through unremitting never-discouraged care for the shape and ring of sentences that an approach can be made to plasticity, to colour, and that the light of magic suggestiveness may be brought to play for an evanescent instant over the commonplace surface of words: of the old, old words, worn thin, defaced by ages of careless usage.

Conrad then made his now famous declaration of intentions, which repeats Henry James's claim that the artist should "produce the illusion of life"—Conrad said: "My task which I am trying to achieve is, by the power of the written word, to make you hear, to make you feel— it is, before all, to make you *see*." The aim is to catch in silence each passing moment and to reproduce that moment so that it arrests the interest of the reader; that function, he says, is the goal "reserved only for a very few to achieve." At that moment, the artistic aims of the creator assume a moral importance—a sense of grandeur and of something fully *done* which captures the moral significance of the moment. This morality of the novelist's integrity is, as with all serious modern artists, his sole answer to society's charges that he has abandoned the common aims of the community.

In varying ways, Conrad's emphasis on the individual artist's conscious mind as guide to his artistic conceptions—an anti-traditionalist position and a throwback to the philosophy of the 1890's, the time of Conrad's apprenticeship—found its counterpart in the statements of Huxley, Virginia Woolf, and Joyce. Conrad was following, in his way, Flaubert's attempt to make the novel a major artistic form, not merely a type of entertainment. Concern with form, a major French preoccupation, did not significantly begin in England, we remember, until George Eliot, Meredith, and Conrad turned to the novel, and only the latter practiced what he theorized. After Conrad, we find several statements of novelistic theory incorporated into the novel itself: as examples, Stephen's sermon on art in *A Portrait*, the remarks in Philip Quarles' journal in *Point Counter Point*, and, indirectly, the tense discussions between Loerke, the devilish creator, and Ursula and Gudrun Brangwen near the end of *Women in Love*.

Looking ahead momentarily to Virginia Woolf's work, we find remarks that gain value when joined to those by Conrad just quoted, and which show further the reliance of the major contemporary English novelists on their French predecessors. Virginia Woolf, harking back to Maupassant, while differing greatly from him in execution, was prepared to reveal the "substance" of life rather than sequences of the details of life. In a speech delivered at Cambridge in 1924, "Mr. Bennett and Mrs. Brown," Virginia Woolf stated her opposition to the Edwardian novels of H. G. Wells, John Galsworthy, and Arnold Bennett, and directly attacked the kind of reality they represented, which was, she indicated, a holdover from Victorian writers. Her main point was that the Edwardians (and Victorians) did not give the reader a sense of *the* character, did not reach into the substance of their people; did not, in effect, give the Mrs. Brownness of the theoretical Mrs. Brown of her title. Each of the Edwardians, she claimed, would merely convey aspects of Mrs. Brown's surroundings, but none would give her essence, her substantial being. Although the forte of the Victorians had been the creation of character, Virginia

Woolf attacks their assumptions even here. These novelists—the above and Dickens, Thackeray, and Trollope—achieved a sort of intimacy with the audience by describing familiar objects—houses, rents, properties, funds—and thus suggesting relationships that everyone can recognize. Character, in their hands, then, only comes alive by their recalling the audience's knowledge of these familiar things. She writes: "They [these novelists] have given us a house in the hope that we may be able to deduce the human beings who live there." In this guise, the character can never be *seen,* and characterization has no felt texture because the novelist is too materialistic to be cognizant of the *thisness* of people.

Virginia Woolf goes on to say that the new novelists, the Georgians like herself, and including Forster, Lawrence, Joyce, and Huxley (Conrad having died in 1911), must reject this type of writing and seeing, and instead visualize Mrs. Brown as more than her house, her rents, and her tangible possessions. What the Georgians need, she indicates, is a new system of communication, a new series of conventions, to transmit their vision. The old system is already worn and obsolete, the conventions ragged and weary. After these admonitions, it is not strange that Virginia Woolf's sense of reality, as we find it in *To the Lighthouse, Mrs. Dalloway,* and *The Waves* differs considerably from the point of view in Galsworthy and Bennett, although the latter's achievements were nonetheless considerable in their way. She closes her indictment with the plea and the prophecy:

But do not expect just at present a complete and satisfactory presentment of her [Mrs. Brown]. Tolerate the spasmodic, the obscure, the fragmentary, the failure. Your help is invoked in a good cause. For I will make one final and surprisingly rash prediction—we are trembling on the verge of one of the great ages of English literature. But it can only be reached if we are determined never never to desert Mrs. Brown.

Mrs. Woolf's main failing here was her inability to recognize that these new tools had already been forged and put to extensive use by E. M. Forster in his early novels, by Conrad as long ago as *Lord Jim* (1900) and *Nostromo* (1904), by D. H. Lawrence in nearly everything he wrote after *Sons and Lovers,* and especially in *The Rainbow* and *Women in Love,* and, most significantly, by Joyce in *A Portrait* and *Ulysses,* the latter published in full two years before her address. It is striking that the person who could write that life is a "luminous halo, a semi-transparent envelope surrounding us from the beginning of consciousness to the end" should be unaware that life was just that to her contemporaries.

Following this same strong concern with a "shimmery reality," Aldous Huxley, through the notebooks of Philip Quarles in *Point Counter Point* (1928), realized that his basic problem as a novelist was how to get beyond external fact. He recognized that one can catalogue objects, as the Victorians and Edwardians had done, and still not create life. "The artistic problem is to produce diaphanousness in spots, selecting the spots so as to reveal only the most humanely significant of distant vistas behind the near familiar object." In short, the problem is to get behind exteriors without creating bizarre distortions and without romanticizing the obvious or making it seem, as he says, "fantastically mysterious."

The twentieth-century novelist, we may safely assume, is concerned chiefly with intensifying aspects of reality; and because he has rejected so many traditional values, he has to recreate for himself what his predecessors could take for granted. When society is reduced to chaos, new systems must be developed, and the novelist's quest is to discover and develop fresh material. This explains in part the originality and individual style of the modern novelist. For full and immediate communication, a novelist must be able to refer, as the nineteenth-century novelist could, to a community of interests, to shared values. Within this community, each novelist's symbols (his means of expressing himself) are at once public and cognitive, recognizable without difficulty. However, destroy the solidity of the community, and the problem of communication arises. The public and the serious writer are cut off from each other, for the latter's symbols now become obscure and personal. Or else, the novelist must forfeit certain of his more complex symbols and nuances of meaning so that the reader can understand him. Already, though, an artificial situation exists. In addition, or instead, he can use one set of symbols when talking to novices and another when in communication with the initiated. Lastly, his alternative may be to direct himself solely to a coterie which has been trained to understand him, and thus forgo a wide audience altogether. In any case, however, the novelist's concern has shifted to technique, to a stress on how to say things rather than only on what to say; and this radical emphasis on technique is something new in the genre in English.

It should be noted that this concern with technical matters does not necessarily mean that the modern novel is better or more proficient than, for instance, the eighteenth- or nineteenth-century novel. D. H. Lawrence is not a *better* novelist than Henry Fielding or George Eliot, although he is a vastly different one. *Lord Jim* is not a better novel than *Tom Jones*, for each speaks with authority, although, again, the Conrad novel is quite different in intention and scope from Fielding's work. It can be said that the technical devices of the modern novel at its best are suitable for *that* kind of novel, if we remember that not all technical devices are necessarily successful just because they are there. For *Tom Jones* to contain the structure of Joyce's *Ulysses* would be nightmarish; but the subject matter of Joyce's novel calls for a technique as daring as the one Joyce uses. Similarly, Jane Austen's subject matter precludes a structure that Virginia Woolf successfully uses in *Mrs. Dalloway* and *The Waves*; in the same way, Aldous Huxley, in *Point Counter Point*, uses an explicit musical structure that would serve no purpose, for example, in *Vanity Fair* or *David Copperfield*. With new subject matter came new techniques; in a good novel, each is appropriate to the other, and we must criticize and analyze largely within the area of the author's intentions and success in carrying them out, no matter what his century. If his intentions are serious to begin with and are artistically realized, if, in brief, he has created something significant, then we can recognize his stature and allow him his seeming eccentricities, however unfamiliar and difficult they are. For the major modern novelist can be described as Edmund Wilson in *Axel's Castle* described the French poets of the nineteenth century:

> Every feeling or sensation we have, every moment of consciousness, is different from every other; and it is, in consequence, impossible to render our sensations as we actually experience them through the conventional and universal language of ordinary literature. Each poet has his unique personality; each of his moments has its special tone, its special combination of elements. And it is the poet's task to find, to invent, the special language which will alone be capable of expressing his personality and feelings. . . .

In trying to travel the rocky literary path between an 1890's "code" of artistic anarchy and a Victorian code of professed didacticism, Conrad, Joyce, Forster, Virginia Woolf, Huxley, and Lawrence took refuge, as had Flaubert and James before them, in that devotion to craft wherein art and morality meet in commitment, responsibility, and lawfulness. By creating the semblance of events lived and felt so that their organization constitutes a completely experienced reality, the artist fulfils his duty to himself and to society. It is, however, solely through projection, through dramatization, that the totality of feeling can be communicated. All these writers concur with Conrad's statement that only the artist—and not the scientist and thinker, who appeal to our commonsense and intelligence—can reach into "life's appearances and forms, the very spirit of life's truth," for only the artist has "a wonderful power of vision."

II

Once we recognize the broad assumptions as well as the diversity and range of the modern novelist, the question then arises as to precisely what he found so congenial in his nineteenth-century French antecedents. For if we trace the dominant trends of this century's prose, together with its poetry, we must return to the French naturalists and symbolists, both of whom exerted considerable influence on English literature. Nineteenth-century French literature was the scene of a series of movements and counter-movements, of manifestoes and counter-manifestoes, of conservatives and radicals, of orthodox writers and wild eccentrics. A time of great ferment in literature, its trends became the major trends of our time, influencing nearly every major writer of this century.

Realism and Naturalism are two sides of the same thing; while Naturalism, as the French developed it, emphasizes cause and effect, is perhaps more "scientific" in its cataloguing of motivations, environmental details, et al., realism is more representative of whole life, less emphatic both on scientific observation and on minute details of character and situation. Each is part of the larger group that reacted against the romanticists as represented by Victor Hugo and the Dumas'. Therefore, for purposes of simplification, Naturalism and Realism will be considered as two parts of the same movement and differentiated solely on the basis of the several authors themselves. The symbolists, in their turn, showed that a major literary force could be developed that was neither realistic nor romantic in a strict sense. Nevertheless, Naturalism had its staunch disciples, not the least of whom was the young Joyce, and its power extended for over half a century into even those who considered themselves strongly anti-naturalistic.

The best-known names in French Naturalism and Realism are Balzac, Zola, Flaubert, and Maupassant, the latter Flaubert's disciple.

Balzac, the earliest of the four, was more a literary social scientist than a scientist, and his claim to Realism is based on his portrayal of actual life against a recognizably realistic background. He can certainly not be regarded as part of any concerted movement, and except for his undoubted influence on later realists his place is secure because of his intrinsic worth rather than for historical importance. Nevertheless, Balzac's vast *La Comédie humaine*, whose novels were to be a panoramic view of every important aspect of French life, could not help but point the literary way for future realists.

Of more importance, historically, in this movement was the work of three non-literary men, Darwin, Claude Bernard, and Auguste Comte. Darwin's theories (*Origin of Species*, 1859) bolstered Zola's later Naturalism with its determinism, its emphasis on heredity, and its simple relationship of cause and effect. Claude Bernard and Comte both applied their knowledge of physical science and the laws of matter to the human species, and their findings, while scientifically negligible, are of great importance in literature; for Zola, as well as Flaubert and Maupassant to some extent, along with the help of the literary historian Taine, built character and situation out of material causes. We remember that Virginia Woolf's comments quoted above were a direct reaction to this kind of reality, which had by her time sifted through, although somewhat transformed, into the work of Wells, Galsworthy, and Bennett.

Perhaps the greatest of French realistic novels is Flaubert's *Madame Bovary* (1857), and, paradoxically, this particular novel has become a source of both symbolical and naturalistic interpretation. Nevertheless, in its naturalistic elements, it shows Flaubert's almost neurotic concern with authenticity, the precise word, the correct nuance of cause and effect; in addition, it stresses the role of environment upon Emma Bovary and explains her downfall with complete impersonality, a type of scientific precision dear to Zola and his followers. Yet Flaubert's type of Naturalism differed in degree, if not in kind, from the type as developed by the Goncourts and by Zola, whose manifesto in *Le Roman expérimental* (1880) showed how far he had left Flaubert behind. The Naturalism of Zola's is distinguished from Flaubert's in its willingness to substitute science, or rather pseudo-science, for art. Zola caught his characters in a vice in which all life was squeezed from them, and their survival depended more on their adherence to a system that would eventually destroy them than on the resources of their inner wills. None of the "inner life" so prevalent in writers like Joyce, Lawrence, Conrad, and Forster could burst through Zola's careful amassing of environmental detail.

In his long essay on the experimental novel, Zola posited society as a vast laboratory in which the novelist could select the various chemicals that would compose each of his characters, adding or withdrawing a certain chemical to determine their make-up. Also, by cataloguing the environmental factors from which no character could escape, Zola was able to chart their rise and fall. This attitude, governed as it is by the laws of heredity, environment, and physiology, must of course force into line any deviations; and it is precisely these deviations that provide the basis for real love and real states of feeling, what Lawrence called "blood consciousness" and what Virginia Woolf labeled the luminous-like halo that makes life real.

Moreover, Zola's very interests provided his novels with only a limited type of reality—the kind found in dismal surroundings fraught with drunkenness, prostitutes, and violence, but withal lacking in individual will and choice. The following passage from *Thérèse Raquin* (1868), macabre in its details, suggests the type of sensationalism and over-statement which characterized much of Zola's work. It should be remarked, however, that Zola's fiction did deviate at times from strict typing and could be effective if one recognizes that a documentary is not of the same order of art as a novel that intensifies life. The passage follows:

Camillus was loathsome. He had been in the water for two weeks. His face still looked firm and rigid; the features had been preserved, but the skin had assumed a yellowish and muddy hue. The head—emaciated, bony, slightly swollen—grimaced; it was turned a little, the hair glued to the temples, the eyelids raised, revealing the staring globes of the eyes; the twisted lips, drawn to one side, had an atrocious, mocking smile; the end of the blackened tongue was visible between the white teeth. Tanned and drawn, as it were, the face remained even more horrifying in its pain and terror by retaining a look of humanity. The body seemed a mass of dissolved flesh; it had suffered horribly. You felt that the arms had almost disintegrated; the collar-bones pierced the skin of the shoulders. On the greenish chest the ribs made broad black lines; the left flank, pierced and open, had fallen into dark red tatters of flesh. The whole torso was decaying. The legs, more resistant, stretched out, stained with foul, pustulant patches. The feet were falling to pieces.

While the reader recognizes Zola's reliance on the bare outlines of Flaubert's novels, in terms of morbid characters and grotesque situations, he also perceives that Zola has changed real understanding of motives into exaggerated sensationalism, and here occurs one of the main differences between Flaubert's Realism and Zola's Naturalism. In one sense of course, all great literature is realistic in that it partakes of incidents that relate to a world recognizable to the imagination, a world that *can* exist and that is probable, if only in certain states of subconsciousness. Zola's naturalistic details, like the English Victorian's material objects, although all readily recognizable, exclude to some extent that projection of life within which imaginative elements are brought together and by so doing exclude diversity and breadth. Thus, although Joyce will use naturalistic detail extensively in *Ulysses* —the novel in one sense is an epitome of the naturalistic novel— *Ulysses* itself is not naturalistic, for Joyce realized the shortcomings of the type and added dimensions of another sort. Similarly, while several of the novels discussed in this volume were influenced by French Naturalism as it worked itself into the English novel, many are *more* than naturalistic, for their authors brought to them an eclectic art in which Naturalism is only one ingredient.

The zenith of Zola's method was reached in *L'Assommoir* (1877), translated into English as *The Dram Shop* or *Gervaise*. Here documentation of laundries, bodily smells, alcoholism, sadism, et al., provides an almost entirely effective novel, unless one recognizes that notes cannot replace art or controlled puppet-like characters real people. Zola's preparations for a novel of this sort were enormous and the documentation authentic; yet when we turn from the details to see a larger plan, we see that the details exist for themselves. There is no inward projection, no shimmer; Naturalism seemed to preclude an interest in the individual's reactions and sensibilities. It was just this neglect of the individual that Conrad had in mind when he wrote Arnold Bennett (in 1902) that the latter stopped just short of being absolutely real because he was too faithful to his dogmas of Realism. He wrote: "Now realism in art will never approach reality." He also advised John Galsworthy that he hugged his "conception of right and wrong too closely," and that the latter's tales lacked air. Similarly, Conrad warned his friend Hugh Clifford that "No word is adequate. The imagination of the reader should be left free to arouse his feeling"—the imagination must do the work after the novelist has provided the guidance.

The limitations of the naturalist school become obvious even in the work of such careful writers as Zola and Maupassant, whose remarks quoted above from his Preface to *Pierre et Jean* seem a composite of

Flaubertian Realism and Zolaistic Naturalism. Maupassant was of course conscious of the necessity of selection, aware that Naturalism would wreck itself on its failure to recognize this; and it is Maupassant's brand of Naturalism—looking ahead as it does to new developments and more flexible than Zola's—that we find intermixed in the major modern English novelists.

Pure Naturalism, in Conrad's remark, lacked the room and air in which its characters could move around and breathe. Just as George Moore was bringing Naturalism to England, appropriately cleaned for late-Victorian eyes, with his novels that imitated Zola's school, *A Mummer's Wife* (1885), *A Drama in Muslin* (1886), *Esther Waters* (1894), the French naturalists were themselves undergoing attack by a new movement, as yet atomistic and disorganized, that was to prove the major literary movement of the century: the symbolist movement, which would give air, room, and space to literature.

As Naturalism in its reaction against Romanticism was an attempt to create orderliness and to form a scientific method, so another group, classical in its assumptions, appeared, called the Parnassians, from whom the symbolists in turn broke away to form an independent movement. The Parnassians, of secondary importance in themselves, are historically significant because they formed the basic ideas in which poets like Mallarmé, Verlaine, and even Baudelaire, were nurtured. Their ideals were to impose orderliness, to project exactness of form, and to write objectively. As materialistic as the naturalists themselves, they presented descriptively phenomena of the external world, while suppressing undue personal emotion. Among the Parnassians, however, were several poets not content with objective realism who, by working along more "spiritual" lines, became the inspiration and forerunner of a counter movement, Symbolism, which was to influence a half century of French and English fiction. Included among the early symbolists were Verlaine, Baudelaire, and Mallarmé, who, along with Rimbaud, inspired the new group, which as yet had no official name.

The symbolists, turning on the romantics, naturalists, and Parnassians—the latter two they found too representative and the former too public—insisted on a world of ideal beauty, convinced that this could be realized only through art. They scrupulously avoided the public and political themes dear to the romantics and disdained the realistic or scientific view of art because it denied the ideal world which was to be the center of their activity. As Mallarmé later put it: "Poetry should not inform but suggest and evoke, not name things but create their atmosphere." To name things is to be a realist, to support causes a romantic, to be concerned with cause and effect a naturalist. The aim of Symbolism was to free French poetry from conventional form, though not by repudiating the objective method of presentation; instead, the goal was to give recognizable external images a spiritual or symbolic value. If we look ahead momentarily, we can find dozens of such images running through the modern English novel: the silver mine in Conrad's *Nostromo* and the sinking of the *Patna* in his *Lord Jim*; the Marabar Caves in Forster's *A Passage to India* and the use of the theme from Beethoven's Fifth Symphony in his *Howards End*; Joyce's merging of water symbolism to the structures of *A Portrait* and *Ulysses*; Lawrence's stress on cathedrals and arches in *The Rainbow*, and the scene with horses at the end of that novel; also, the scene in which Birkin scales stones into the lake in *Women in Love* —moreover the wrestling episode and the African statuettes in the same novel also serve symbolic, not realistic, purposes. Similarly, one could point to the lighthouse in Virginia Woolf's novel, or to the use of chimes in *Mrs. Dalloway*, or to the bicycle at the end of Huxley's *Antic Hay*. Some of these symbols are, of course, more effective than others, for one author could invest his symbols with greater potential by charging their context with more significance. The more profound the context, the more far-reaching, obviously, the symbol.

The French symbolists themselves opposed description for its own sake—thus the clean lines and spareness of their work; literal directness they replaced with suggestive indirectness—thus the emphasis they placed upon the careful choice of words, upon the colors, tones, and rhythms of their phrases. In their poems, words become subtle forms of communication, and connotations are more important than simple denotation; or else denotation itself becomes unclear, as in many of Mallarmé's poems. Even though the symbolists favored individuality, they did not stress egoistic emotions—thus their interest in impersonality, in control, in surface orderliness, some of the qualities they had carried over from their Parnassian heritage.

Put another way, Symbolism in literature is a form of expression, at best approximate, in which unseen reality is apprehended by the consciousness. The symbol represents without reproducing; through it the infinite, or some degree of it, is revealed and embodied, and the infinite is made to blend with the finite. As Moréas, in a virtual symbolist prose, wrote in his symbolist manifesto (1886):

Enemy of explanation, of declamation, of false sensibility, of objective description, symbolist poetry tries to clothe the Idea in a palpable form, which, nevertheless, is not an end in itself, but which, while serving to express the Idea, remains subject to it. The Idea in its turn does not let itself be seen without sumptuous trains of exterior analogies; for the essential character of symbolic art consists in never going to the conception of the Idea in itself. Thus in the art, pictures of nature, actions of men, concrete phenomena are not there for their own sake, but as simple appearances destined to represent their esoteric affinities with primordial Ideas.

Moréas claims that Symbolism is a reaction of the soul in literature against all those literary movements which represent things that only visibly exist, exactly as they exist. It is, he says, a reaction against a type of language that *says* rather than suggests. Symbolism, in practice, would free literature from the bondage of rhetoric, externals, regular beat in poetry, from the cataloguing of nature and the chance accidents of daily life, freeing the literary arts of all elements of materialism, which hitherto had prevented the disengagement of the ultimate essence of soul from its insignificant externals. Literature can, in these terms, attain liberty and authentic speech, becoming, as its English interpreter Arthur Symons put it, "a kind of religion, with all the duties and the responsibilities of the sacred ritual."

Apparently, such a doctrine would alienate the artist completely from the general public. The poet or writer becomes a priest-like person, a seer, one who receives light or inspiration from God, and whose manner of expression disallows easy communication. No longer can he be read by the same public oriented to Dickens, Victor Hugo, Jane Austen, or Voltaire. The very surface of his work, seemingly clear, is a deceptively contrived pattern in which the aim is *to be* rather than to express. As Arthur Symons wrote, "To name is to destroy, to suggest is to create." Now, a public educated by authors who define and explain will accuse the symbolist poet and novelist of using private symbols or of fostering a coterie in his attempts to be exclusive, different, and eccentric. The writer himself can only answer with another work in which he evokes and suggests ideas in a seemingly arbitrary way, in which his words become, as it were, spiritualized in their capacity for allusion and in their role as correspondents between the visible and the invisible. Moreover, undaunted by his unpopularity, he will continue to create incomplete scenes and suggest evanescent themes which recur in various shapes, only to become increasingly vague unless the reader has been alert to earlier clues. His method of working, in addition, will include seeing resemblances between things that hitherto seemed dissimilar. Aware that the imagination is a "putting-together" faculty, what Coleridge in his *Biographia Literaria* had called the shaping and modifying power, the symbolist writer is constantly working and re-working his material until constituent ingredients, point of view, words themselves become garbled and renovated by fresh meanings. Thus the reader will be further alienated and the gap between public and creator widened. Thus Joyce's work, particularly *Ulysses*—the epitome of the symbolic novel—even now, more than thirty years after its publication, reaches only a limited audience of initiates and remains almost unintelligible to the less serious reader.

What, one may ask, are the sources of symbolist doctrine? what are the poems like in which sound color, taste—the whole range of the senses—are expressed through words which no longer tell a story or point a moral? Charles Baudelaire, perhaps the finest French poet of the nineteenth century, was the origin of many symbolist ideas, although no one person can be said to have originated the movement. His *Les Fleurs du Mal* (1857) demonstrated a new voice in poetry, and his sonnet, *Correspondances*, suggested many of the ideas that later became symbolist dogma. The poem reads, in a literal English translation:

Nature is a temple from whose living pillars
Confusing words are sometimes permitted to come forth;
Man wanders there through these forests of symbols
Which observe him with familiar stares.

As long echoes which from afar are mingled
Within a gloomy and profound unity,
Vast as the night and vast as the light,
Perfumes, odors, and sounds correspond.

There are some perfumes fresh as children's flesh,
Gentle as oboes, green as prairies,
And others, corrupt, rich, and triumphant,

Having the expansion of infinite things,
As amber, musk, benjamin, and incense
Which sing the transports of spirit and sense.

One other poem, "The Albatross," is also illustrative of Baudelaire's "new" poetry:

Often, to amuse themselves, the boat crew
Will snare some albatross, vast bird of the sea,
Who follows, indolent companion of voyages,
The ship gliding through bitter gulfs.

Hardly is their victim deposited on board
Than that king of the blue, clumsy and shy,
Piteously abandons his great white wings,
Like oars dragging alongside.

This winged voyager, how awkward and feeble!
Lately so lovely, now how comic and unsightly!
One torments his beak with a pipe,
Another mime, limpingly, weakens him that soars.

The Poet is similar to that prince of the clouds
Who haunts the storm and mocks the archer;
Exiled on the ground amidst the shouts,
His giant wings impede him from walking.

In "Correspondances," Baudelaire presented his now familiar doctrine of synesthesia, familiar because of the symbolist stress on it, in which the senses are mixed, i.e., colors can be seen, or sounds have color and taste. This intermixing of the senses was of primary significance to the symbolists, for if the concrete object or sense was merely the guide to a transcendental experience, then the ramifications of the correspondence were infinite because never stated. When art is a symbol of eternal beauty and truth, as the symbolists believed, then there is a mystical experience in which all restrictions are abandoned, and an albatross can be compared to the poet, or colors and sounds can correspond, or perfumes can lead to God. If, furthermore, as Baudelaire believed, beauty is in the artist and not in the object, the artist is free to make of the object what he will. The artist must, so to speak, unfold the mysteries of the universe, exiled and unmanned as he is by the shouting street crowds. For in this doctrine, the imagination is a divine faculty which perceives intuitively the secret and hidden connection between things, the eternal "analogies" which are the only fabric of art. Therefore, for the symbolists, music was the supreme art because by eliminating the denotative restriction of words it was completely analogous and had infinite meanings. Thus, poetry was to approach the condition of music, a doctrine found soon after in Walter Pater that would become a staple of literary criticism with Conrad, Virginia Woolf, and James Joyce.

Following Baudelaire's poetry, Arthur Rimbaud developed his idea of the poet as *voyant*, or seer, who would become the shadow of the eternal mind by being assimilated to the eternal creative power of the universe. From Plato's time, the poet has been believed to derive his powers from God, and the symbolists, consequently, made the poet into a miniature deity himself who connects man to the Universal Intelligence. In this way, everything that man sees is an imperfect image of some invisible unity.

For this kind of poetry, which would be unified, harmonious, and expressive of the spiritual and philosophic problems of the age, new forms were necessary; and this, again, in large part suggests the experimental nature of contemporary English fiction and explains how each of our major authors felt that he had to break through the technical limitations of the novel to express his ideas. The French-speaking Conrad sensed the atmosphere and prophesied that imaginative prose work would be in a new form, but "a form for which we are not ripe as yet." In an earlier comment reminiscent of Rimbaud's theory and the statements of the other symbolists, Conrad lamented fiction as a career and emphasized the unearthly nature of the enterprise: "One's will becomes the slave of hallucinations, responds only to shadowy impulses, waits on imagination alone. A strange state, a trying experience, a kind of fiery trial of untruthfulness." Shortly afterward, James Joyce, in just this fiery trial, began *A Portrait of the Artist as a Young Man*, and E. M. Forster was to write four of his five novels, while Conrad himself was to go from experiment to experiment, in *Nostromo* (1904), *Chance* (1914), and *Victory* (1915).

Symbolist doctrine was perhaps brought closer to its completed form by Stéphane Mallarmé than anyone else. The surface of Mallarmé's poetry is so elusive that almost no evident symbols are provided; a rhythm or tone may convey the sole suggestible element of the poem. Often, his symbol is a sensuous atmosphere with as few external references as possible, or else the symbol will lead only to the void and the vacant, or turn in upon itself as a symbol of the mind trying to understand itself by creating symbolist poetry. The following sonnet, "All the Soul Summed-up," is built upon an extended metaphor in which poetry and smoke are compared. But is it poetry? life? or what? Why a "choir of songs"? why exclude the real?

All the soul summed-up
When slowly we exhale it
In several puffs of smoke
Suppressed in other puffs

Proves that some cigar
Burns knowingly for little
That its ash is separated
From the clear kiss of fire

Thus the choir of songs
Soars to your lip
Exclude if you begin
The real because base

Its too precise sense will overwhelm
Your vague literature.

The poem itself becomes smoky, veiled, vague, full of possible meanings, yet possibly with no meaning at all. We can suggest that Mallarmé is talking of the poet and poetry that make life glow just as smoking a cigar makes it glow with the "clear kiss of fire." Further, we can suggest that the cigar has no worth except for its smoke or ash, just as the base of poetry must be its soul, not the words themselves. We can, in brief, suggest many possible interpretations, all of which will be suitable and consistent with what Mallarmé provides, but which is correct? The answer must be all, for the poet's conscious elusiveness expressly enforces vagueness on the poem and destroys "prose reality" in favor of transcendent ambiguity. Similarly, in the sonnet called "A Lace Curtain," Mallarmé ranges from a window curtain to bed curtains, from birth images to the birth of poetry, and ends with an image of creativity, the result of love:

A lace curtain is suppressed
In doubt of the supreme Game
Unfolding as a blasphemy
On a bed eternally absent.

This unanimous white conflict
Of a garland with its like
Fleeing to the wan glass
Floats more than buries.

But where dreams become gold
Sadly sleeps a mandola
Musician in the empty nullity

Such that towards some window
Depending on no bowels but its.
Filial one might be born.

Mallarmé, like Wagner in his music drama, tried to attain a synthesis of the arts and to make verse into music, which is the least denotative of the arts. Therefore, in Mallarmé's work, each object seems to lose its form and identity and to merge into a blurred vision that works in time rather than space. Each word is weighted with allusions, and word order is consciously inverted to build a structure of sensations. Mallarmé's quest was for the absolute—to encompass all time and even all space in the suggestibility of his verse. Following Wagner, he believed that poetry consisted of words plus music; so he wrote poetry whose content was word-drama and whose form was musical, hoping this way to approximate his ideal.

Symbolism itself passed into England almost fortuitously; that is, its leading French practitioners were examined solely for elements congenial to the English temperament. Thus, Swinburne made Baudelaire into a sadistic and sluggish poet, the same Baudelaire that Oscar Wilde transformed into a symbol of exotic beauty, a martyr to the bourgeoisie's fear and hatred of art. While Swinburne in "Ave atque Vale" and Wilde in *Salomé* were making of Baudelaire and the symbolists what they wanted, George Moore, now turning against Naturalism, saw in Symbolism the possibilities for a future literature, and although he too distorted Baudelaire's work, he did bring symbolist ideas into England with something of their original intention. Moore was personally acquainted with Mallarmé, attended his famous Tuesday night literary discussions, and translated some of his prose-poems. The former naturalist also caught correctly the doctrine of synesthesia, and was the first to write essays in English on Verlaine, Rimbaud, and Laforgue.

Moore, furthermore, was friendly with Édouard Dujardin, a minor writer whose novel *Les Lauriers sont Coupés* (freely translated into English as *We'll to the Woods No More*) gave James Joyce his ideas for the interior monologue or stream-of-consciousness technique, in which reality is sifted through the mind of the character-narrator. Moore talked about Dujardin's novel in Dublin, and the knowledge of this small work while never widespread did cross the channel from France. By acknowledging Dujardin, Joyce by implication acknowledged his debt to the symbolists, for Dujardin was a frequent visitor to Mallarmé's Tuesday evenings.

The symbolists, however, had so far reached only those English writers looking for a way out of Naturalism, and it was not until Arthur Symons' *The Symbolist Movement in Literature* (1899) that the French movement reached a wider audience. Through reportage, critical comment, evaluation, and translation, Symons brought to England the discussions he had heard at Mallarmé's gatherings. His essays, of markedly varying worth, on Gérard de Nerval, Mallarmé himself, Rimbaud, Verlaine, Huysmans, Villiers de l'Isle Adam (whose *Axel* strongly impressed William Butler Yeats, and also Conrad, in *Victory*), and Laforgue (whose manner is obvious in T. S. Eliot's early work) showed more understanding than Moore's sketchy work and, at the same time, emphasized the ideas necessary for a true comprehension of Symbolism. In his essay on Mallarmé, actually the heart of his book, Symons showed how these writers considered words as living things, as evocators of visions, the word as a liberating principle through which the human spirit is extracted from matter. Poetry created this way *is* the new consciousness of the invisible in which words strive to achieve infinite suggestibility. Symons also stressed the symbolists' ability to trace resemblances between unlikes where others saw only divergences; in this way, they created an ironic manner in which the pathetic and the ludicrous appear side by side. This notation helped squeeze excessive rhetoric, false eloquence, and cloying sentimentality from the typically inflated prose and poetry of romantics like Hugo and the Dumas'. Moreover, Symons saw their dedication to art as a priestly affair in which the artist sets himself off from worldly concerns and lives for his work. In practice, the decadent movement in England was undoubtedly influenced by the French symbolists, but the latter's authority lasted long after English decadence had become a historical curiosity. After Symons, the major French writers had crossed the channel and successfuly invaded English literature.

Evidently, the practices of the French symbolists differed considerably from those of previous authors who had also used symbols, diverging in their consciousness of practice, in their planting symbols for poetic effects rather than for purposes of narrative, in their removing story line and thrusting the novel forward through the interaction of the symbols themselves. Conversely, when Edmund Spenser, for example, used the symbol of a fire-eating dragon, he was using it for direct meanings on moral, political, and personal grounds; the dragon *meant* things tangible. It *signified* several things that Spenser wanted to say, and after they were said, no residue of dragon remained, so to speak, which would suggest more. The dragon, despite its several meanings, is denotative.

Put another way, the symbolists, as one critic has stated it, renounced "the causal connection between meaning and image; it [Symbolism] gives the image a transcendent meaning." As the symbol of the symbolists has only a negligible causal function, it is present almost solely as a way of evoking relationships far beyond those of cause and effect. In the realistic novel, on the other hand, the symbol has a realistic function, and while it may also function as a transcendental image, it is nevertheless tied to its real use. In reading symbolic novels, however, one must also be aware that no novel lives by virtue of symbols alone. The stuff of the genre, as we have often been reminded, consists of manners, morals, class structures, tensions between characters, et al. The symbols merely help to organize and extend this material, which is itself the sole basis of any meaningful discussion of the novel.

The French symbolists, as well as their twentieth-century followers, used symbols in many different ways. A minor symbol, for instance, will have only situational importance; that is, it may recur for one or two (possibly more) scenes while relating the characters and their actions and making clearer certain aspects of the total situation. If we take a modern practitioner, Conrad, as he develops a minor symbol, Miss Haldin's veil, in *Under Western Eyes*, we can see that the veil works as a complement to her feelings toward Razumov: the initial raising of the veil by Miss Haldin is her way of opening her heart; when she drops the veil at her feet she means Razumov to open his heart to her; after she recognizes his guilt, her veil—like her feelings— lies dormant and still; Razumov's sudden seizing of the veil conveys his strong feelings for her, for after this he makes of it something of a fetish; and the veil finally becomes the covering for Razumov's journal in which he reveals his daily life since his betrayal of Miss Haldin's brother. Through Conrad's use of the veil in relation to Razumov and Miss Haldin, a tangible object suggests a psychological comment; the veil is a minor symbol which gives greater intensity and drama to a significant scene. This particular application of the symbol is little different from its use by Victorian or earlier novelists. Thackeray, for instance, in *Vanity Fair*, has Mr. Osborne, at the moment he plans to disinherit his son, George, open the family Bible with its frontispiece representing Abraham sacrificing Isaac. Now the suggestion of this sacrifice of sons runs through the book—sons sacrificed to fathers, to property, to country, to materialism, but Thackeray never consciously plays with the Biblical image or the idea again, and the Abraham and Isaac scene itself has no more than momentary interest.

A major symbol, on the other hand, is not only important for the immediate situation but also provides a spine to the entire book. These symbols reverberate to a far greater extent than do the minor symbols, and provide an all-important order for both the form and content of their respective novels. If, for example, we take two major symbols, fog in Dickens's *Bleak House* and water in Joyce's *A Portrait*, we can see how they work in each book and how Joyce's use is in the line of French symbolism while Dickens's is a traditional way of holding the novel together. In brief, a traditional symbol—Dickens's use of the fog—works inward, restricts the range of activity; conversely, the twentieth-century type of symbol suggests more, works outward, is itself partially hidden, and *includes*. The fog in *Bleak House* recurs throughout the novel, representing the opaque net of confusion which Chancery has thrown around England's legal system. The fog, furthermore, covers the shady background of Lady Dedlock and the unclear lineage of Esther Summerson. The fog demonstrates that a pall has been cast over everyone's life, and that until the Jarndyce case is resolved, the sun cannot penetrate to hearts now damp and cold. At its broadest, the fog, along with the law, is, as Edgar Johnson says, a symbol "of all the ponderous and murky forces that suffocate the creative energies of mankind."

The fog here, central though it is, has a definite meaning—it can be restricted, and what it suggests is finite, is caught within the terms of the novel, is not a means of extension beyond what Dickens provides in character and situation. The fog, therefore, is dramatically necessary but not transcendental. In Joyce's *A Portrait*, one of the major recurring symbols is water in its various guises as the water of bed-wetting, dirty ditches, bathroom sinks, as well as holy water and the water of creativity. Stephen Dedalus, Joyce's protagonist, reacts to water with disgust (a theme that will recur in *Ulysses*; for Stephen, cleanliness is next to bedevilment), and suddenly water stands for Ireland, family, middle-class life, the church—everything, in fact, that Stephen must reject in order to assert himself as an artist. Water, in this context, is a form of death, for it destroys the creative self, the only *live* thing that Stephen has. Yet, conversely, water, the baptismal water or the water of refreshment, brings life, and, accordingly, Stephen must plunge into the waters of baptism at the very moment he dedicates himself to a life of art and creativity. Water, then, enfolds all of life.

from bed-wetting, in which it prefigures all the unpleasant aspects of a watery life, including the parents who are the closest thing to the infant, from this to the waters of creativity, and, finally, to the waters that one must disdain, for they may bring immersion injurious to the pure artist, or even death. Yet Joyce does not talk about water the way Dickens repeats the word fog; Joyce merely indicates the incidents or situations in which water is present and lets the imaginative reader make the connections and see for himself that water becomes one of the important links of the novel's various motifs. Whereas Dickens, anxious that the fog is not missed as a symbol, constantly brings it before the reader's eyes and impresses him with its symbolic value.

The difference between the two is one of emphasis, and in that area we have, perhaps, the chief difference between the traditional use of the symbol and the twentieth-century application. In that area, we can ascertain one of the difficulties the modern reader has when he comes to A Portrait, or Ulysses, Mrs. Dalloway, The Waves, Women in Love, Nostromo, et al. without any awareness that these novels will proceed differently from the ones he is probably accustomed to. More carefully arranged novels, he comes to realize, need more careful readers. The modern novelist often merely gives the materials and lets his symbols and other devices suggest whatever the reader can make of them. Furthermore, his symbols themselves will not always be clear—they may be in many different forms: short incidents, casual images, broken conversations, minor characters, peripheral scenes. And as the novelist gains in imaginative power and maturity, he refines his symbols and makes their importance more subtly provoking. For the novelist realizes that as new areas of knowledge open up, new symbols are needed for expression; so the reader must be on close guard or a major theme or motif may be lost; and in novels like Nostromo, A Portrait, Ulysses, Point Counter Point, and A Passage to India, which proceed by motifs and recurrent themes, one loses entire sequences if he is not completely alert to what the novelist is doing.

Defining these new areas of knowledge, some of which were suggested above, is of great importance in trying to trace the intentions of the major contemporary novelists, for the novel readily responds more fully and faster than any other art form to new ideas. The biggest single influence was in psychology—Freudian, Bergsonian, William Jamesian, among others. At the same time the modern novelist was beginning to use symbols to reach outward and include more of the possible universe, the modern psychologist was beginning to use new techniques to probe inward and define more clearly man's motives. Symbolism, with its ordered surfaces and disordered complexity of meanings, can be seen as a psychological movement in its own way, psychology being complementary to Symbolism in its attempt to shun the restrictions of surface reality by probing further into the unknown. In another way, both placed the creative artist at the center of the universe, the symbolists in their doctrine of the artist as seer in direct communication with the Creative Intelligence, the psychologists in their making the patient (artist) the focal point from which fantasies, dreams, and inner states of feeling can emanate. As much as Darwin's *The Origin of Species* upset the preconceptions and changed the artistic purposes of the late-Victorians, so did Freud, Jung, and the several schools that followed them stir the atmosphere in which the twentieth-century novelist worked.

Moreover, both Symbolism and psychology served a further purpose in providing anti-materialistic support for novelists already rejecting the Victorian writer's concern with a moneyed and propertied society. The whole paraphernalia of a bourgeois society—the emphasis on wills, suitable marriages, incomes, estates, benefices, et al.—all this has disappeared from the major contemporary novel as a matter of theme. With this large area of emphasis cut away, the novelist of course had to turn elsewhere; so rather than probe man's possessions, he probed man. Therefore, we find that although the Victorian novelists created great fictional figures—Dickens's David Copperfield, Mrs. Gamp, Pip, Pickwick, Sam Weller, Joe Gargery; Thackeray's Becky Sharp, George Eliot's Dorothea Brooke, Meredith's Sir Willoughby Patterne, Trollope's country parsons, Emily Brontë's Heathcliff, and so on—despite this achievement, the vast welter of detail the novelists accumulated is piled on the *exterior* of their characters. Time and again, we reach scenes or situations in which a new method is called for, in which the character could only be realized through an interior probe, and that area is precisely where the Victorian novelist is lacking, despite his great attainments in other ways. Novelists like Forster, Lawrence, and Huxley, not to mention Conrad, Woolf, and Joyce, along with their lesser contemporaries, could, however, show their post-Victorian disenchantment through more analytic means than their predecessors. Thus, Huxley works through character and situation doubles to approximate counterpointing ideas; or Forster, through a musical theme, suggests the layers beneath human consciousness and reveals areas that more traditional methods would leave buried.

Furthermore, the new psychology of Freud and his followers gave the modern novelist new themes almost ready made for artistic dramatization and new means to conceive these schemes. Freudian psychology precluded the nineteenth-century conception of the soul as an entity in which a character was either "good" or "bad," a view that often resulted in melodrama and/or sentimentality. After Freud, the soul, or man's personality, was seen as having a multiplicity of aspects, which the novelist uses to demonstrate the controlled disorder of the human mind. Thus, new techniques and new ways to present information had to be discovered, and psychology offered suggestions here too. Accordingly, the novelist in attempting to approximate the discontinuity of the mind uses discontinuity in the novel—for instance, a series of free associations of ideas which follow in random, not logical, order. The sole logic is the one enforced by the novelist to obtain certain results, but his logic is usually effective only when it creates the semblance of illogical reality. So the novelist must plan his effects two or three times removed from the reality of the reader, and this planning leads, often, to a stress on method which sharply diverges from Victorian practice.

Along these lines, we can find several psychologically-oriented devices which serve the novelist's purpose: frequent accidental interruptions of conversations or situations; lack of concern with completing a given action or following it through to its logical end; recurrence of themes, a whole rhythm of repetition, of doubling of motifs, characters, even words and syllables; a kind of poetic lyricism that results from a careful use of words for musical effect as well as for meaning, an impressionism in which repetitive sensations create an atmosphere from which the author, nevertheless, remains impersonal and removed; a de-emphasis of logical reasoning, a type of anti-intellectuality in which reason is denied because it can never explain human behavior, in which diversity and complexity are the twin stuff of emotional, not rational, man.

Many of these ideas came from Freud and his followers and many from the writings of Henri Bergson, the influential *fin de siècle* French philosopher, whose anti-materialism worked its way into Proust, Gide, and into a whole generation of English novelists. Bergson, in his logical attempt to break up a mechanistic world, complemented the work of the early psychologists, and his emphasis on the *merging* of time is significant in any discussion of the modern novel, his influence appearing in *Nostromo, The Waves, Mrs. Dalloway, To the Light-*

house, Ulysses, A Portrait, Point Counter Point, and several minor novels. Melting time, we realize, was not a surrealist discovery. The difficulty of measuring experience, the interpenetration of moments of consciousness by unexplained memories, the impossibility of analysis without distortion and alteration—all these ideas, implicit in Bergson, help to define a modern theory of the novel and provide part of the base beneath modern technical experimentation. In the Bergsonian world, time is heterogeneous, always in motion, fluid, evershifting, and things in it are indistinguishable. Space, conversely, is homogeneous, still, measurable. Time, furthermore, cannot be characterized by separate moments—to do this, as some have attempted, is to measure what is indistinguishable and to replace time by space.

Through *durée* (durational or psychological time), Bergson asserted a disbelief in the surface reality of life and stressed a time in which the clock is artificial and mental time is natural. In Bergson's "duration of time," one is in that stream of non-thinking impulse which constitutes life. One is "inside the object" by means of intuition, an irrational process, rather than surveying the object from the outside, from a window, which is an intellectual and rational process. Bergson's idea of reality conceived the world as a flux of interpenetrated elements unseizable by the intellect. This anti-mechanical mode of thinking places all time—all the past, as well as the present moment— in what one critic has called "one concentrated *now.*"

Bergson's theory of time was appealing for several reasons. Based, like modern physics, on the relativity of historical and philosophical truths, the time theory, in literary terms, signifies the relative nature of human experience. Most modern novelists, but especially Proust, Conrad, Woolf, Joyce, and Faulkner, deny absolutes in human relationships, and the structural format of their work, in its emphasis on fluctuating time, mirrors this belief in the non-absolute quality of experience and history. Nowhere more than in Proust's *Le Temps retrouvé,* in part a treatise on time, are these melting relationships analyzed. Marcel, in this seventh part of Proust's novel, experiences those moments of insight and revelation (what he calls privileged moments) which project the flotsam and jetsam of the past into his mind and provide tension with his contemporary surroundings. This tension gradually melts into a continuity between past and present, an endless interpenetration of time which can only be "clocked" by art. Marcel says:

And then a new light dawned with me, less brilliant, it is true, than the one which had disclosed to me that the work of art is our only means of recapturing the past. And I understood that all these materials for literary work were nothing else than my past life and that they had come to me in the midst of frivolous pleasures, in idleness, through tender affections and through sorrow, and that I had stored them up without foreseeing their final purpose or even their survival.

Only art can stop the flow of time and, as it were, contain it, the whole present and past in one solid form.

What Proust wrote under Bergson's strong influence was repeated in various ways by every major English novelist. Bergson, Proust, and their English contemporaries were using time in much the same way the psychoanalysts were using memories and experiences from the past as indications of present actions. Moreover, Bergson further paralleled evidence from psychology and natural science when he claimed that the intellect in dealing with a certain aspect of reality distorts it in a mechanical direction by remaking it in its own image. To obtain a complete picture of reality, another faculty of the mind—what Bergson called intuition—is necessary. Just as there must be a category which deals with matter, there must be one that can deal with the immaterial. This latter faculty is intuitive, vital, instinctive. Accordingly, Bergson's philosophy helped break the hold of scientific positivism and empiricism which had provided the base for the naturalists, and worked with symbolist doctrine to create the atmosphere for a new literature.

Replacing belief in religion, progress, and materialism with the Oedipus complex (*Sons and Lovers*), with the hunt for a father (*A Portrait, Ulysses, The Waves, To the Lighthouse*), with new gods (*The Rainbow, Women in Love, The Plumed Serpent, Nostromo, Brave New World, Eyeless in Gaza*), with self-analytic heroes and heroines (all the above plus *Victory, Under Western Eyes, Point Counter Point, Antic Hay, Mrs. Dalloway, Howards End, A Passage to India*), the modern novelist strove to recreate a world that he himself had smashed. All these relatively new concepts relate to the peculiar development of the contemporary "hero," in whose eccentricities we have another clear indication of what direction the novel has taken. In Conrad's Axel Heyst, Joyce's Stephen Dedalus and Leopold Bloom, Lawrence's Paul Morel, Huxley's Philip Quarles and Mark Rampion, Virginia Woolf's Mrs. Ramsay, Forster's Mrs. Wilcox, and several others, the "hero(ine)" has undergone changes that require the word itself to appear in quotation marks. He has become, in some instances, trivial, comic, self-conscious, pitted with vices and faults, in short, almost an anti-hero in his failure to achieve stature and in his disdain of the classical virtues. Yet how mature and understanding he seems to us! And the reason he seems sympathetic is that, like us, he has inherited a world which since the Renaissance has disallowed heroes, in fact, has made them ludicrous and melodramatic.

Several of the scientific discoveries of the last century have worked together to remake man's vision of himself, to turn heroes into fallible men. From Darwin's evolutionary theories through Freud to Max Planck and Einstein, the nature of the universe has undergone a number of different interpretations. Darwin upset man's egocentricity and made the individual merely a speck in the historical sweep of biological changes. No longer could man be considered even the highest mammal, but now, merely a transitional figure in an evolutionary process. Further, the new physics, as demonstrated in part by Planck's quantum theory (1900), merely fortified man's new role by shattering cause and effect (the basis of any rational view of the universe) and by emphasizing discontinuity and the seemingly irrational. Modern science, born when Galileo tried to explain *how* things happen rather than accepting Aristotle's explanation of *why* things occur, suddenly found it could no longer explain the "how" with certainty. As scientific horizons broadened, the unseen and the unknown became more significant; the chief mysteries of nature seemed to dwell in realms furthest removed from man imprisoned by his senses. While a theory like Max Planck's computation of the radiant energy given off by a heated body—the bits being measured in what he called *quanta*—tried to explain certain phenomena by mathematical abstraction, it still could give no real explanation of the mechanism of radiation. Nevertheless, his quantum theory suggested a breakup of continuity—the bits or portions, or *quanta*, became in literature the bits of characters, scenes, and life itself. Reality, as science gauged it, was broken into pieces, and all the arts somehow reflected this change in perspective. It became increasingly difficult for a "hero" to control the world when Man suddenly realized that with all his knowledge and equipment he still proceeded by irrational means.

Einstein, recognizing the importance of Planck's quantum theory, postulated that all forms of radiant energy, including light, heat, and x-rays, travel through space in discontinuous *quanta*. No longer was man even sure of light, which he had hitherto taken for granted; now,

Einstein spoke of light particles. These physical theories, both coming at the turn of the century, and coinciding with Freud's most important work, helped further demolish man's complacency by destroying his belief in causality and determinism; the fundamental idea that nature exhibits an inexorable sequence of cause and effect was soon abandoned. The very base of French Naturalism no longer existed, and this fact drove its influence still further from the twentieth-century English novel, leaving the way open for literary theories that encompassed the metaphysical, the irrational, and the unknown.

An even more important result of Einstein's work was that man could no longer "see" objective reality with any clarity; for now, because of the unsureness of his own senses, he distorts reality in the very process of observing it. As man's perceptions of actual phenomena are not reliable, he must recognize that his world is based on a mathematical system which is merely symbolic of things that cannot be visualized or observed.

The former reliance on fixed points of reference which had once utilized man's perceptions was no longer valid when Einstein developed his theory of relativity. All things hitherto seen as fixed and stable were now observed in relation to other things. The important word is relation(ship), in physics as well as in literature, for relation (of objects, scenes, motifs, characters, symbols) describes Virginia Woolf's and James Joyce's world as much as Einstein's. With relationships, both the modern novelist and scientist stopped looking for absolutes, and with this change in point of view, the novelist stood of course on different ground from his predecessors. No longer is a romantic hero possible in which he manipulated a stable world that responded to his forceful will. Now the will itself is under attack. If man's perceptions are too insecure to allow the observation of phenomenon, then man himself is too insecure to claim an important role for himself. Thus, Stephen Dedalus is incomplete, Leopold Bloom lacks manhood, Nostromo is destroyed by pride and greed, Decoud and Heyst perish for trying to escape a menacing world, Mr. Ramsay is merely the thinking half of a man, Septimus and Mrs. Dalloway must together form a single human being, Will Brangwen can find solace only in his cathedrals, not in life, Conrad's Jim must run from his fears, Philip Quarles realizes that he lacks feeling, Paul Morel cannot love Miriam because of his mother's opposition, and so on through the major characters of the twentieth century.

As the quantum theory and the theory of relativity tended to upset many previous beliefs about the nature of the universe, Freud and Jung were delving into man himself and showing new relationships of the adult to his childhood, of modern man to the beginning of culture. Freud, surely more than Planck and Einstein, appealed to the novelists, for several of his theories on sex and psychopathology had always been the commonplaces of literature and were now interpreted by many as literary, not scientific, doctrines. It is striking that the novelists with whom we are concerned did not on the whole absorb Freud's ideas so much as take to an atmosphere in which the development of character and personality had been transformed into something new. Freud's theory of the psyche allowed the imagination to probe areas that reason had once dictated as off bounds for moral scruples. His recognition that below the sane mind there lay a swamp of irrational motives involving sex, parental authority, fixations, repressions—the whole paraphernalia of the unconscious—gave freedom to the literary artist in his search for new ways of describing human behavior. Furthermore, Freud's definition of the psyche in terms of a duality which he termed the Ego and the Id, the Ego as the logical aspect of the mind, the Id as the predominantly irrational unconscious aspect of the mind—in this division Freud created a tension between rational and non-rational motivation which was the very stuff of characterization. Then with Freud's definition of the Super-ego, the moral judgment which holds the Id in rapport with society, the novelist found an idea which had all the suggestivity of a vast symbol that could be projected on several levels at once.

Furthermore, Freud's interpretations of symbols showed that no image or symbol has one meaning alone, for it carries with it at least its opposite in the unconscious or in dreams. In the latter, several images with only single or dual meanings can expand into manifold significance. The literary use of symbols which derived from the nineteenth-century French movement joined here with Freud's examination of the psychological importance of symbols to create new aspects of personality and motivation. Sexual images either from dreams or reality were given psychological significance and thus removed from the cloak of secrecy imposed by the Victorians. Sexual fantasies, as well as new frankness in the discussion of marital problems and the dramatization of repressions and half-hidden wishes, became the stuff of novelists like Lawrence, Huxley, and Joyce. Even in Conrad, Forster, and Virginia Woolf, where sexual themes were less evident, the undercurrents of a new attitude toward sex were forming, although they do not dominate as in Lawrence's *Sons and Lovers*, Huxley's *Antic Hay*, or Joyce's *Ulysses*.

Among Freud's disciples, perhaps the most important is Jung, who denied Freud's interpretation of sex as the basic psychological drive in western culture. Jung's own theory posited the collective unconscious of the race as the repository of its taboos. In this collective unconscious, which is the inheritance of everyone born into the culture, we can discover the origin of neurosis and myth. So modern man is related to primitive man by a common cultural tie. The importance of this tie for literature cannot be overstated, for it allowed still another relationship, this one in time, and permitted the alert novelist to dredge up old myths and reinterpret them in the light of modern experience. These myths, which even though old continue to affect our culture, allow points of historical reference and comparison for the novelist. The use of myth provides related ideas of situation and character and gives the novelist a ready-made framework through which he can comment. The most famous of mythmakers was Joyce, whose *Ulysses*, built upon Homer's *Odyssey*, contains constant parallels to the archetypal epic. Bloom's trip across Dublin is Odysseus's journey home from the Trojan War, and Stephen's unsure wandering through Dublin's streets parallels the wandering of Telemachus in search of his father. The faithful Penelope of Homer is transformed into the lively Molly of Joyce. With wit, irony, parody, and verbal genius, Joyce created a modern *Odyssey*, which speaks for us as much as Homer for his day.

The use of myth was not, of course, limited to Joyce, for the mythological world was also in the minds of many of his contemporaries. New discoveries in Troy, Egypt, and Crete, plus the work of Frazer and Tylor, and several others, had turned modern man to the past to find vestiges of his continuing culture. We see a concern with myth running through Lawrence's novels, particularly in *The Plumed Serpent*, but also in *Women in Love*, in which Birkin and Gudrun find African sculpture to their taste; or in his *The Man Who Died*, in which Jesus is resurrected and converted to life. In Forster, the mythical elements of vitality and animism contrast natural primitive man with desiccated modern Englishmen, especially in *Where Angels Fear to Tread* and *The Longest Journey*. Aldous Huxley, in *Brave New World*, tried to create a myth of modern man in which automation makes man as we know him obsolete. Natural man, in the form of the Savage, is a mythical person upon whom the future world will look with curiosity and distaste. We notice that "naturalistic" in twentieth-century literature refers to natural man, the primitive being of myths, and not to the literary movement in which cause and effect predominated. Novelists like Conrad, Lawrence, and Forster, sickened by the world industrialism had nurtured, turned to creating protagonists who contain the mythical virtues of integrity, unity, and belief in personal values. The new discoveries in myth, science, and psychology turned the modern character in upon himself, for he somehow realizes that survival must come from within.

A striking omission—and evidently a conscious one—on the part of the contemporary English novelist has been his neglect of political issues *per se*. That is not to say that the novels have not been political—the work of Conrad, Lawrence, and Forster, as well as George Orwell and Graham Greene would refute this claim—but rarely political in the sense of party politics, specific issues, even a strong political stand. Not political in the sense of Meredith's *Beauchamp's Career*, George Eliot's *Felix Holt*, or several of Disraeli's novels. Marxism, for example, seems to have been a minor influence indeed on our novelists, with the exception of Orwell. Perhaps one reason for this neglect on the part of a novelist interested in the complexity of life is the realization that a character created according to Marxist standards would be wooden, not lifelike, and that the atmosphere would be naturalistic, not symbolic. Marxism missed the first wave of naturalists, and when it finally came to England it stood little chance of influencing writers who had long since rejected the "scientific" development of characters. Even Huxley, perhaps more interested than any of his contemporaries in the novel of ideas (as opposed to the novel in which ideas are dramatized), in his major novels ignores large political movements in favor of man's condition as a whole. With all the great novels that English writers have produced, there has never been a major one treating political revolution, and the modern novel is no exception. England's political system, with its flexibility and adaptability, has not been conducive to the kind of revolutionary violence common to the French and Russian novel. Moreover, the modern novelist's emphasis on states of feeling rather than states of mind would seem to preclude any systemized political doctrine from figuring large; when a political figure does come along, like the fascist Webley in Huxley's *Point Counter Point*, the author has him killed as part of a larger plan.

The lack of apparent systematization in a carefully planned novel, the contemporary novelist realized, is one way of suggesting the complexity of life. This belief in controlled disorder accounts for the great amount of technical experimentation already indicated, and, accordingly, one finds the novel borrowing devices from other arts, in particular from the motion pictures and from music. From the latter, we find recurring motifs, verbal harmonies, polyphonic development in which separate melodies or themes combine in contrapuntal interweaving, an emphasis on tones, rhythms, et al. From the motion pictures, we find an even more extensive borrowing, for the modern novel and films have developed together, with the latter's plastic freedom allowing for numerous innovations in focusing upon reality. Thus the most important of contemporary innovations, the stream-of-consciousness technique, is closely connected with the motion picture devices of cut-back, dissolve, and montage. In the use of montage, especially, one finds the basic ingredient of the interior monologue: that past and present time can be telescoped into one image that is all *present* at once. The film flashback, moreover, has now become a staple of the novel, and as well the shift in perspective which in films became known as fade-in and fade-out. The close-up, the speed-up, or ralenti, the angle or point of view, among others, are all devices common to both media.

There is little evidence that the borrowing was all on the part of the novel from the films; rather, that the novel, extremely sensitive to all other artistic expressions and the most inclusive of arts, borrowed and loaned devices interchangeably. Thus, cubism, expressionism, even surrealism in art, together with dissonance, broken chords, interrupted development in music, find their counterpart in the novel. Picasso and Braque were coming into their own when Stravinsky's "The Rite of Spring" was first performed in Paris and Joyce was writing A *Portrait*. In 1910, a showing of post-impressionist paintings (of Cézanne, Van Gogh, Picasso, and Matisse) in their first London exhibition meant a break from Impressionism in art; at about the same time, Arnold Schönberg was breaking with Wagner's influence in music and beginning his own studies that resulted in the twelve-tone system. In literature, Conrad was trying to remake various aspects of the novel, Joyce was foreshadowing his revolution in fiction; in poetry, Imagism was readying for its break with nineteenth-century poetry, and T. S. Eliot had written "The Love Song of J. Alfred Prufrock," while William Butler Yeats was beginning to write the kind of poetry that showed a reversal of nineteenth-century diction, tones, and rhythms; meanwhile D. H. Lawrence was drawing the curtain on the Victorian compromise in sex.

All these movements had one thing in common: they show renewed interest in individual experimentation, with the resultant rise in deviations from the "traditional." As much as Impressionism and Naturalism had stressed the environment, Symbolism and Expressionism emphasized the individual. Yet withal the stress on the individual author, the modern novelist felt a distinct need to remove himself from direct relationship with his readers. Accordingly, he tried to gain distance by creating a spokesman or a narrator who gave the author an unseen omniscience. Joyce, following Flaubert, wrote that the "artist, like the God of creation, remains within or behind or beyond or above his handiwork, invisible, refined out of existence, indifferent, paring his fingernails." And Conrad created Marlow, a middle-aged sailor, who could direct and arrange the material of the narrative while Conrad in turn controlled him. The novelist, in brief, arrived at the dramatic by using the dramatist's chief advantage over the novelist: impersonality and objectivity in presenting his materials.

The use of the narrator, which is not new but merely a traditional device moved to new contexts, permitted the author to include much without forgoing form. Like a character in dramatic poetry, the narrator can be inclusive in his range of ideas while still controlled by the author. Moreover, he further made it possible for the author to move the plot forward in terms of situation and scene and not from a personal point of view. In addition, the narrator becomes a chorus-like figure of the world-at-large who both arranges the images the reader should see and adds his comment on what is seen. By bringing to bear as many eyes (*I's!*) as possible upon his narrative, the novelist hoped, literally, to make the reader *see*.

A writer like Conrad, who was unable to get beyond surface realism through a tour de force technique like the stream-of-consciousness, could, through a narrator, convey psychological associations by outside detail. He could, by means of Marlow, create a matrix of physical images which bore in toward the subject while carefully defining and particularizing their effects. He could, further, create different levels of reality, the one between author and narrator, between narrator and other characters, between author and other characters, and, finally, between all these various elements and the reader.

The use of a narrator also brought about a situation dear to the modern novelist—with a spokesman he rarely had to face a climax squarely. A climactic scene could be narrated rather than dramatized; the big scene that in the Victorian novel often became sentimentalized or, worse, melodramatic, could be reported rather than presented. But even if the novelist wished to write the big scene directly, the narrator would become responsible for its tone, and its possible melodrama or sentimentality would in part be his and not the author's. Furthermore, the narrator permitted the novelist to alternate between squarely meeting big scenes or reporting them; this method in itself, while breaking up a certain monotony of narrative, gave the novelist a chance to work on rhythmic repetitions, on recurrences of characters, situations, and themes. In short, the narrator is a freedom-making device for the novelist; it frees him from doing things only one way, from being forced into any situation with a single alternative.

The stream-of-consciousness technique is, in several ways, closely connected to the use of a narrator. For the stream, or interior monologue, becomes a kind of narration at least once removed from the author. When Leopold Bloom, in *Ulysses*, free associates tag ends of information in an interior monologue, the burden of conveying the narrative is, as it were, on him and no longer on Joyce. When Septimus, in *Mrs. Dalloway*, surveys his states of feeling in an interior monologue, he alone, in this way, controls both his own character and the narrative. The narrative becomes the free association of the characters as their personalities evolve. Consequently, Joyce and Virginia Woolf gain distance and objectivity. Using this method, the modern author is the furthest removed from his material in comparison with Thackeray or Trollope, for instance, or with any other of his Victorian predecessors.

The modern novelist, in his attempts to achieve impersonality and objectivity of point of view, conceives of a little world in itself, and unlike the novelist before him he feels that his "little world made cunningly," as John Donne said, must remain intact. Each component, including the use of a different time scheme from that in the world of reality, the emphasis on recurring symbols and images, the self-analyzing character, the central narrator, the verbal by-play, the repetition of themes, characters, and sequences, the attempt to build rhythms entirely out of the materials in the novel, each of these is merely another ingredient in the making of a solid block of experience compact in itself and air-tight.

The major modern English novelists with few exceptions refused to see the novel as a fiction in which the novelist can interfere at will because he assumes the reader to be involved in a novel and not in life. Fielding, for example, could manipulate Tom Jones as he saw fit, for he was manipulating a character of his own making, not one who had the reality of life. Nineteenth-century novelists, like Thackeray, Dickens, Eliot, and Trollope, followed the same reasoning. With the advent of Symbolism, however, the novel became separated much further from life, in the sense that it acquired reasons of its own for existence. When the novel suddenly obtained a life independent of real life, the novelist realized that this independent body must have inner consistency and harmony. With that in mind, he tried to create a novel that was self-intact, all the while drawing upon other disciplines and new areas of knowledge. The inclusion of new material from the social and natural sciences, as well as the desire to keep the novel at least once removed from everyday life, forced the serious novelist to seek new ways of presenting his material. This situation made experimentation a necessity, and thus the modern novel seems "so different, so difficult, and so apart from reality."

The "apartness" is intentional, the "difficulties" those that are met in any original work, and the "differences" a combination of a changing world with a re-emphasis of several traditional ideas. At its best, the modern English novel has its great characters, its great scenes, and its great themes which can compete with those in the greatest novels of the past. Its range includes the finest of comedies as well as the most effective of tragedies. In Joyce, Lawrence, and Conrad, the modern novel has three writers who have already become of great intrinsic and historical importance. And in Forster, Virginia Woolf, and Huxley, the age has produced three novelists whose fiction as a whole just misses greatness, but whose fine individual works are the kind that serve as interstices in every century between the peaks of achievement.

Despite the emphasis on experimentation in the contemporary novel, technique rarely becomes an end in itself. The devices of *Ulysses,* once understood and assimilated, seem only to make that book's great humanity shine forth even more brightly; the time shifts of *Lord Jim* make Jim seem caught in a world that will constantly lash him for his mistakes in the past; the deliquescent manner of *The*

Waves seems to wash personalities against each other so that meanings become merged rather than blurred; the cathedrals and rainbows of *The Rainbow* give profound weight and depth to the lives of the characters; the mysterious caves of *A Passage to India* provide a suitable background for human relationships that will always remain confused by misunderstandings and mixed motives. In each novel, technique allows for a manner of expression, a new way of approaching reality. When the reader realizes that the major contemporary novelists were attempting to be "more real" than reality, then understanding will follow. The novels are there; what they yield is up to the reader

Introduction: SELECTED BIBLIOGRAPHY

ALDRIDGE, JOHN W., ed. *Critiques and Essays on Modern Fiction, 1920–1951.* New York: Ronald Press, 1952.

BEACH, JOSEPH WARREN. *The Twentieth-Century Novel: Studies in Technique.* New York: Appleton-Century-Crofts, 1932.

BROWN, E. K. *Rhythm in the Novel.* Toronto: University of Toronto Press, 1950.

BRUMM, URSULA. "Symbolism and the Novel," *Partisan Review,* xxv (Summer 1958), 329–342.

DAICHES, DAVID. *The Novel and the Modern World.* Chicago: University of Chicago Press, 1939.

FORSTER, E. M. *Aspects of the Novel.* London: Edward Arnold, 1928.

LANGER, SUSANNE K. *Feeling and Form.* New York: Scribner's, 1953.

LUBBOCK, PERCY. *The Craft of Fiction.* New York: Peter Smith, 1947.

MENDILOW, A. A. *Time and the Novel.* London: Peter Nevill, 1952.

O'CONNOR, WILLIAM VAN, ed. *Forms of Modern Fiction.* Minneapolis: University of Minnesota Press, 1948.

POULET, GEORGES. *Studies in Human Time.* Baltimore: Johns Hopkins Press, 1956.

PRITCHETT, V. S. *The Living Novel.* London: Chatto & Windus, 1946.

TINDALL, WILLIAM YORK. *The Literary Symbol.* New York: Columbia University Press, 1955.

TRILLING, LIONEL. "Freud and Literature" and "The Meaning of a Literary Idea," *The Liberal Imagination.* New York: Viking, 1950.

WELLEK, RENÉ and AUSTIN WARREN. *Theory of Literature.* New York: Harcourt, Brace, 1949.

WILSON, EDMUND. *Axel's Castle.* New York: Scribner's, 1931.

Joseph Conrad xx Life

When Stein in *Lord Jim* spoke about the necessity of immersing one-self in the destructive element of life, he was not only pointing the way for the redemption of modern common man but also for that of the modern artist. To plunge into life while endeavoring to interpret it, is the ordeal every serious artist must face, an ordeal that Conrad fully recognized in the Preface to *The Nigger of the "Narcissus."* It is not unusual that the former Polish seaman should have taken litera-ture seriously and conformed to exacting standards, for his entire life had been a preparation for serious trial. His personality was earnest and his nature dogmatic; as his letters testify, he would not tolerate nonsense either in art or life. His serious standards were acquired as a youth; the broad range of his career reflects a man who faced up to reality and immersed himself thoroughly in life.

Conrad's father, Apollo Korzeniowski, was a scholar, an intellectual, a man whose strong principles became translated into revolutionary action, an idealist whose ideas forced him, along with his wife and child, from Poland into exile in Russia. Aside from his political activi-ties, Apollo Korzeniowski had a lively interest in French and English literature, ably translating Victor Hugo, Shakespeare, and Alfred de Vigny into Polish. Five years after Conrad's birth on December 3, 1857, Apollo came to Warsaw to start a literary journal, to be called the *Fortnightly Review.* Ostensibly, Apollo's activities in Warsaw were literary, but his real interests were political, specifically to in-crease resistance to Russian oppression, with the final aim of winning back Polish independence. He helped organize the secret National Committee which met frequently in his own home. But even before the famous 1863 insurrection in Warsaw against Russian rule, he was arrested and condemned to exile. Conrad's mother, the former Evelina Bobrowski, was a well-educated and sensitive woman who fully entered into her husband's interests and requested permission for herself and her child to follow Apollo into exile in Perm, not far from the Ural Mountains. Once in exile, Mme. Korzeniowski, frail, sickly, and poverty-stricken, became steadily weaker and died less than three years later at the age of thirty-four.

Apollo himself was a gloomy and defeated figure; without sufficient money to support himself or the young Joseph, he was wholly dependent upon his brother-in-law, Thaddeus Bobrowski. He retained, however, through all his misfortunes a love of literature. At this time he translated *The Two Gentlemen of Verona* and Victor Hugo's *Travailleurs de la Mer* into Polish. Removed from politics and immersed in literary work, yet broken in health and spirit, Apollo died in Cracow in 1869, only seven years after he had arrived in Warsaw as an active partisan against the Czar. The young Conrad, living in his father's world of lost hope, occupied his lively imagination with books, which were his only companions. Certainly a large part of Conrad's later emphasis on individual responsibility and his own strict self-control can be traced to his lonely childhood.

At eleven, Conrad was enrolled at St. Anne High School in Cracow, where he studied classics and German. By this time, he was familiar with French, in which he became fluent in his later years. From 1870 to 1874, his studies were supervised by a young student of the University of Cracow. It was during these years that Conrad confided to his uncle-guardian, Thaddeus Bobrowski, that he wanted to go to sea. All attempts to dissuade him were futile; no doubt his early love for the sea was a literary love, for in his father's personal library he had read a wide selection of sea and travel books. Conrad was early possessed by the desire to see other countries. There is the now familiar story of his putting his finger on a blank space in a map of Africa and saying, "When I grow up I shall go *there*." The *there* was the Belgian Congo, and Conrad's trip became the basis of "Heart of Darkness."

On October 14, 1874, two months before his seventeenth birthday, Conrad left for Marseilles and a sea career, armed with a few introductions and a small monthly allowance from his reluctant uncle. Shipping out from Marseilles, Conrad voyaged on French ships to the West Indies and to Central and South America; the frail factual basis of *Nostromo* was formed here, and it was on the *Saint-Antoine* heading for South America that he had his first experience with gun-running. While in Marseilles, Conrad met several Royalists, and these meetings led to his smuggling activities on behalf of the Carlist cause, activities which he related in *The Arrow of Gold* (1919). After four years in the French merchant service, four years in which he drifted from one berth to another with no idea of advancement, Conrad shipped out on the English steamer, the *Mavis*, on April 24, 1878, bound for Constantinople.

On the return of the *Mavis* to Lowestoft, Conrad first stepped on English soil, hardly understanding a word of the language. Little past his twentieth birthday, he decided, as he points out in A *Personal Record*, that if he was to be a seaman, he would be an English seaman and no other. It was, he said, "a matter of deliberate choice." After two years, in 1880, he passed his examination for third mate, and subsequently in 1883 and 1886, for mate and master. Two years later—and ten after entering the English merchant service—he had his first command, the *Otago*, from January, 1888, to March, 1889.

Just when Conrad started to write is not clear. But when he began his first novel, *Almayer's Folly*, in 1889, he was still a seaman and not by any means a dedicated writer. Conrad himself said:

> The conception of a planned book was entirely outside my mental range when I sat down to write; the ambition of being an author had never turned up amongst these gracious imaginary existences one creates fondly for oneself at times in the stillness and immobility of a daydream.

It was just after Conrad had begun *Almayer's Folly* that he was made second mate on a Congo steamer (in late 1889), an expedition that became the source for "Heart of Darkness," and perhaps had as much effect on maturing his outlook as the trip to the Sakhalin Islands had on Chekhov's. The Congo voyage, Conrad's biographer believed, turned him from the sea to a literary career. Broken in health by malarial fever but impressed by the desolation and meaninglessness of what he had seen, he continued to write while recuperating.

When his health permitted, he returned to sea on the *Torrens* until mid-1893. It was as chief of the *Torrens* that Conrad first met John Galsworthy, and with this meeting their close friendship began. It was on the same ship that Conrad, on his last voyage, showed the manuscript of *Almayer's Folly* to a young Cantabrigian, W. H. Jacques, who encouraged him to finish the novel. When Conrad left the *Torrens*, he was never to go to sea again, although it was not for lack of trying. *Almayer's Folly*, meanwhile, was finished and submitted **to**

T. Fisher Unwin on July 4, 1894, where Edward Garnett, then a young publisher's reader, was greatly impressed with the manuscript. The novel was accepted, and Conrad, encouraged by Garnett, soon turned to writing another. While the evidence shows that Conrad was trying to obtain a command as late as September, 1898, he nevertheless continued to turn out nearly a volume a year for the next thirteen years.

Conrad's writing life extended for twenty-nine years, from 1895 until his death in 1924; during this time he wrote thirty-one volumes of novels, short stories, essays, and plays, besides many volumes of letters. The novels include: *Almayer's Folly* (1895), *An Outcast of the Islands* (1896), *The Nigger of the "Narcissus"* (1897), *Lord Jim* (1900), *The Inheritors* (1901, with Ford Madox Ford), *Romance* (1903, with Ford), *Nostromo* (1904), *The Secret Agent* (1907), *Under Western Eyes* (1911), *Chance* (1914), *Victory* (1915), *The Shadow Line* (1917), *The Arrow of Gold* (1919), *The Rescue* (1920), *The Rover* (1924), *The Nature of a Crime* (1924, fragment with Ford), *Suspense* (1925, uncompleted at death). The short stories: *Tales of Unrest* (1898), *Youth* (1902, including "Heart of Darkness"), *Typhoon, and Other Stories* (1903), *A Set of Six* (1908), *'Twixt Land and Sea* (1912), *Within the Tides* (1915), *Tales of Hearsay* (1925). Among his important non-fiction are: *The Mirror of the Sea* (1906), *Some Reminiscences* (1912, published also as *A Personal Record*), and *Notes on Life and Letters* (1921). Conrad's letters to Edward Garnett, Richard Curle, and Marguerite Poradowska, as well as those in Jean-Aubry's *Life and Letters*, contain his most significant remarks on art and life.

Even with growing popularity, however, Conrad remained isolated from the principal writers and movements. For a major novelist, his circle of friends, although intelligent and devoted, was curiously limited to those of the old guard, conservative and safe. There were of course some exceptions—H. G. Wells and Henry James among them—but they were never in the circle in the same sense as Edward Garnett, R. B. Cunninghame Graham, John Galsworthy, W. H. Hudson, Hugh Clifford, or Edmund Gosse. Conrad remained almost entirely unaware of Freud's work and the new advances in science, and completely ignorant of Joyce, Lawrence, Woolf, and other modern experimenters in the novel; among contemporary authors of the first rank he knew only Gide and Proust.

Despite his relative isolation, Conrad formulated through his own knowledge of the novel as a potential art form a kind of fiction in which concern with the shape of the novel complemented a strong belief in man's innate dignity and worth. At the beginning of Conrad's literary career, there was, perhaps, little more than force of will and an ability to draw upon all experiences and memories from the past. His great power, like George Eliot's, lay in his ability to fashion strength of will into moral idea; and his life's work was devoted to "seeing" the moral idea from as many aspects as possible, until the idea became, as it were, the thing itself. In his desire to make the reader "see," Conrad placed himself in the main line of modern novelists who dramatize what their predecessors often merely verbalized. And in his ability to saturate his work with moral ideas, he offered his only response to the charges of artistic irresponsibility leveled against the writer dedicated solely to his craft. For Conrad, the ordeal of the sea became the ordeal of art, and his best work is an indication of his devotion to the truth of both.

Joseph Conrad xx *Works*

The major work of Joseph Conrad provides a transition from the best of the Victorian novelists to the best of the moderns. Conrad was that kind of author who seemed, almost unconsciously, to intuit nearly every important development that the novel would take after him. Serious, dedicated to his craft, like Flaubert he turned dissatisfaction with existing forms into new ways of focusing upon reality. He drew his literary methods from writers as disparate as Sterne, Richardson, Dickens, Dostoevsky, Flaubert, and James, among others, and to these he added his own insights and techniques. Although several of the literary devices Conrad used appear in his predecessors, only James had explored the relationship of technique to content as thoroughly as he. His realization that the novel needed new life and his willingness to experiment, together with his defense of the genre as a serious and mature undertaking, gave new dimensions to what he thought was the tired late Victorian form and managed to create a change of atmosphere in the novel.

Judging from Conrad's two earliest novels, *Almayer's Folly* (1895) and *An Outcast of the Islands* (1896), one can see little or no departure from the late Victorian models he was evidently still influenced by at this time. In fact, these two works demonstrate that Conrad was fully occupied with *fin de siècle* mannerisms, tones, and language. The novels, as befitting their background, are ones of decadence and breakdown, pageants of retreat, of dreams, of filmy torpor and fatigue. Conrad's settings in *Almayer* and *An Outcast* are exotic, full of jungle scenes, semi-civilized natives, and violent emotions. These images and attitudes—the basic stuff of his early work—are found later in new settings transformed into the storm images of *The Nigger of the*

"*Narcissus*," the natural description of "Heart of Darkness," *Lord Jim*, and *Nostromo*, the city backgrounds of *The Secret Agent* and *Under Western Eyes*, and the island backdrop of *Victory*. In neither of these two early novels, however, was Conrad able to project misery into tragedy or transform a dramatic scene into a tragic situation.

By the time Conrad came to write the Preface to his third novel, *The Nigger of the "Narcissus"* (1897), he apparently was confident that he was heading in a new direction. Both the Preface and the novel show Conrad's interest in symbolism, in suggestion, in shaping a novel as a tight world of its own. With its action at sea, *The Nigger* allowed Conrad, like Melville before him, to recreate a microcosm of a universal situation, that is, the inarticulate confusion of men of vague convictions when confronted by fear and superstition. Conrad's concern at this time was with the ever-shifting relation between the individual and society, and the role that each must play in conflict with the other. James Wait, the Negro protagonist of the novel, stands as a symbol of the ethical demand that human beings in distress exert upon others, for Wait's predicament upsets the solidarity of the crew and creates a disturbance that can be reconciled only in moral terms. This is somewhat like the situation in *Lord Jim*, reversed though it is in emphasis, in which the crew without any sense of honor or integrity—deeply rooted as it is in merely personal justification—causes and abets Jim's defection from the *Patna*. Wait, in his role of sea-going confidence man, finds his counterpart in the fraudulent Donkin and in the vague fears and susceptibilities of an ignorant and superstitious crew. How Conrad develops this relationship, how the nature of Wait's illusory attraction conflicts with a crew rooted in reality and survival, becomes the theme of the book.

Working in the same vein of the illusory versus the real, Conrad, in "Heart of Darkness," turned to his own travels in the Belgian Congo and wrote what has since become a classic novella in which greed, selfishness, and materialism replace all ethical values. As a study in human degradation and wretchedness, "Heart of Darkness" demonstrates what the terrible consequences of the loss of responsible heart can be in an individual, here in Kurtz, and later in the chief characters in *Lord Jim*, *Nostromo*, *The Secret Agent*, *Under Western Eyes*, *Chance*, and *Victory*. Kurtz's tragedy becomes, in Conrad's world, a universally tragic experience.

This novella, working on the accumulation of images which when grouped all contribute to the main theme of human corruption, also proceeds by means of a series of contrasts: for example, Kurtz vs. Marlow, Kurtz's native "goddess" vs. his English fiancée, and Marlow's and Kurtz's initial idealism vs. the reality of the Congo. Conrad's conception of the material in images seemingly disconnected and tangential and in the constant contrasts of elements allowed him to relate the bare narrative to more general aspects of experience. Therefore, "Heart of Darkness" can be read on several levels at once: the simple narrative of Marlow's journey to the Congo and his experiences there; the psychological level in which Marlow himself matures as he recognizes for the first time real evil in the world; the political level in which Conrad suggests, ironically, how reputations are made and maintained contrary to the facts; the historical level in which imperialism is attacked as a corroding evil that destroys both conquered and conqueror. Finally, we recognize that Conrad has found both a theme and a style that will henceforth penetrate all his major work. Kurtz himself will continue to reappear in various forms, and the theme of moral honesty versus moral corruption will engage Conrad for the next twenty-five years.

LORD JIM: THE RUNAWAY SLAVE

Corruption in its various guises haunts Jim as he runs further and further from his own past. Accordingly, the spine of the novel is formed by the three decisions of increasing intensity that Jim must make, each one showing him as a romantic hero who is a failure. Jim is a youth of excellent motives possessing a mind drenched in ideals, a youth enticed by a vision that constantly eludes him. Unable to make the right decisions at the opportune time, he commits mistakes in judgment and makes hairline decisions dictated by predisposition and by the exigencies of the moment. In this way, Jim progresses through three successive stages, each of which is sharply defined by the necessity of decision.

The first is the training school incident, which in itself conferred neither shame nor dishonor, but did instill a subconscious guilt that with enlarging circumstances in later years proved self-destructive. When Jim first missed his opportunity for heroics—he stands still while others rush to a rescue—he romanticized his vagaries, and then, as Conrad says, "felt angry with the brutal tumult of earth and sky for taking him unawares and checking unfairly a general readiness for narrow escapes. . . . he exulted with fresh certitude in his avidity for adventure and in a sense of many-sided courage."

In Jim's hierarchy of decisions, the second is of course his abandonment of the *Patna* under the influence of the morally degrading ship's company. Jim's dreams of a heroic role slip from him as he moves from a purgatory of indecision into an active vision of hell when he jumps into the lifeboat, that "everlasting deep hole" which means eternal self-castigation.

The terms of Jim's third decision are far removed in time and space from those of the earlier two, but in its circumstances this decision is a natural development. In letting the predatory Brown escape from Patusan, Jim recognizes that a forceful decision cannot be made by an imperfect being and that his tainted past precludes making strictures against even a criminal. "Let us agree," says Brown, "that we are both dead men, and let us talk on that basis, as equals." Conrad comments that through their sparring there ran a "vein of subtle reference to their common blood, an assumption of common experience; a sickening suggestion of common guilt, of secret knowledge. . . ."

This hierarchy of decisions forms the frame of *Lord Jim* and creates an ever-expanding circle of adhesive material. Much of this material is brought together by means of the fugue-like quality of certain scenes, a quality conveyed by dissimilar sequences running parallel in time to each other. Conrad, here, was interested in making traces of past time react upon and combine with present circumstances. As suggested above in the Introduction, Conrad was using time in much the same way psychoanalysts use memories and experiences from the past as indications of present actions.

In *Lord Jim*, some of the narrative difficulties are eased when we recognize that Conrad used seemingly isolated fragments and portions of sequences that in succeeding pages he develops through repetition until the entire sequence finally becomes clear to the reader. This type of narration helps simulate the polyphony of several voices counterpointing each other. For example, once the novel has moved less than half-way into the first part, Conrad, at one point, is expanding five sets of circumstances, none of which has as yet been fully developed:

(1) The frame and its setting: Marlow as he narrates the story and comments upon it to his listeners.

(2) The setting of the initial conversation between Jim and Marlow.

(3) Jim's version of the *Patna* incident.

(4) The gap between the "facts" of the court story and the "real" circumstances on board the *Patna*.

(5) The novelist himself in the background controlling Marlow.

If we compare the chronological sequence of events in one column with the novelist's conception of the sequence in the other, we can see how Conrad tried to tell his story:

The Chronological Order	The Novelist's Order
1. The *Patna* voyage.	7. Jim as water clerk.
2. Hitting the derelict.	1. The *Patna* voyage sketched.
3. Desertion of the *Patna*.	2. Hitting the derelict.
4. Court of inquiry.	4. Court of inquiry.
5. Jim's sense of defeat.	6. Marlow's interference in Jim's
6. Marlow's interference in Jim's	life.
life.	5. Jim's sense of defeat.
7. Jim as water clerk.	3. Desertion of the *Patna*.

Conrad, however, went further than to keep each element in suspension while he worked part by part. Using a sequence of direct juxtaposition of several elements, he placed the initial meeting between Jim and Marlow against the background of a ridiculous assault and battery case in the courtroom. The whole confusion of Jim's case fans out, becoming one of universal misunderstanding, symbolized by his misinterpretation of Marlow's intentions taken together with his mistaking the chance remarks of a bystander—and ever in the background the natives involved in the assault upon a money-lender.

The question of course arises, what did Conrad hope to gain by a narrative that keeps the reader almost constantly off balance and disallows any of the "easiness" common to the nineteenth-century novel? Through varying the ways in which his characters are *seen* by the reader, for example, Conrad hoped to catch their plasticity, their life-in-motion. He wanted to make them visible, fully observed, and this, he felt, could only be effected by making them alive in several ways. To Conrad, "alive" meant that he had to catch the inner flow of personality, and lacking a technique like the stream-of-consciousness, he probed from the outside to strike inward. Thus, dramatically and psychologically, each situation and each character provides a relevant statement about Jim's state of mind and position. More than merely buttressing the story, these characters are molded to the rhythm of the novel; frequently, they assume the narrative function. In this way, we can explain Brierly, Brown, the French officer, the German skipper of the *Patna*, Jewel, Marlow, and Stein.

Brierly's suicide is a way of identification with Jim's failure. Brierly is a successful Jim who recognizes that failure is a condition of life and who destroys himself while still in good fortune, with his ship on course and his log up to point. Marlow realizes that Brierly had looked into himself when faced with Jim's defection and found there "one of those trifles that awaken ideas . . . with which a man . . . finds it impossible to live."

Similarly, Brown's treachery is equated in psychological terms with Jim's defection on the *Patna*; the French officer's sense of honor is Jim's dream now reduced to dust; Jewel's loyalty, as her name implies, is of a solidity and perfection which contrast with Jim's tainted past; the German skipper of the *Patna* is the reality principle at its cruelest, and this is what Jim in the midst of his dreams succumbs to, realizing in action his sub-surface fears and sense of failure.

If the German skipper represents the harsher side of reality, then Marlow himself stands for a gentler but ever staunch sense of reality; his attitude, in its almost dogmatic rejection of romance, is in sharp contrast with Jim's persistent spirit of adventure. Even when struck down by the *Patna* experience, Jim is still able to see it as a chance missed—" 'Ah! what a chance missed!' " Marlow's comment is derisive: " 'Ah, he was an imaginative beggar! . . . With every instant he was penetrating deeper into the impossible world of romantic achievement.' " Whenever Jim dreams of the might-have-been, whenever his imagination recreates his dreams and not the actuality, the ever-realistic Marlow pulls him back almost cruelly, almost sadistically, to his former tragic decision and to the fatal consequences of withdrawal from reality.

If Jim is constantly punished for his withdrawal from reality, it is not surprising that the very center of the book is devoted to that scene of great consequence between Stein and Marlow. Against man's imperfections, a mankind perhaps spawned by an artist who "was a little mad," Stein offers the perfection of nature, particularly the beauty and delicacy displayed by the incomparable butterfly. Then in a statement central to Conrad himself, Stein speculates on the relative merits of the butterfly and man. The butterfly clearly accepts reality, but man "wants to be a saint, and he wants to be a devil"; in short, man sees himself as he can never be. The question, adapting Hamlet's, is how to be; and the answer is to follow the dream which is self-destructive, to submit to what is an eternal condition of man, and in the submission, temporary though it is, lies the only relief, the only salvation.

This doctrine is a recognition that man is limited by his own inferiority in an inexplicable world, a realization that violence and destruction are a concomitant of the will to live, and that the loss of self-protective illusions is the surest way to self-destruction. As Robert Penn Warren pointed out in his fine essay on *Nostromo:* "The last wisdom is for man to realize that though his values are illusions, the illusion is necessary, is infinitely precious, is the work of his human achievement, and is, in the end, his only truth."

Nowhere else has Conrad created a "god" figure like Stein, who can order human destinies through his superior wisdom and infinite capabilities. In his combination of the active and the scholarly, Stein more than any other Conradian character becomes not only a model of what the twentieth century wants, but also a wistful reminder of what the complete man could be. Strong man among Conrad's intellectuals, Stein has abilities the lack of which destroy Decoud (*Nostromo*), Heyst (*Victory*), and Razumov (*Under Western Eyes*), those men of excessive intellect with but jejune illusions.

While surrounding Jim with different narrators and piecing the narrative together as it would happen in real-life experience, Conrad was able to create a central character who *seems* to be more than he really is. Even when, for purposes of examination, we simplify Conrad's narrative technique, we can see how involved method is with matter. For example, the first three chapters are narrated by the omniscient novelist, who in chapter four then shifts to Jim and shortly afterward introduces Marlow as the one who remembers Jim's story. In chapter five, Marlow takes over the narration from the novelist and continues in direct command through chapter thirty-five, about three-quarters of the novel. Chapter thirty-six begins a new narrative method, a letter that Marlow sends two years later in which Jim's affairs are continued. The recipient of the letter—who is introduced by the omniscient novelist—then relates the letter, itself a patchwork of Marlow's observations over a period of time and lacking in real continuity. In chapter thirty-seven, Marlow's letter is presented, and he reveals that his source for his information about Jim comes from someone else, the villain Brown. Marlow's letter proper ends, and his story of what happened now begins in chapter thirty-eight. This narrative, beginning with Marlow's comment that "It all begins . . .

with the man called Brown," continues to the end of the novel with Jim's death and Stein's waving "his hand sadly at his butterflies."

These are the main narrative divisions within the novel, but within each there occur the further complications of several simultaneous events and a ranging back and forth into time past and past perfect, while Jim himself breaks in with comments as reported by Marlow to his audience; so that chapter twenty-five begins with words by Jim and then shifts back and forth between Jim and Marlow and ends with comments by the latter. Five chapters later, Marlow relates the story, what we shall call the present, of two events in the past, both at different times: the assault that Jim made on Sherif Ali's forces and the meeting between Jim and Cornelia that took place before the assault. We have here, then, a present, a present perfect, and a past perfect, all held in suspense at the same moment by Marlow. Then, as this narration continues, Marlow's sources become increasingly fragmentary: Brown, who was mentioned above; Marlow's own experiences; the re-entrance of Stein; a Malay named Tamb' Itam; and the girl Jewel.

A great deal of the later narration is, however, merely cover-up for the relatively simple story of Jim's decline and fall. In the first part of the novel, that relating to the *Patna* episode, the technical complications are effective, while here they seem to exist merely to disguise Jim's shallowness and immaturity. The lack of strong central guide occasions the hollowness and stringiness of the Patusan section. In the *Patna* section, we see so little of Jim that we believe more about him than we actually know of him. Conrad's method of indirect narration keeps us at a distance; and while Marlow himself is not excessively stimulating, the result is an idealized Jim seen almost solely from without. But in Patusan the situation has changed. The method, despite superficial complications, is really simpler, more direct, and our eye is upon Jim. Yet withal the rich language, as well as the evocative scenes of adventure, love, and fidelity, not even the dramatic Jamesian dialogues can dissemble the simple surface reactions of the sailor-boy Jim. We know all when we know a little, and for Conrad to tell more is to go around Jim and not to penetrate further into him. By burdening Jim with so many crucial choices, Conrad weighed down a callow youth with the decisions only a god could make.

Only Stein could have sustained a consistently tragic view, and it is evidently a tragic view that Conrad intended the reader to take. We can judge from Conrad's particular use of natural description in the novel that tragedy awaits Jim. What first looks like an Edenesque setting in Patusan turns out to be an anti-Eden in which the constant struggle in nature sharply underscores the conflict in man's affairs. Natural man—if such a thing existed for Conrad—is often equivalent to savage man or corrupted man who lacks the gentler tones of a moral character. Under natural conditions the will to survive unmasks every desire for decency and propriety. Even the sea, often a source of renewed energy and human solidarity, becomes the background of hate and treachery when man's natural fears are touched.

It is not the sea, however, but the jungle, that primitive repository of stagnation and torpor, which symbolizes man's hopeless struggle to keep afloat in life. The ominous jungle which surrounds Jim is not an earthly Eden; it is, instead, filled with fatal temptations, with the "stumps of felled trees," with flowers destined for "the use of the dead alone," with "smells like that of incense in the house of the dead," with "white coral that shone like a chaplet of bleached skulls," and over all is a silence "as if the earth had been one grave."

The haunting presence of an indifferent or belligerent nature of course further isolates the human aspects of life and suggests tragic dimensions. The displacement of Jim from human society and his effacement in an anti-paradise afford ironical comment on a doomed anti-hero trying to become a tragic hero against a backdrop that would frustrate the efforts of even a god. The unheroic surroundings contrast with Jim's futile quest for respectability and a sense of status. His continual failure to recognize that anonymity is impossible makes his quest lose its rationality; and his self-destructive actions become those of a compulsive neurotic who seeks suffering while hoping that through physical and mental masochism he may efface what reason would tell him is a hopeless situation.

Conrad's attempt at tragedy must, however, fail, for the very terms of Jim's quest preclude a tragic sense, simply because he never knows exactly what he is doing. He acts from the top of his emotions, and the simple view he takes of his plight prevents any countering struggle. To the stimulus of criticism, Jim responds by running. Perhaps our only concrete memory of Jim can paradoxically be his absolute vagueness, the image that Marlow carries of his last sight of Jim:

> He [Jim] was white from head to foot, and remained persistently visible with the stronghold of the night at his back, the sea at his feet, the opportunity by his side—still veiled. What do you say? Was it still veiled? I don't know. For me that white figure in the stillness of coast

and sea seemed to stand at the heart of a vast enigma. The twilight was ebbing fast from the sky above his head, the strip of sand had sunk already under his feet, he himself appeared no bigger than a child—then only a speck, a tiny white speck, that seemed to catch all the light left in a darkened world. . . . And, suddenly, I lost him. . . .

Jim, as we leave him, is a man of self-conceived romance and misplaced imagination who is perforce a failure. Suffering as he does from an excess of imagination—Stein, with his German background, recognizes the type—he resembles that greatly-admired hero of Conrad, Don Quixote. Conrad called Jim a romantic, and perhaps he saw him as Henry James saw Emma Bovary—as of romantic temper and realistic adventures. Jim is clearly in the line of those romantic heroes whose awareness of reality never catches up with the roles they have conceived for themselves.

Stein, conversely, suggests reality, control, forethought. His advice that one must immerse in the destructive element—a loose paraphrase of Novalis' "Most men will not swim before they are able to."—conveys his realization of man's limited powers. *Realization* is perhaps the key word in *Lord Jim*, as much as it is a key to tragedy. But only Stein, not Jim, *realizes*. The latter, because he beats against life without ever recognizing his role, will always consider himself a failure—and tragic heroes are made of other stuff. Stein's presence detracts from Jim's centrality, for the former's multifarious activities—his controlled romanticism, his grasp of reality, for example—allow alternatives to Jim's compulsiveness, and the alternatives, had Jim acted upon them and still failed, would have provided the stuff of real tragedy.

The novel, even if it lacks the tragic sense, still remains, of course, a rich and varied experience. Jim, in his semi-articulate and stumbling way, in his sense of almost complete failure, in his inability to act powerfully and wisely, is a compelling guide to the modern temper; and his frustrated quest for personal salvation in an evil world is Conrad's distressing prophecy for the twentieth century.

NOSTROMO: THE REALITY OF SILVER

Throughout his early fiction, we see Conrad struggling to find an adequate form for his work. The object was to isolate and dramatize, to gain distance between the material and the creator. Marlow, or an equivalent narrator, was important but not sufficient; all explanations of Marlow—his presence for purposes of dramatization, for the collaboration of narrator and listener, for the entrance of the reader into the creative process, or for getting the story started—all these ways of explaining Marlow only define one part of Conrad's method of working. The process of objectivity is more subtle.

When we come to *Nostromo*, we see all the early lessons have been learned. The novel comes to us as the very stuff of human experience, with an intensity of impression that shows Conrad to be, in Henry James's words, "one of the people on whom nothing is lost." Although *Nostromo* may seem in parts to be a hangover from the Victorian novel, Conrad referred to it as a "great fraud" and an "audacious effort," by which he meant to suggest it as an ambitious and daring experiment. As in *Lord Jim*, here too the chronological sequence controls the flow of experience. To cite an example: the flight of the Costaguana ruler, Ribiera, is used as a reference point, first mentioned in Chapter 2; referred to at the end of Chapter 8, in the context of a large cluster of related details; hinted at in Chapter 1, Part 2, with some additional background details; further explained in Chapter 3, Part 3, in Captain Mitchell's narrative. Ribiera's flight is just one of the time pegs on which Conrad suspended the narrative; the ever-present silver mine itself weaves in and out of the narrative and helps to create a distinctive undercurrent of rhythm. Through these reference points, among others, all scrambled in a conscious time sequence, Conrad was able to control the flow of action. These "jumps" in time remove the onus of direct narration from the author, with its possibility of sentimentality, and place it on the reader, who, with varying degrees of difficulty, must reconstruct the action.

The somewhat unorthodox narrative also functions in other ways. Nostromo himself—in this respect like Molière's Tartuffe—is a "constructed" character: that is, one who is seen from outside, created almost apart from his physical being, and then presented in person at the climax of his acts. In *Nostromo*, we hear of the titular character in a fragmentary manner, but we know a great deal about him by the time he assumes central importance. Through an encircling time sequence that shuttles between the novel's present and various shades of the past, Conrad is able to surround his characters with comments and actions which construct, if only partially, their personalities for us.

In another way, the narrative of *Nostromo* exemplifies part of Conrad's own philosophy, for the historical sense—that awareness of history in the making—enters into the very constructive processes of the novel. History is made, Conrad implies, by every person with a point of view, whether verbalized or muted. Each point of view reflects an opinion, and each opinion carries with it action or denial of action. By juxtaposing different points of view in the form of narrators, and by letting each narrator participate in "making" the novel, so to speak, Conrad conveys that confused and irregular sequence of events which we call history. History is what we do as individuals or as nations, and therefore each detail and each character is significant in the chain of events. Conrad, by refracting his material through a series of narrators arranged in different time sequences, has created in *Nostromo* a world that is constantly in flux; and by making his characters act as narrators, he assured himself of a variety of stories whose total effect is always greater than the sum of individual narratives. Some of the narrators include (1) the author as omniscient narrator; (2) Captain Mitchell's early narrative; (3) Decoud in his long letter; (4) Dr. Monygham's reflections; (5) Captain Mitchell's summation of the revolution; (6) Nostromo himself.

Through the omniscient author and the several narrators, the novel —up to and including the saving of the mine—comes to us in retrospect. The beginning of Chapter 5 through the end of Chapter 8, a total of one hundred pages, gives background for the uprising that Conrad has already mentioned in Chapters 3 and 4. As we proceed in Part 2, "The Isabels," the filling in of the past continues until Chapter 7 in which Decoud's long letter picks up another element of the past—first suggested by Ribiera's flight in Chapter 2 of the first part— and brings the narrative into another aspect of the past. Still in past time, the narrative, through a whole series of narrators (Hirsch, who talks to Sotillo, and Dr. Monygham to Mitchell, and then to the reader) finally reaches the reader's present, first introduced in Chapter 3, before twenty pages of the novel had passed.

Then, after a short interval in which the narrative moves ahead, not, however, without interweaving minor flashbacks, the story returns, by Chapter 8 of the third part, to Nostromo's past actions; Chapter 9 of this part goes back to a period before 8, until, midway through, the time sequence of the previous chapter returns. Then the revolution itself is recounted by Captain Mitchell (Chapter 10) in a fragmentary conversation with visiting dignitaries, with a break to allow the omniscient novelist time to relate what has since happened to Nostromo. The novelist, consequently, shifts to Decoud's end before bringing everything up to date. The short section after the revolution, beginning with Chapter 11, is all in the present, and this section, in which Conrad is at his most direct, is, incidentally, the weakest in the novel.

Running as an insistent theme throughout the labyrinths of the twisting narrative is the ever-present silver mine, which provides a focus for the plot and all other major elements of the novel. The silver, in short, provides the same center for *Nostromo* as the ivory for "Heart of Darkness" and Jim's failures in *Lord Jim*. Conrad was himself anxious to point out the significance of silver in a long letter to Ernst Benz, an early admirer and critic of his work:

I will take the liberty to point out that *Nostromo* has never been intended for the hero of the Tale of the Seaboard. Silver is the pivot of the moral and material events, affecting the lives of everybody in the tale. That this was my deliberate purpose there can be no doubt. I struck the first note of my intention in the unusual form which I gave to the title of the First Part, by calling it "The Silver of the Mine," and by telling the story of the enchanted treasure on Azuera, which, strictly speaking, has nothing to do with the rest of the novel. The word "silver" occurs almost at the very beginning of the story proper, and I took care to introduce it in the very last paragraph, which would perhaps have been better without the phrase which contains that key-word.

The dramatis personae of *Nostromo* are many and varied, representing numerous social classes as well as different nations and races (American, English, Spanish, Italian, Jewish), but the nature of each character, no matter what his position, is defined in terms of his reaction to the mine. Early in the novel, Conrad described the mine as a way of life in which "its [the mine's] working must be made a serious and moral success." The mine is central to character and theme, and an analysis of how it attains psychological, moral, and political significance becomes an analysis of nearly every major theme in Conrad's work as a whole. The mine is Conrad's most persistent symbol; pervading the novel from the first chapter to the last paragraph, almost indeed to the last word, it increasingly acquires meanings which themselves enlarge in succeeding circumstances. The mine, godlike in its omniscience, goes on, said Conrad, "as if neither the war nor its consequences could ever affect the ancient Occidental State secluded beyond its high barrier of the Cordillera."

The idea of treasure first enters in the third paragraph in the legend of gringos who perished while searching for "heaps of shining gold." This short account of the disaster presages the central tale of the silver mine. For the mine—from which, as Conrad said in the Preface, "there is no escape in this world"—literally becomes one of the Furies of the world. A testing ground for man's ideals as well as for his ability to handle reality, it is a symbol of progress for Charles Gould, who apart from it would have no existence; it results in loss of family for Mrs. Gould; it creates diversion for Holroyd, the American who backs the enterprise; it provides a way of gaining Antonia Avellanos's love for the disenchanted Martin Decoud and a means to reputation for the swaggering Nostromo; it is ever a source of greed and power for the Central American politicians; and, finally, it becomes, paradoxically, the means of regeneration for Dr. Monygham. The mine is the public symbol of each private failure; as cause and effect, instigator and outcome, it is the symbolic embodiment of personal neuroses.

At its most literal, the mine represents a handy means to personal wealth and materialistic power. Like the ivory in "Heart of Darkness," it partakes of man's selfishness and pays tribute in dubious rewards. As Kurtz had an ivory head, so Gould has a silver heart. Strictly speaking, the silver is metallic, crass, and vulgar, although it can force heroic, even spiritual, responses. Psychologically, the mine reaches into the subconscious of each character. Surrounded by material interests, all except Mrs. Gould have little self-control. While Gould and his cohorts deal with the solidity of the mine and its various compensations, she is concerned with human problems, with feelings that perforce run counter to the mine. It is no accident in the psychological make-up of the novel that she becomes sole repository of Nostromo's admission of greed for the silver. The silver is, in addition, a political and economic force, for its possession is the key to control of Costaguana. Conrad recognized that material wealth meant political power, and that personal ambition could be translated into political terms.

In his relation to the mine, Gould, despite his obvious materialistic interests, is an idealist, while his wife, on the contrary, is a realist. Her anti-materialistic humanity is opposed to Gould's philosophy of "I make use of what I see." Gould naively believed material interests themselves would eventually create stable conditions in which they could thrive and that the result in time would be better justice for all. Psychologically, this belief is a necessity for him, for he would surely be nothing, would have no prop, without his idea. This eagerness for attachment—a typical nineteenth-century identification with progress of a sort—is an eagerness to assert what he considers best in himself and to strip away any encroaching uncertainties. An artist only in his sedulous devotion to his work, Gould possesses an imagination that is as prosaic as the silver itself.

Mrs. Gould, on the contrary, is first in a line of sensitive and feeling twentieth-century women who are the opposites of their materialistic husbands; she foreruns, for example, Mrs. Ramsay (Virginia Woolf's *To the Lighthouse*), Lawrence's Lady Chatterley, Woolf's Mrs. Dalloway, Mrs. Moore (Forster's *A Passage to India*), and Mrs. Wilcox (Forster's *Howards End*), without manifesting their non-intellectual smugness. In her hands, Gould becomes a child; she treats him, Conrad points out, "as if he were a little boy."

Nostromo's reaction to the silver is more complex than Gould's, and therefore more fraught with doubt. For the latter, the mine is both means of existence and way of life; but for Nostromo, the mine is only one of any number of possibilities for building his reputation. Because he is not closely involved with the success or failure of Gould's mission to continue the flow of silver, his goals are quite different and the silver can corrupt him with small inner struggle. Nostromo, with the possible exception of Decoud, is least fixed, least rooted, of all the characters—both float, as it were, beyond the confines of any given situation. Not being dedicated to the mine and its functions, each in his way is more liable to deviation than Gould, Dr. Monygham, Don Jose Avellanos, or Captain Mitchell.

Dr. Monygham's relation to the mine is relatively simple, although he is surely one of Conrad's more interesting minor figures. In his devotion to the mine, Monygham, next to Gould, is perhaps the most selfish; for the only way he can expiate his past is through saving the silver and this by outwitting the piratical Sotillo. His motives remain simple and clear—if he is to survive psychologically, he must relate himself to the effort to save the silver. To Dr. Monygham, the mine is Mrs. Gould; to regain his dignity he must feel accepted by her, and the mine is his only agent. He has the full sense of being, as he admits to himself, the "only one fit for dirty work," but emasculated by his past he sees his weakness recurring in every action. Fully aware of what Conrad calls "the crushing paralyzing sense of human littleness," Monygham recognizes that his attempt to attain psychological stability means participating in the very type of action he disdains. In his reaction to Nostromo's heroics—which he can view only with contempt—Monygham demonstrates his own limitations, the result of his morbid past. What is a means to reputation for Nostromo is a psychological necessity for Monygham.

Decoud is caught by the silver in a situation in which he must write and print what he does not believe, what with his skepticism and intelligence he could not possibly believe. The silver has corrupted his sense of indifference; confounded by the illusion of love, Decoud must play the game of silver. For him, he says, "life is not . . . a moral romance derived from the tradition of a pretty, fairy tale," as it is, for instance, for Charles Gould. The reality of his own situation can cause only banter; the seriousness of the mine is fit sport for his irony. Yet Decoud is caught more firmly perhaps than the others, for unlike Gould, Nostromo, and Dr. Monygham, he cannot hide the actual situation from himself by disguising his true motives and interests. The mine, as *he* knows, is a farce; yet because of Antonia Avellanos he finds himself committed to something he can only scorn. Mocking the idealists and contemptuous of the realists, Decoud must still admit that his actions, like those of the others, are also "clothed in the fair robes of an idea"—his love for Antonia.

Conrad did not only relate each character in *Nostromo* to the silver both psychologically and physically, but he also connected each character to another or to more than one other, with the silver of course never far from the conflicts of each. Through the silver, several of the characters find affinities for each other; in a sense they complement other figures in the novel, forming loose but apparent character doubles. Through this recurrence of similar characters, Conrad was able to create a dimension beyond verbalization. Perhaps it is these rhythms and half hints that caused one critic, Edward Crankshaw, to comment: "Before the hundredth page is reached the reader is aware of infinitely more than he actually knows and is free to watch the psychology of the innumerable characters as they are revealed."

The most important pair of doubles is the complementary Nostromo and Decoud: Decoud, a nihilist, who denies even the value of his own feelings, and Nostromo, an egoist, who denies the existence of others except as their opinions increase his own sense of worth. Nostromo realizes that his finest moment—the moment when he had saved the silver—means nothing to the others; "Betrayed! Betrayed!" he cries and with great loss of confidence admits that "No one cared" about his great deed. Similarly, Decoud, after admitting his devotion to Antonia, cannot believe seriously even in his own being and destroys himself while silently mocking his attachment, exactly as

Nostromo was later to mock his own reputation. As Conrad comments, Decoud in recognizing only intelligence had "erected passions into duties"; in like manner, Nostromo had believed so strongly in his emotions that when he found even they had failed him he was easily corrupted. Feeling the weight of solitude which follows upon dishonesty, Nostromo is engulfed by the same fears that had destroyed Decoud. As much as Decoud, the brilliant boulevardier who, "weighted by the bars of San Tomé silver, disappeared without a trace," Nostromo, the slave of San Tomé silver, "felt the weight as of chains upon his limbs. . . ." The two men, despite their many differences, combine, with the silver never far from either. Disbelief, nihilism, and reputation all fall victim to the voracious silver, which as fast as it draws victims destroys them physically and spiritually.

Even in death, Nostromo and Decoud are brought together through the silver. When old Viola mistakenly shoots Nostromo, the spirit of Decoud still lives in the air, conscious, as it were, that the Italian Capataz should perish in the same spot for almost the same reason. Conrad writes: "The tree under which Martin Decoud spent his last days, beholding life like a succession of senseless images, threw a large blotch of bleak shade upon the grass." Destroyed by the silver, Nostromo joins Decoud, Mrs. Gould, and the hapless businessman, Hirsch, all victims of the power of the mine. Only Dr. Monygham and Gould are benefited by the silver, and they stand alone, straddling the smashed remains of a past which will nurture, Monygham is sure, an even more destructive future. "It'll [the mine will] weigh as heavily, and provoke resentment, bloodshed, and vengeance," says Dr. Monygham, "because the men have grown different." A cynic like Monygham can see the mine's true course, and only a fool like Captain Mitchell can believe that it will be a force for good. In corrupting the "incorruptible Capataz," the silver has shown that its possibilities for contamination are limitless. Victimized by four missing ingots of silver and by a world that is too busy to praise his cleverness in spiriting away the treasure, Nostromo worships at the altar of silver: "And the spirits of good and evil that hover about a forbidden treasure understood well that the silver of San Tomé was provided now with a faithful and lifelong slave." By reducing to nonsense Nostromo's one fixed idea, his reputation, and by forcing Decoud into actions completely contrary to his temperament and design, the silver has turned everything to its own shape. The epitaph for the silver can be no more final than Conrad's epitaph for Decoud:

A victim of the disillusioned weariness which is the retribution meted out to intellectual audacity, the brilliant Don Martin Decoud, weighted by the bars of San Tomé silver, disappeared without a trace, swallowed up in the immense indifference of things.

It has been remarked that Decoud signifies thought and Nostromo action; that when, however, they reverse their roles they ruin themselves. Although this is a partial simplification of their qualities, both characters are evidently incomplete, in the way that Jim and Heyst (*Victory*) are incomplete. Decoud lacks the belief in illusions that maintains Nostromo, destroying himself when he realizes brain is not sufficient; while Nostromo literally destroys himself when he recognizes his illusions are no longer real. After the loss of illusions for both, there follows a quick loss of life—Stein's warning to Marlow is repeated.

Dr. Monygham, on the other hand, is a realist among the illusionists; he understands by mind what Mrs. Gould knows through feeling Sentient, sympathetic, and knowing, she is the Doctor's idea of perfect woman, one who would buttress a man's loneliness and sense of duty with understanding tenderness. Similarly, Monygham's own nature, says Conrad, consisted in "his capacity for passion and in the sensitiveness of his temperament . . . [lacking] the polished callousness of men of the world. . . ." These qualities find appreciation in Mrs. Gould, who becomes sole repository of Dr. Monygham's faith. Isolated by the mine and by her husband's dedication to its success, she is as alone as Monygham, whose past puts him psychologically beyond human companionship. Treading the fringes of lonely lives, they reach across to each other in a moment of common commiseration.

Mrs. Gould's role as comforter affects even Nostromo. When he wants to divulge his deception, it is she whom he wants; the ever-sympathetic woman, "cloaked and monastically hooded over her evening costume," assumes a priestly role in the confessional, and like a priest maintains the secrecy of her oath. When the dying Nostromo says the silver has killed him, she recognizes that it has as well killed her, and her note of compassion takes the form of a similar confession: "I, too, have hated the idea of that silver from the bottom of my heart." Then she adds about the lost silver: "No one misses it now. Let it be lost for ever." Later, while commenting on Nostromo's relationship to Giselle Viola, Mrs. Gould says that as she herself was forgotten by Gould, so too Nostromo would have forgotten the girl for treasure. Across the pitiless and soulless mine, arms reach in condolence and understanding, while many of the characters join psychologically in similar wants and needs.

Even Dr. Monygham and Decoud—otherwise unlike in many ways —meet in their awareness "of the crushing, paralyzing sense of human littleness." But while the Doctor at least believes in Mrs. Gould, Decoud can believe in nothing, not even in his own emotions. On a lesser scale, many of the minor characters play complementary roles; the figure of heroic Viola with his antiquated principles is placed, for example, against "heroic" Gould with his "modern" ideas; the terrified Hirsch in the foreground suggests Monygham's own terror at the hands of Guzman Bento; as a barely suggested double, the charming Decoud is now and then in mind as complement to the priggish Gould.

All these characters, through either partial or complete identification, create the meanings as well as the rhythms of *Nostromo*. But the meanings of this novel, as of every major novel, are numerous. Conrad believed in the far-reaching power of evil, although he also believed that evil, even more than virtue, could not be simplified or explained. If the silver was evil, it also brought prosperity; if Nostromo became corrupt, it was because he lived among self-seekers who lacked courage to probe the motives of their inner convictions; and if Decoud could only banter when inner conviction was needed, it was because he recognized that each conviction contains the seeds of an almost equally convincing counter-conviction. No one is to blame for evil; it is a condition of life, a part of the rhythmic flow which Conrad tried to catch in the novel.

As a political institution, the mine forms a documented allegory of the cyclical rise and fall of a Central American republic. Gould's naive belief that the flow of silver would create a stable economy, one in which resulting prosperity would make possible conditions under which the mine would continue to flourish, comes under serious attack in Conrad's ironic arrangement of material in the latter third of the novel. Not unintentionally, Conrad has the triumph of Sulaco narrated by Captain Mitchell, a dullard whose own accomplishments are a pompous display of the English colonial mind at its worst. In his almost senile report, the success of the silver mine becomes an ironic tale with two sides. The civilization it has brought Sulaco is prosperity tempered with inherent vulgarity which portends an even worse future. Only Dr. Monygham fully understands the cycle of events and foresees what the mine will come to mean; material interests, he says to Mrs. Gould,

> have their law and their justice. But it is founded on expediency, and is inhuman, it is without rectitude, without the continuity and the force that can be found only in moral principles. . . . the time approaches when all that the Gould Concession stands for shall weigh as heavily upon the people as the barbarism, cruelty, and misrule of a few years back.

When Gould dies, as Dr. Monygham realizes, all semblance of moral principle, no matter how righteous and short-sighted it really is, will die with him, and anarchy will once more disrupt Sulaco.

Mitchell's narrative, then, relates the triumph of self-righteous bourgeois mediocrity. In the new Sulaco, Mitchell is official guide, the parvenu Don Juste Lopez is Chief of State (Mitchell calls him "a very generous man . . . a first-rate intellect"), and Hernandez, the ex-bandit, is Minister of War. Sulaco is rapidly being modernized—a café has replaced the sale of wine on streetcorners, while wealthy tourists are increasingly drawn to the American bar. And presiding over all is the local bishop. As a final irony, in claiming that Nostromo was originally his protégé—"The sailor whom I discovered and, I may say, made, sir."—Mitchell wants full recognition for this depressing triumph to fall on himself. Perhaps society at the end of *Nostromo* is preferable to that at the beginning—order has been restored to a lawless land and poverty has been replaced by at least a façade of prosperity. But, as Robert Penn Warren shrewdly commented, materiality can work two ways; it is only a phase and not an end. The sky is still foul at the end of *Nostromo*, and the foulness will without doubt persist.

The San Tomé mine, then, has manifold possibilities which depend upon the point of view of the person involved; the mine gains new aspects each time it appears. In its psychological and political connotations, the mine suggests at least two sides of Conrad's belief in moral principle; it demonstrates that sustained moral principle can work toward bettering man while also containing, paradoxically, the seeds of its own destruction. If *Nostromo* is a view of human destiny at a certain historical moment, then the mine is one of those half-forgotten forces which form society into what it is and help define the individual as well as collective nature of man.

As already suggested, it was Conrad's ability to combine different elements in *Nostromo*—the symbol of the mine and varying character complements, for example—that gives the novel its distinctive rhythm. Working together with the mine and with character is setting, comprising those natural forces which seem to define man's psychology as much as the silver itself. The setting of the novel gives both the limitations and possibilities of Sulaco, of man lost in nature while trying to attain a *modus vivendi* in what he cannot possibly understand and surely cannot control. The great difficulty Conrad had in writing the early pages on Golfo Placido, which extends from Punta Mala to Azuera, and in describing "The Isabels," which rest in the calm of the Gulf, testifies to his concern about this particular setting.

The early passages on the Gulf and "The Isabels," as well as the description of the Cordillera range and the "white head of Higuerota [which] rises majestically upon the blue," are an organic part of the novel; for nature is implacable, and its ever-present ruthlessness helps to define, like the silver, each character it touches. The Gulf provides an appropriate background for Decoud's suicide, Nostromo's deception, Dr. Monygham's near martyrdom, and the collective greed of the local diplomats. In the central scene of the novel, the ever-present and silent Gulf generates an overpowering darkness that swallows the lighter on which Nostromo and Decoud are trying to save the silver. The oppressive darkness fits the spirit of negation in Decoud's own mind, and the stillness of his natural surroundings is a public sign of his inner failure. Its deathly calmness, "like a wall," drives Decoud back into himself, isolates him as much as it has isolated Sulaco from the rest of Costaguana. The blackness of the Gulf is most suitable for this "imaginative materialist," as Conrad calls him, who inexplicably is caught in a situation that demands idealism and selflessness.

Nature conveys the loneliness of the characters, with the mountains on one side and the Gulf on the other crying "Separate" to the area and its inhabitants. Sulaco, like its inhabitants, is truly "distinct and separated," isolated, Conrad writes, "as if within an enormous semi-circular and unroofed temple open to the ocean, with its walls of lofty mountains hung with the mourning draperies of clouds." The bare face of the Cordillera range, "immense and motionless, emerging from the billows of the lower forests like the barren coast of a land of giants," combines with hovering clouds and bands of silent water on the Golfo Placido to reduce man's existence to that of an animal. Against this setting, Nostromo is manifest as part of nature itself, "as natural and free from evil in the moment of waking as a magnificent and unconscious wild beast."

In his brief but evocative description of "The Isabels," the three uninhabited islets opposite the entrance to the harbor of Sulaco, Conrad was able in the first chapter to suggest several of the attitudes that would appear later in their full importance. He wrote:

That last is no more than a foot high, and about seven paces across, a mere flat top of a grey rock which smokes like a hot cinder after a shower, and where no man would care to venture a naked sole before sunset. On the Little Isabel an old ragged palm, with a thick bulging trunk rough with spines, a very witch amongst palm trees, rustles a dismal bunch of dead leaves above the coarse sand. The Great Isabel has a spring of fresh water issuing from the overgrown side of a ravine. Resembling an emerald green wedge of land a mile long, and laid flat upon the sea, it bears two forest trees standing close together, with a wide spread of shade at the foot of their smooth trunks. A ravine extending the whole length of the island is full of bushes; and presenting a deep tangled cleft on the high side spreads itself out on the other into a shallow depression abutting on a small strip of sandy shore.

With this, Conrad introduces the tone of the novel through an indifferent nature whose cruel relentlessness rejects man's persistent efforts to conquer it. The image of the witch-like palm tree rustling its dead leaves above a bare rock foreshadows Decoud's own bare existence on the Great Isabel. The witchery of the tree creates a distinctive and precise image of desolation and forlornness which will recur in different forms throughout the narrative. The ravine on the Great Isabel presents a deep-tangled cleft into which the silver will be secreted, the same ravine that becomes the site of Decoud's desolation and Nostromo's decision to "grow rich very slowly." Already, nature was spreading, so to speak, an opaque curtain between man's eternal yearnings and his pitiable fulfilment.

Conrad used more than the symbolic presence of nature as a means of illuminating his central theme of man's striving, almost futilely, against forces which shatter both the idealist and realist. Even when man decides to follow Stein's advice and immerse himself in the destructive element of life, his aims are frustrated and his lot is painful isolation. Life itself corrupts under any circumstances: that is man's ultimate wisdom. Certain scenes in the novel immediately present themselves in which man's efforts are suddenly reduced to pygmy size even though necessary for his survival. In the description, for example, of the desolate Custom House (Chapter 9, Part 3), deserted except for Hirsch's tortured and twisted body, we have the dismal solitude of a "man struggling with natural forces, alone, far from the eyes of his fellows." The House, a witch of a structure, is full of weird clicks of doors and latches, the rustling of torn papers, and gusts of wind passing under the high roof. Here is the entire desolation of the Sulacan situation, an epitome especially of the mental processes of Decoud, Nostromo, and Dr. Monygham. Hirsch, having died tortured and disregarded, is a reminder to the Doctor of his own fears; while the lonely house emphasizes Nostromo's change of attitude, his realization that he is applauded only because he is needed. Off in the background is the deserted Decoud, who had "lost all belief in the reality of his actions past and to come."

Later in the novel, the lighthouse near the Great Isabel where Nostromo has stored the silver serves an ironic as well as strictly functional purpose. It becomes a symbol of disclosure, lighting up Nostromo's secret fears and his inner disgrace. That Nostromo, who had once lived in the light of the "admiring eyes of men," should now be afraid of light is the ironical position materialism has placed him in. He has now become a self-admitted pariah, outwardly honest, but inwardly marked by the dark of his secret. As a sexual symbol, the white lighthouse—"[which], livid against the background of clouds filling the head of the gulf, bore the lantern red and glowing, like live embers kindled by the fire of the sky"—comments most ironically on Nostromo's choice of Linda, who controls the light, and his rejection of Giselle, whom he really loves. The lighthouse literally and symbolically searches out every detail of Nostromo's corruption, affecting even his choice of a wife and inevitably leading to his death.

These scenes and images—as well as several others—allowed Conrad to dramatize his narrative and to cast new meanings on his subject. *Nostromo* as a finished novel becomes more remarkable when we recognize that Conrad's basic story is relatively simple; and yet by relating people and objects in several combinations, and casting all in a time sequence that in itself suggests further meanings, Conrad was able to write a novel that comes with the fullness of reality realized. As a story, *Nostromo* is concerned with a revolution that takes place in order to control the silver mine; the conflict is between two forces, each drawn by various motives, but neither too dissimilar to the other. Gould, with his idealism, and the pirates, with their rapacity, are further apart in their relative respectability than in their intrinsic aims. Grouped around each are characters of diverging interests, none of whom would by himself command much attention. The colorful natural descriptions, also, would be of isolated interest had not Conrad integrated nature to man and shown the growth and structure of the latter in conjunction with the former. The water of the Gulf, the overhanging and brooding natural surroundings, the mobs that follow either Nostromo or the petty tyrants of Costaguana—all in combination with the silver itself—provide that distinctive rhythm which results from fusion of scene and character. This fusion, revealing itself, as Coleridge wrote in the *Biographia Literaria*, "in the balance or reconcilement of opposite or discordant qualities: of sameness, with difference; of the general with the concrete; the idea with the image; the individual with the representative; the sense of novelty and freshness with old and familiar objects. . . ."—this interrelation of elements is the highest act of the imagination, and it characterizes *Nostromo*. For Conrad transmuted mean elements into gold and realized every possibility in drawing from material in itself of small worth a world of relevant meanings.

UNDER WESTERN EYES: THE DECLINE AND FALL OF A WOULD-BE HERO

A consistent irony runs through Conrad's work commencing with *Nostromo* and continuing through *Victory* (1915). The influence of Flaubert, whose characters have little or no belief in themselves or society, was never stronger and is now supplemented by a fuller recognition of Henry James's use of irony. Typical Jamesian characters, particularly those in his later novels, suffer self-distrust while still maintaining moral belief, and by creating a tension between principles and the ability to live up to them, the novelist has a situation which is pregnant with ironic possibilities. Conrad's works contain a long line of such characters, including Nostromo, Razumov (*Under Western Eyes*), Heyst (*Victory*), Kurtz, Jim, among others. By equating individual moral necessity with the realm of social and political facts, Conrad in this period of his work was dealing with material that is central to man's existence.

If we follow the symbols and motifs from "Heart of Darkness" and *Nostromo* through *The Secret Agent* to "Il Conde" and then on to *Under Western Eyes* and *Victory*, we find Conrad ranging back and forth through the major themes of the twentieth century—colonialism, the condition of European culture, the nature of political man, and the ethical posture of contemporary civilization. He suggests all the tensions of historical and social tragedy in the form of symbolic characters and scenes. The political novel of our time, especially the work of Graham Greene, Arthur Koestler, and George Orwell, is a phenomenon that in fact began with Dostoevsky's and Conrad's insights into the modern political mind. Conrad's way of working, however, was not to make a frontal assault on a particular issue, but to allude to, and suggest through symbols, the generic situation of which a particular issue would be only part. *Under Western Eyes* is just such a work. Its surface is always human, and its dramatic climax is resolved in human terms, but the political meanings are now common coinage in the contemporary intelligence.

Razumov in *Under Western Eyes* tries to pry himself from human solidarity in order to go his own way, a position that inevitably proves self-destructive. Conrad rarely equated self-imposed isolation with independence or individualism. Freedom from others is burdensome, an incubus and not a release, and in most cases it leads to personal catastrophe. Conrad's conception of the individual is, ironically, a person who, once thrown out of society, must recognize the terms of his existence and then try to re-enter or else be overcome by a hostile world. His way of re-entry, in so far as he has a choice, can be through conquest or renunciation. Razumov renounces, and paradoxically this leads to both his destruction and acceptance, in each case by the same people.

This overt theme, however, is surely not the sole importance of *Under Western Eyes*, for Conrad not only pioneered the political detective novel in English, but he also knew how to provide effective psychological drama. *Under Western Eyes* is full of subtle devices which by appearing at nearly every turn in the novel replace a direct narrative line and provide psychological depth for otherwise superficial political and social activity. As in "Heart of Darkness," *Nostromo*, *Lord Jim*, and *The Secret Agent*, Conrad in *Under Western Eyes* attained psychological depth through certain professional touches: the placement of a crucial image, the sudden shift of narrative, the use of a large symbolic scene which draws together various elements of the plot, or simply an ironic comment which cogently suggests another dimension.

By the use of three sources in the construction of *Under Western Eyes*—(1) Razumov's diary, (2) the old teacher of languages, and (3) the omniscient author himself—Conrad was able to integrate numerous time shifts into a semblance of orderly experience. In the ninety-nine pages of the first part of the book, eight distinct shifts are made between Razumov's diary and the language teacher—Razumov as participant and activator in the historical scene, and the language teacher, in turn, commentator and peripheral participant. Through a Marlow-like narrator taken in combination with the old-fashioned device of a diary as a source of information, Conrad achieved time shifts that convey an historical awareness of *how* events happened.

We find in *Under Western Eyes* another attempt at the Tartuffe-like character development of Nostromo, but with this difference: Razumov is presented early, rather than late, in the plot and his precarious position is dramatically defined at the outset. Once the hopelessness of his situation is made clear to him, Razumov disappears from active participation in the novel for nearly two hundred pages. So ends Part One. Conrad then shifts sharply from the Russian setting to Geneva, where Razumov inevitably is to arrive as a counteragent. Before we meet him again, however, Conrad has circled closer and closer *around* his situation, introduced us to the Haldins in Geneva, and created the personalities of that revolutionary world who are first to raise Razumov to great success before dropping him to his doom. Razumov, accordingly, becomes a character created by circumstances. Therefore, despite a group of characters that lacks the variety and range of those in his other major novels, Conrad was able to convey in *Under Western Eyes* a thickness and density of tragic event and an awareness of the complex things of this world which we usually find only in great literature.

The conclusive element in *Under Western Eyes* is perhaps its irony —not the pervading ironic comment of *Nostromo* or *The Secret Agent*—but an irony, rather, that is evoked through the pointed juxtaposition of people and objects, an irony less of word than of scene. One can cite, for instance, the scene (Chapter 4, Part 3) in which Razumov retires to the islet in Geneva guarded by the statue of Rousseau, and while sitting under the enthroned author of *The Social Contract* meditates his position and begins his diary.

For this scene, however, to possess more than momentary interest, the whole unfavorable situation of Razumov must first be examined. When he is taken into Haldin's confidence, his world of security is suddenly shattered, and he must deal nakedly with all the forces he had hitherto chosen to ignore. He becomes a guilty man exposed upon an open craft which is at everyone's mercy, and because of his realization of guilt, a man unable to function for himself. The everyday world is left behind—food, clothes, marriage, the niceties of societal intercourse, even the leisurely and relaxed moments a person intermittently allows himself—all these necessities of sane living are pushed into the background. Razumov recognizes himself as a Sisyphus who, morally speaking, can never escape his burden. Lacking roots and with nothing to fall back upon but himself, he is perforce isolated and introspective. Agonizingly, he feels the necessity of moral support; as Conrad says, "No human being could bear a steady view of moral solitude without going mad." Decoud, Razumov, Renouard ("The Planter of Malata"), and Heyst (*Victory*) to some extent all feel the want of human encouragement and recognize the "naked terror . . . of true loneliness" which destroys the will to live.

Sensing the terror, Razumov, at the very moment of betraying Haldin, feels the need to embrace the revolutionary "in an incredible fellowship of souls," a feeling of hysterical insecurity in which he momentarily wants to embrace the personification of everything he fears, in which he momentarily wants to assume the form and character of another person. As Razumov later points out to Haldin, the latter has family connections to fall back upon, while he, Razumov, has no one; he is just "a man with a mind." He says: " 'I have no domestic tradition. I have nothing to think against. My tradition is historical . . . you [Haldin] come from your province, but all this land is mine—or I have nothing.' " After Haldin leaves, to fall into the police trap, Razumov again identifies with the now equally isolated revolutionary, and in their common rootlessness they become spiritual brothers; "After a moment he [Razumov] thought, 'I am lying here like that man. I wonder if he slept while I was struggling with the blizzard in the streets. No, he did not sleep. But why should I not sleep?' " Razumov truly has nothing but himself; his solitary and laborious existence has been destroyed by Haldin's intervention, and wherever he goes he must go alone. " 'Where to?' " asks Mikulin (end of Part 1), for Razumov, as the State Councillor realizes, has lost his direction in life.

Two hundred pages later, Conrad answers the rhetorical question, and we find Razumov in Geneva sitting under the statue of Rousseau. The irony of the scene on the islet can perhaps be seen now in clearer perspective, for the exiled Russian eventually finds peace only on that isolated islet which is the home of the "exiled" Frenchman. Watched over by this exponent of human freedom, Razumov, alone and morbid in spirit, writes his own diary, a virtual record of conformity, an anti-social contract. The companionship of the two is made even more ironical by the physical parallel: both sit near the bridge looking for possible passers-by; both are ready to greet visitors, Rousseau in honor, Razumov to dispel suspicion. The Russian student has found the perfect place to write his diary, to explain his own desolation while sitting in the loneliness of this small piece of land as the current breaks against the corner of the islet. All his hopes and dreams are centered here—" 'Extraordinary occupation I am giving myself up to,' he murmured." Like Decoud, his brother in gloom and wretchedness on the Great Isabel, Razumov is cut off from all human intercourse; his only companion is a bronze statue, and his only concern is himself and his own safety. After hours of introspection, he finally leaves the island, confident that "there is no longer anything in the way of [his] being completely accepted." Later that night he confesses to the revolutionaries and is hopelessly crippled for life.

Why should Conrad, one may ask, have chosen Rousseau as a companion for Razumov? Surely, the choice was not fortuitous nor solely to impart historical depth to the novel. The reason, we may speculate, was more intimate, was posed more in terms of irony and feeling than for reasons of historical or philosophical magnitude. Conrad was, as he always claimed, a writer of feeling, interested more in colors and tones than in strictly intellectual appeal. Razumov, on the other hand, has been a faithful believer in the intellectual life and has always tried to regulate his activities in accordance with a strict logic of profit and loss. Now in his decline, when intellectuality, as he realizes, cannot even begin to sustain him, he turns to the image of Rousseau, that lifelong exponent of the emotional and the sentimental, and within his shadow finds temporary peace. The spirit of Rousseau, manifest in the bronze statue, spurs Razumov to conduct himself with other than intellectual assumptions. Once Razumov recognizes that a pact with logic is a pact with the devil, he becomes spiritually cleansed, and his confessions, first to Miss Haldin and then to the revolutionaries, are the fruits of his conversion.

The scene on the islet, meaningful as it is, does not, however, exist in isolation, for Conrad worked through reduplicating situations; and this present scene between Razumov and Rousseau harks back to an earlier one that related Razumov to another statue, and more directly to Haldin himself. In that earlier scene, Razumov has gone to see his patron, the Prince, and has told him that Haldin is hiding secretly in

his room. The two then go to the General's palace, one corner of
which is filled by a bronze on a pedestal, a quarter-life-size statue of a
running adolescent figure, Spontini's "Flight of Youth." As the Prince
comments upon its lines, Razumov stares semi-hysterically at the
statue, transfixed by its resemblance to the "running adolescent"
Haldin, now in his room. Conrad writes: "He [Razumov] was worried
by a sensation resembling the gnawing of hunger." When Razumov
finally returns to his own room, he sees Haldin, "already at the door,
tall and straight as an arrow, with his pale face and hand raised
attentively, [who] might have posed for the statue of a daring youth
listening to an inner voice." When Haldin becomes identified with
the "Flight of Youth," he is forever fixed in Razumov's mind as a
personal Fury that can never be exorcised, a Fury that bedevils him
until his repenting confession before Miss Haldin.

The recurring scenes of the statues bring together in sharper identification Razumov and Haldin themselves and through this acute
psychological doubling enrich the narrative. The revolutionary Haldin
initially enters Razumov's life at the moment the latter has decided
to enter an essay contest, the psychological moment when he is ready
to strike for fame. Thus Razumov is even more than usually interested in self, while Haldin, on the contrary, has just committed his
most selfless act for the revolutionary cause. Each one, at first meeting, has been pushed to the limits of his particular personality; yet
such is their reaction upon each other that they approach similar
psychological conditions. In a moment of desperation, Razumov is
tempted to embrace his opposite, but instead embraces the police, as
logic tells him to do. Then he almost at once recognizes that Haldin
is sincere and that the police and the General are despicable—he
senses that Haldin's sympathies should have been his. He realizes that
life without happiness is impossible, and that his own way leads not
to personal happiness but only to a tainted success. When he suspects
that Haldin, in his way of life, was happy, he reaches to him as to his
double. Razumov's logical program of "History not Theory, Patriotism
not Internationalism, Evolution not Revolution, Direction not Destruction, Unity not Disruption" fulfills only the public and not the
private man. From Razumov's initial meeting with Haldin until his
confession in Geneva, he acts always in the shadow of Haldin.

His betrayal of his fellow student destroys himself rather than
the revolutionary, for Razumov's existence is never his own henceforth. He exists only because of the memory of Haldin, only because

Haldin exists for the people in Geneva. Rather than gaining self, Razumov has completely lost whatever personality he once had. He still has no life of his own; once an exile in his own country with only an historical tradition to look to, now he has forfeited even that prop. Completely rootless, completely exiled from the niceties of life, he must assume Haldin's family as his own. He is an extension, a physical corollary of Haldin's spirit and idealism. As he eventually comes to realize, *he* is the victim, not Haldin; the great Cosmic Joke, as Conrad called man's destiny, had been using him as its butt. In betraying Haldin, as he suggests himself in his confession to Miss Haldin, he has most basely betrayed himself. Conrad's juxtaposition of Haldin and Razumov, first through the recurrence of the statues and then as spiritual brothers in conflict, gives thickness to the novel through incidents and characters that recall antecedents from other contexts. This is a key part of Conrad's novelistic art.

In still another way, Razumov is doubled by the hapless Tekla, whose existence in isolation parallels his. Her only use is to help others, and still she is shunned; a virtual pariah, she says: "No one talks to me, no one writes to me. . . . I have no use for a name. . . ." Earlier in her life she had nursed another crushed and tortured spirit, a revolutionary, Andrei, who during a beating had let out some information. Only Tekla would assist Andrei, as only Tekla would take care of the crippled Razumov after his confession. Nameless, sexless, treated like a beast, Tekla is Razumov's fate; in her idiotic slavishness, she becomes the sole means for survival for this ex-student with intellectual pretensions.

Closed in by Haldin on one side and by Tekla on a second, Razumov is still far from being defined. There remains a third side, the drunken driver, Ziemianitch, who is incapable of action when he is most needed and who commits suicide, it is thought, because of inconsolable remorse for having failed Haldin. Razumov, who likewise is incapable of an audacious decision, believes that Russia must decide between two basic types: the Ziemianitches, drunken and unable to perform their duties, and the Haldins, who have the dream-intoxication of the idealist and are unable, in Razmuov's view, to perceive the true character of either men or the world. Razumov, ironically, flatters himself that he falls into neither category. But there is a third category which Razumov cannot, fails to, or does not want to see—that is, his own fluctuating and indeterminate position. In his way similar to all three—a failure like Ziemianitch, a nameless and homeless cipher like Tekla, and an idealist like Haldin—Razumov fits neatly into no category and consequently must forfeit any hope for personal status. In the eyes of society, a Haldin, a Ziemianitch, even a Tekla, have status of a sort, no matter how low; but Razumov is a nonentity because he is unidentifiable. His confessions to Miss Haldin and to the revolutionaries, when he finds peace is unobtainable, are, then, ways of identifying with Haldin and with the drunken sled driver as victims. For in this world, the ex-student realizes, even the victims are a class with status. To attain this is, for Razumov, a way of success.

In discussing Conrad's method in *Under Western Eyes*, it is important to remember his injunction in the Author's Note written in 1920. He said: ". . . [it is] my primary conviction that truth alone is the justification of any fiction which makes the least claim to the quality of art. . . . I have never been called before to a greater effort of detachment: detachment from all passions, prejudices and even from personal memories." He said his chief problem was to gain a view of the characters as they appeared to the western eyes of the old language teacher. The teacher himself, a Marlow-like character who remains static during the course of the novel, is useful as chorus, as confidant to Miss Haldin, and, most of all, as a means of unfolding the narrative.

The narrative, without possessing the complicated chronology of *Nostromo* or *Chance*, or even *Lord Jim*, is unfolded amidst what we now identify as Conrad's typical involutions of time. Conrad perhaps tried to construct the plot entirely on Razumov's personal diary and the narrative of the language teacher, but certain scenes do not fit easily into either and must be ascribed to the author's own direction of the novel. But by interchanging all three possible means of information, Conrad was evidently able to juggle the narrative to his artistic satisfaction. He was chiefly concerned with providing ready and plausible sources for his information: the confession scene, for example, is reported by Laspara, one of the revolutionaries present, and it is he, Conrad is careful to point out, who originally chronicled Razumov's startling move. The full story of Razumov's confession, however, is later told to the narrator by Sophia Antonovna, who had heard it from Razumov himself; the rest of the narrator's information comes from the diary.

By using Razumov's diary to provide the principal facts of the story, Conrad was of course employing a device as old as the novel itself.

Earlier, in *Nostromo*, he had used Decoud's long letter to his sister to bolster the narrative at a crucial point, and later, in *Chance*, he was to throw together all the traditional devices of the novel—Conrad evidently did not forsake a novelistic trick solely because of its traditional utility.

By casting the narrative of *Under Western Eyes* in a somewhat involved time sequence, Conrad brought freshness to well-worn material and conveyed an irony of form and content. By ending Part 1 with the sardonic question, " 'Where to?' " and then shifting to Geneva to sketch the group that is waiting for Razumov as Haldin's friend, Conrad created the situation neatly and tersely. A technical comment like this informs a scene that most previous novelists, Flaubert excepted, would have verbalized to their own detriment.

Another, and more significant, example of technique working with content comes toward the end of Part 3, when Razumov is sitting in anxiety and meditation on the islet containing Rousseau's statue. Having placed Razumov on the islet, Conrad suddenly shifts to his motives for coming to Geneva and for the first time recreates his plight immediately after Haldin's capture and execution. The ironic juxtaposition of the Geneva location with the agent heightens the absurdity of his position and the absurdity of all people involved in conscious or unconscious duplicity. Everyone literally becomes a fool: Mikulin with his short-sighted wisdom, Haldin with his savage energy, Razumov's princely patron with his aristocratic complacency, the red-nosed student who is willing to starve for a misconceived ideal, the playboy Kirylo who is anxious to steal from his own father to aid the revolutionary cause—all become less than human in Razumov's eyes, all become ridiculous buffoons who are "always dazzled by the base glitter of mixed motives." The biggest fool of all is of course Razumov himself, who must play out the game with deadly seriousness, while recognizing, as he communes with Rousseau, that he is dealing with dangling puppets in matters of life and death. This is the stuff of Conrad's irony, and it is attained here succinctly through a structural framework.

Structure, however, can break down even in major novels, and any discussion of the narrative in *Under Western Eyes* inevitably brings one to the climax and then to the eleven-page coda which completes the novel. Leading up to this coda is a series of episodic events that comprise half of the novel although they last only one day. The events themselves are in the form of a number of linked scenes between

Razumov and several individuals, broken only by the episode on the Rousseau islet and the short flashback to Russia. Yet the nature of these episodes caused Conrad to make a number of false moves which partially reduced the seriousness of the novel, for the ending lacks proportion and fails to make sense dramatically. After the close of the action proper—that is, after Razumov's confession to the revolutionaries—ten distinct fragments of information are presented that account for everyone while tying together all loose ends.

(1) Miss Haldin is to return to Russia.

(2) The faithful Tekla cares for Razumov in a hospital.

(3) Miss Haldin makes a farewell speech to the language teacher, who has since received Razumov's diary in the mail, a speech full of love and forgiveness in which she hopes some concord will eventually spring from the earth soaked in blood and struggle and watered by tears.

(4) Sophia Antonovna, an ardent revolutionary, has made a secret excursion into Russia and has seen Miss Haldin.

(5) Sophia has seen Razumov also in a small town in Russia.

(6) She mentions that some of the revolutionaries always visit Razumov when passing through his area.

(7) Sophia admits that Razumov was "safe" when he made his confession, and then praises his character for recognizing his own ignominy.

(8) She informs the language teacher that Nikita, the crippler of Razumov, was also a police spy who killed in both camps.

(9) She tells of Councillor Mikulin's meeting with Peter Ivanovitch, the spiritual adviser of the Geneva revolutionaries, in a railway carriage in Germany, a meeting in which Mikulin hints about the true nature of Nikita's activity.

(10) And Sophia closes by telling of Peter Ivanovitch's marriage to a peasant girl, and remarks that both are now living in Russia apparently under the eyes of the police.

Many of these events are incredible if the story is to maintain its artistic realism. That Sophia Antonovna, an ardent revolutionary, and her comrades would visit the counter-agent Razumov after he has admitted betraying Haldin and spying on them, is, in the sequence of the novel, impossible to believe. When she goes on to praise Razumov's character in glowing terms, she destroys the illusion of the revolutionaries as a serious group and reduces them to ridiculous actors in a make-believe drama. If Conrad has succeeded in making his revolutionaries seem ridiculous, then Razumov's feelings of guilt, along with his dramatic self-effacement in their presence, all become meaningless. If they are contemptible, one may ask, how can they be Haldin's heritage? If we do grant, nevertheless, that the revolutionaries have, up to the present point, stayed just this side of sanity, then we can see that in this hasty summation they and their activities become nonsensical. For it is incredible that in the meeting between Mikulin and Peter Ivanovitch the former should divulge Nikita's true identity. This makes a farce of Razumov's inner tensions as he fluctuates between Mikulin, who represents Russian power, and Peter Ivanovitch, who is the revolutionary guide. Then to be told further that Peter Ivanovitch is now living in Russia, is to be outraged by what Conrad had done to the novel. The latter part of the story, by introducing factors outside the realm of the possible, clearly works to the loss of dramatic intensity in the entire book.

One could perhaps claim that Conrad's political prejudices—his inability to see anarchy and revolution at their strength—invalidated the dramatic denouement in which Razumov and the reader must take the revolutionary world seriously. The faultiness of the latter part of the novel, however, would seem not to be a result of Conrad's political prejudices but an aesthetic flaw in which he seriously misjudged the true climax of the story. If Razumov's confession to Miss Haldin and *not* to the revolutionaries is seen as the dramatic climax, then all the later business at Laspara's house becomes superfluous. It is Miss Haldin who causes Razumov's confession; his love for her and his feeling of guilt toward the revolutionaries leads to his inner conflict. The most telling passages in the novel are those in which Razumov's personal struggle engages us, and the least convincing are those concerning the conspirators. Conrad had always disdained both the ability and the desire to create a realistic revolutionary world, and if we take him at his word then the personal elements in the novel must remain paramount.

But even so, the conspirators, while obviously neither heroic nor savory, can be granted some credibility. In their lack of organization and in their mixed motives, they seem the very type that Razumov could efficiently deceive. Give them efficiency—for instance, the organization of a modern bureaucratic spy system—and Razumov's dissembling would have been impossible. Their pigheaded egoism and lack of cohesiveness make plausible Razumov's movement among them. The looseness of their activity would also seem to bolster the speculation that Conrad beyond a token effort never tried to develop their role in the novel. The conspirators are sufficient, nevertheless, as background for Razumov's conflict with regard to Miss Haldin; it is only when Conrad tried to give importance to their hold upon Razumov that he went wrong aesthetically, and showed that as a political writer he was not Dostoevsky's peer.

After Razumov's confession to Miss Haldin, even a more cogent ending could not have retrieved the novel aesthetically, for Razumov's devotion is clearly to her and through her love he realizes he must spiritually cleanse himself; only then can he be worthy of her and only then can he gain forgiveness. Not unlike Raskolnikov in *Crime and Punishment*, who finds that his crime is doubly abhorrent when faced by Sonya's love, Razumov recognizes his own impurity confronted by Miss Haldin's trust. Through love and trust, Razumov attains self-knowledge and realizes that in betraying Haldin he has most basely betrayed himself. His contempt for others, a sense of scorn which now extends even to himself, has become a viper in his soul which can be exorcised only by confession. After Razumov recognizes this point and abases himself before Miss Haldin, the rest is explanatory and not dramatic necessity. When Conrad failed to develop this change in Razumov as the *sole* climax of the plot, as *the* psychological inevitability of Razumov's story, then he committed many grievous errors aesthetically, the worst of which is the summary.

From Conrad's failure to conceive the story along its own inevitable lines, there ensue many awkward and obvious touches. All these defects, significantly, are connected with Razumov's relation to the conspirators; none relates to his feeling for Miss Haldin. For example, the storm symbolism of *Under Western Eyes* occurs at two distinct times, both of which are crucial in Razumov's development: initially, during the snow storm in Russia, he decides to betray Haldin, and later, during the rain storm in Geneva, he decides to confess. These acts are the twin nodes of Razumov's behavior, and both are carried out to the violent accompaniment of the elements. Yet the second is that kind of evident device which adds little to the novel and what is more likely an affront to the serious reader. As Razumov's resolution to confess becomes stronger, the rain increases in intensity; as the storm cleanses him physically, so his confession is to cleanse him spiritually; as he nears Laspara's house where the revolutionaries are meeting, a single clap of thunder heralds his arrival; and after he is deafened by Nikita and thrown into the street, the violence of the outer world can no longer touch him—his confession has truly led to serenity of mind and spirit. As a psychological comment, the storm is senseless, for Razumov's own conflict must be powerful enough by now to give his decision sufficient thrust of its own, and as a physical medium of expression, the storm is more melodramatic than dramatic.

Another weak attempt at the obvious parallelism of situations concerns the stoppage of a watch. When Haldin leaves Razumov's room to go to his doom, the latter's watch stops at midnight; time literally stops for Razumov at this point. It is at midnight in Geneva, then, that he goes forth to confess, to make his absolution an exact duplication of Haldin's martyrdom. Once again, Conrad seemed afraid to let Razumov's conflict speak for itself without these unnecessary decorations which inevitably cheapen a novel filled with great psychological insights.

The ending itself, as suggested above, is a concomitant of this need to "dress up" the novel, to give completion to the various personages introduced in the course of the story. By forcing Razumov into a second confession, a clear breach of the dramatic inevitability of the plot, Conrad flawed the book and forced himself into a succession of false steps. The incredible last eleven pages have almost nothing to do with Razumov; if he is the central figure of the book, these pages are evidently superfluous. So much of *Under Western Eyes* is powerful and compelling, intuitively driving to the heart of serious moral problems, that one is dismayed to see Conrad frustrating the dramatic force of his theme with irrelevances and encumbrances. This was his way, however, in several of his major novels, and when we come to *Victory* we are faced by a similar aesthetic defect.

The years from 1908 to 1911 were a period of great activity for Conrad. Having finished *Some Reminiscences*, an autobiographical memoir, he returned to work on *Under Western Eyes*, while also writing "The Secret Sharer" and correcting proofs of the French translation of *The Nigger of the "Narcissus."* He had also been holding *Chance* in abeyance (since 1906) and about five months after finishing *Under Western Eyes*, he sat down to modify and conclude that novel, which began to appear in the early part of 1912. During the summer of 1910, while still busy with *Chance*, he wrote "A Smile of Fortune" and shortly afterward, "Freya of the Seven Isles." These two stories, along with "The Secret Sharer," appeared in the volume *'Twixt Land and Sea*, which was published in 1912.

Of these stories, only "The Secret Sharer" need command our attention. "The Secret Sharer," though surely not so profound and far-reaching as "Heart of Darkness," is for several reasons one of Conrad's major stories. Writing to Edward Garnett, Conrad revealed his feelings about the tale:

> I dare say Freya is pretty rotten. On the other hand "The Secret Sharer," between you and me, is *it*. Eh? Every word fits and there's not a single uncertain note. Luck my boy. Pure luck. I knew you would spot the thing at sight. But I repeat: mere luck.

"The Secret Sharer" deals principally and simply with the theme of apprenticeship-to-life, which is the same theme of growing up and maturing that Conrad handled from "Youth" through *Lord Jim*, *Under Western Eyes*, *Chance*, *The Shadow Line*, and *The Arrow of Gold*. Therefore, the recent excessive emphasis on the psychological phenomenon of the alter ego belabors what is surely the most obvious and least important part of the story. If Conrad stressed any one thing, he stressed the resemblance, both physically and psychologically, between the Captain and the fugitive, Leggatt. The constant parallel descriptions of the two men, the use of doubles, doubling, second half, secret self, other self, and so on, are emphasized so that Conrad's point cannot possibly be lost.

"The Secret Sharer," once this aspect has been noted, is the other side of *Under Western Eyes*: the Captain is a Razumov who does not betray his trust, and Leggatt is a Haldin who escapes his oppressors. The two works taken together pose a double question and show the consequences leading from both answers: what happens when you betray a trust?, and what happens when under duress you remain true to your secret? It is the Captain's recognition of these points that sustains the dramatic interest of the story.

Morton D. Zabel, in his well-known essay "Joseph Conrad: Chance and Recognition," remarked that the crisis in every one of Conrad's novels and stories arrives when by accident, decision, or error a man finds himself abruptly committed to his destiny. As with Razumov and Lord Jim, this recognition occurs here through a series of steps: isolation of the character from society; his recognition of his situation in a hostile world; and then, once self-knowledge is attained, his way of either solving or succumbing to his problem. This is also the problem of the artist; and Conrad through his particular way of developing "The Secret Sharer" was able to relate the psychological and moral contradictions in human nature to the ambivalence of reality as art embodies it, and finally to a searching analysis of value itself. Commensurate with this search for value in life, another way of looking at "Heart of Darkness" suggests itself, with "The Secret Sharer" also in mind: the journey of Marlow-Conrad into the Congo is a means of gaining self-knowledge in which the crucial experience is a process of maturation into both adulthood and artistry; once the journey into this turmoil of experience has been resolved, the survivor is able to proceed to live and create. The experiences of Marlow-Conrad in the Congo, together with the Captain's experience on his ship, are forms of initiation which all must undergo, but which only the true artist in life or fiction can successfully sustain.

Self-knowledge is as much a key to survival as it is to artistic creation; and self-knowledge is one of the chief ingredients in the apprenticeship novel. Jim's tragedy is that he unconsciously continues to romanticize a situation that can be alleviated only by a stauncher view of reality. As a successful Jim, the Captain in "The Secret Sharer" is faced by the stern materials of his salvation, disguised though they are, and is courageous enough to act on his problem once he has intuitively formulated its substance.

This story, then, becomes a microcosm of Conrad's major themes; but for all its suggestiveness, it is, paradoxically, one of his most straight-forward and obvious works. Its narrative is a model of clarity. In giving the terms of initiation into maturity and/or art, Conrad was travelling very familiar and sure ground. His only fault was in making every point a stated point and every psychological-ethical commentary a labored verbal explanation. When Conrad, getting away from the obviously good story he had to tell, forced the obvious physical parallels between the two men, the narrative often loses its thrust in a welter of amateur behaviorism.

Although "The Secret Sharer" does not have the cosmic significance of "Heart of Darkness," *Nostromo*, or even *Lord Jim*, perhaps because its surface narrative *is* its entire significance, its import resembles the others, for it is concerned with the arrival of the Captain at a degree of maturity in which he gains self-respect and confidence. As an initiate, the Captain has the recognizable qualities of Conrad's other isolated individuals who must demonstrate responsibility in the face of challenge. As a stranger to his ship as well as to himself, he is insecure and untried. But he is a realist, and therefore he can recognize the challenge when it comes. In order to dramatize the demand that is made upon the Captain, an analogy was necessary, and it is here that Conrad introduces the Captain's psychological double. If the symbol of threat is a fugitive (Leggatt) who has killed, then a similar "fugitive" quality must be found in the Captain. Conrad quickly establishes the Captain's insecurity as his strangeness on board ship (the crew had been together for eighteen months or so), his youth (second youngest aboard), and, most of all, his desire to be faithful to an ideal conception of his personality. Clearly, then, like the knights of old, he must go through an ordeal. His ordeal is simply to protect Leggatt, and this forms the narrative of the story. As doubles in secrecy, they are of common size, common origin, common age, and even wear common clothes. This close identity between the two was of course necessary for realism, for without it the Captain's attachment to Leggatt, except perhaps on some sexual basis, would contain no substantiation. But once this rapport is clear, then the two become interchangeable, and the success of one depends upon the other. In their relationship, Conrad shows his grasp of the psychology of guilt, of man's secret self, of the dark elements in man's character, although his insights here are not to be compared with those in his major novels.

In the connection between the two men, one point deserves further comment: the meaning attached to the floppy white hat which the Captain almost desperately thrusts upon Leggatt. Conrad writes: "A sudden thought struck me [the Captain]. . . . I snatched off my floppy hat and tried hurriedly in the dark to ram it on my other self [Leggatt]." The hat is given fortuitously, and yet it is this very object which provides the marker that saves the ship from grounding. If the Captain's entire previous efforts were to have been wasted without the last-minute gift of the hat and if his daring attempt to meet a personal challenge was all in vain unless the hat had found Leggatt's head in the dark, what then is Conrad's point? Seen in this light, the meaning of the story can go many ways: is it that personal courage means relatively little in a world in which chance rules heavily, and that to meet a challenge successfully one must combine personal fortitude with cosmic luck? or is it Conrad's point that in giving the hat, the Captain was really following a logical turn of mind derived from his original decision to hide Leggatt? If the latter, then the fortuitous giving of the hat only *seems* an act of chance, but is indeed an integral part of the Captain's complete identification with and giving of himself to Leggatt. These two possibilities, while not necessarily opposing each other, become the chief ambiguity of the story and lead directly into Conrad's last major novel, *Victory* (1915).

VICTORY: HEYST AND THE OTHER WORLD

With *Nostromo* and *Victory*, Conrad must stand or fall as a major novelist, although the reader may surely not react to both with equal fervor. While *Nostromo* for many years did not receive its just critical praise, *Victory* was from the beginning one of the critics' favorites, but rarely for those reasons we would now applaud. Hailing Conrad's power, his imagination, and his insight into the bizarre and the eccentric, the contemporary reviewers failed to see in *Victory*, as in *Nostromo*, those social and political implications which give it major stature.

Conrad's Note to the volume in the Collected Edition gives few clues to its subject. Only in one respect does he suggest a major theme, and that in his discussion of the personality of Axel Heyst. Heyst, he says, "in his fine detachment had lost the habit of asserting himself"; Conrad then continues in a general statement: "The habit of profound reflection, I am compelled to say, is the most pernicious of all the habits formed by the civilized man. . . ." Heyst's flaw is his penchant for reflection, an "unbalance" which, as in Greek tragedy, must lead to his undoing. Heyst's attitude is a clear indication of certain late nineteenth- and early twentieth-century ideas, which strongly imply that before 1914 man could make a pretense of detachment, but that, eventually, everyone must become involved in life. In Conrad's prophetic novel, Heyst's trouble on the island amid the violence of the predatory Jones and Ricardo is, so to speak, his own world war.

To bring together all the diverse elements of *Victory*, Conrad used, in the figure of Axel Heyst, a human symbol of large dimensions, analogously, in the novel's setting, in its shifting chronology of narrative, and in its various subsidiary symbols of sight and sound, Conrad has made the book a model of arrangement and suggested meanings.

The problems entailed in the construction of both *Victory* and *Nostromo* were similar, and the beginning of one recalls that of the other: each starts with a description that is organic and meaningful; each comes to its main figure indirectly and through the eyes of others; and in each the major themes of the novel are summed up in the first five or six pages. Such is the first chapter of *Victory*, which ends with the words, ". . . there was no reason to think that Heyst was in any way a fighting man." Then, the smoking volcano, ironically juxtaposed to Heyst in these pages, prefigures the sudden violence that is to engulf· him and Lena. Beginning *in medias res*, the reader comes to Heyst in the same way that reality catches up with this "Hamlet of the South Seas."

From the hints thrown out in the first chapter, Conrad moves in ever larger concentric circles while developing his main character and introducing episodically the derelict, Morrison, the innkeeper, Schomberg, and his wife, the omnipresent Davidson, and through recurring references the much-persecuted Lena. For the first sixty-two pages— Part 1 of the novel—we see Heyst only indirectly. Built up and filled in by seemingly scattered details, Heyst comes to the reader just as Nostromo did earlier, but with this difference: Heyst's activities *are* the center of a book which directly or indirectly he dominates in a way that Nostromo does not dominate *Nostromo*. What Heyst does and thinks determines *Victory* on all its levels at once. He is the central figure as well as the central symbol. *Victory*, therefore, seems a more unified book. With a single basic situation, capable though it is of great extension, *Victory* has none of the problematical development of the more diverse *Nostromo*. In four hundred pages, Conrad was able to develop the novel fully. Its melodramatic coda aside, *Victory* ends when it must, with Heyst's recognition of the active role he should have played in the human scene. There amid the wreckage that he has helped create, he finally recognizes Lena's triumph as the victory that has regenerated even while destroying him. The rest is truly silence.

Part 1 of *Victory* provides the sources and materials of the novel; Part 2, so to speak, the novel itself. In the first part Conrad was careful to account for his sources, while in the second and succeeding parts he assumed the role of omniscient narrator. The chapters, like those in the long *Anna Karenina*, are short and deceptively convey the sense of a less lengthy novel. Conrad, despite continued verbal opposition to Russian writers, had their method of elaboration—a delving into attendant and antecedent circumstances to produce the effect of power, not speed. This is, in fact, one of Conrad's major developments from *Almayer's Folly* through *Nostromo* and *Victory*. The images themselves take on a precise and calculated effect, as Conrad shows his ability to work imaginatively within a tightly-knit frame of reference. Entirely applicable to *Victory* are his later remarks on matters of form:

> I am a man of formed character. Certain conclusions remain immovably fixed in my mind, but I am no slave to prejudices and formulas, and I shall never never be. My attitude to subjects and expressions, the angles of vision, my methods of composition will, within limits, be always changing—not because I am unstable or unprincipled but because I am free. Or perhaps it may be more exact to say, because I am always trying for freedom—within my limits.

"Within limits" describes the form of *Victory*, for it is by means of a strict formal arrangement that Conrad was able to shift the novel from one point of view to another, from the generality of the opening to the particularity of Heyst, and then finally to Lena, who comes to assume a central and pivotal role.

This circling method suits Heyst, for in his incapacity for attachment, he himself literally circles: the method and the man are one. Lena, too, is only reached obliquely, and although Conrad writes more directly of her than of Heyst, she is, as well, "circled" and "found out" piece by piece. In the early chapters, Conrad went back into Heyst's past and by means of short narrative portions began to fill in, but as he progressed toward the reader's present, the chapters lengthen considerably and slow up the pace of the novel. There is frequent juxtaposition of two different times in the past or of past with present time; so that Heyst as he was and Heyst as he is, are both simultaneously before the reader. Heyst is reconstructed historically by the omniscient author at the same time Heyst's contemporaries are commenting upon his present activities—all this before we have met him in his own right on the island with Lena. We have Conrad narrating Heyst's past, we have Heyst in relation to his father, we have Schomberg slandering the now departed Heyst; in addition, while we know that Lena and Heyst have already run off together, in the foreground of the novel they have only met. Intensified in six pages (Chapter 3 of Part 2), this story within a story continues with additional sequences and digressions until Part 3 of the novel. By this time, the reader has met Heyst in all his possibilities: as a detached creature of the past caught in a human situation, responsible through his own efforts for a helpless girl who is completely dependent upon him.

The method of the novel, then, posits a conflict between events of the past and those of the present, just as Heyst's problem—the overt theme of the book—is a personal conflict between dictates of the past and necessities of the present. By catching Heyst in a narrative sequence circling between present and past, Conrad was able to suggest technically the two nodes of Heyst's behavior, and to make narrative method an organic part of the novel's theme. How much more significant the narrative involutions of *Victory* than of *Chance,* with its superficial complexities!

Victory, we recognize, is as much a clash of cultures as a conflict of personalities. The two sides of Axel Heyst—his desire to withdraw from society and live in himself on the one hand, and his latent sense of responsibility on the other—are twin aspects of the late nineteenth and early twentieth century. The strong pull from the past is in the form of the elder Heyst whose late nineteenth-century spirit is the temporal ghost of the book as it influences Axel himself. The conflict in Heyst is between his father's pervasive doctrine of indifference and its evident inadequacy in the face of everyday exigencies. The tension in the novel is created, then, by a theoretical point of view applied to a practical situation; and the breakdown in Heyst can be viewed in terms of how strong a hold the past retains on his sense of direction; how he is, in effect, lamed by the past.

Those frequent flashbacks in which father and son combine, virtually become one idea and one being, are symbolized by the father's books, his portrait, his furniture, as well as by his voice from the grave whispering advice to Axel. Axel is caught up by the elder Heyst's negativism tinged with pity; in the father's words of "universal nothingness" and "strange serenity," we find the key to Axel's own behavior. This voice from the past, as it works on and influences the present, acquires political and social consequences, the voice of historical necessity which is establishing grounds for a new conflict. The elder Heyst clearly speaks as a representative of an outmoded *fin de siècle* point of view. His philosophy of "look on—make no sound" is self-destructive in a situation that calls for a Stein-like commitment to reality. The crippling influence of his father forces Axel into inaction, into indecision, and finally into indifference even to his own doom. The father, that "silenced destroyer of systems, of hopes, of beliefs," has fathered an age, the early 1890's, which narcissistically can only look inward and "cultivate that form of contempt which is called pity" under pretense of personal indifference. Retreating into himself, Axel tried, like Villiers' Axel, to avoid the compromising contamination of human matter. But unlike Villiers' Axel, he even disbelieves in the efficacy of spiritual perfection; his despair is secular, heaven holds no reward and hell no punishment for his disenchantment. What is not dust is ashes; love is vanity, and attachment is momentary weakness. The pure life, the perfect life, is not for him a positive ordering of virtuous acts, but a complete negation of action.

Conrad has made Axel and his father into historical counters who act out their "capacity for scorn" and their "mastery of despair" on a world-wide stage as participants in the vast drama that preceded World War I. Their spirit of withdrawal, particularly that of the elder Heyst, should be stressed, for it extends from the individual to society at large. Thomas Mann remarked about *The Magic Mountain* what can also be said of *Victory:* that each character in the novel is a person and yet symbolically each is more than himself; and that Hans Castorp in his double role as individual and society must go, Mann says, "through the deep experience of sickness and death to arrive at a higher sanity and health; in just the same way that one must have a knowledge of sin in order to find redemption." So Heyst must be chastened into realization. The narrative of his chastening is the allegory of an age that chose detachment in the face of violence. Heyst realizes, though too late to save himself, that immersion in the realities of life may indeed be melancholy advice, but it is, nevertheless, the only way to survival.

In another way, Heyst's conflict within himself is a dramatization of certain obvious aesthetic ideas—the role every artist faces of a life of social consciousness versus a life of so-called pure art, even though the conflict is rarely cast precisely in these terms. Conrad was concerned with the problem of art for itself as early as the Preface to *The Nigger of the "Narcissus"* when he attempted to divorce the serious artist from the ivory tower by demonstrating that devotion to craft transcends any temporary formula of pure art. "In that uneasy solitude," he said, "the supreme cry of Art for Art itself loses the exciting ring of its apparent immorality." Writing in the summer of 1914, Henry James, in *The Ivory Tower*, asked the same question: whether a person of Graham Fielder's sensitivity can survive in the corruption and insensitivity of his day. Fielder's is responsible detachment, we are led to believe, for his achievements are yet to come, no doubt in literary achievement. But like Heyst who cannot come to terms with life, Fielder is unable to exist in a predatory and moneyed background; and just as Heyst, recognizing his incapacity, destroys himself, so James, perceiving Fielder's bleak future, perhaps "destroyed" the novel by not completing it. Both Fielder and Heyst sensed the bleakness and mercilessness that are behind the great possessions of the world, and unable to abide the world, they chose to leave it. When violence does come to Heyst, his defenses cannot be changed, and unlike Prospero he has no magic wand to do his bidding.

The reference to *The Tempest* is not fortuitous. Conrad had always shown a close awareness of Shakespeare, not only by using epigraphs from three plays but also by the repetition of certain cadences and by early experiments with blank verse prose. Conrad had been acquainted with Shakespeare from childhood, both in his father's translations and also from reading he did during twenty years of sea voyages. Heyst has affinities, which should not of course be forced, with both Hamlet and Prospero. An early reviewer called Heyst a veritable South Seas Hamlet, but essentially a Hamlet of our day, and this remark was later repeated by James Huneker, the American critic, in his appreciative chapter on Conrad. In the common tensions of Hamlet and Heyst between detachment and involvement, between a destructive idealism and a violent reality, and between the pulls of the past and present which each tries to synthesize, the two figures must face similar problems in a way that eventually proves fatal to both. In the carnage that clears the stages of *Hamlet* and *Victory*, the protagonist of each succumbs to the forces of destruction. The melancholy Swede perhaps speaks for the early twentieth century as much as the melancholy Dane speaks for Elizabethans three hundred years before.

In *Victory*, Heyst's idyllic retreat, like Prospero's in *The Tempest*, is suddenly invaded by violence, deceit, and dissembling outer-worlders. Lacking magic, Heyst must call upon his own resources, which are unable to respond; and so, unlike Prospero, he cannot command the scene. But while differing in their respective abilities to reach decisions and to carry them out, both the weary Heyst and the aging Prospero possess an emphatic awareness of self. Both see in foreign intrusion a blow at personal equilibrium, and both find their existing worlds too heinous for participation. The result for each is a way of life in which self is supreme, in which important decisions are minimized or postponed, and in which peace can be obtained only by evading action. As Prospero must protect Miranda, so Heyst is responsible for Lena; but while Prospero through magic can hold in abeyance the uncivilized Caliban and the civilized intruders, Heyst is unable to handle either the savage Pedro or his perverse masters.

After the violence has ended, Prospero is left to live in peace and quiet, while Heyst, ineffectual and surely a failure, dies, although, it must be recognized, with his dignity intact.

Much as Heyst dominates the material of *Victory*, he is by no means the sole figure of interest. Conrad was able to move away from Heyst frequently, for example to Jones and Ricardo or to Lena, because each one partakes of a psychological segment of Heyst himself. Technically, Conrad was repeating his use of doubles in *Lord Jim* and *Nostromo*. Through this technique, the principal character hovers over the scene as a spiritual or psychological presence even when physically absent. By means of a carefully worked-out system of character shifting, Conrad maintained the unity of *Victory*.

In the fourth part of *Victory*, the narrative distinctly shifts from Heyst to Lena in the foreground of action. By the time the situation on the island has been fully developed, Lena is the center of the novel, and everyone except her in one way or another is being deluded: (1) Heyst himself is being misled by Lena concerning Ricardo; (2) Jones, duped by his man-servant, Ricardo, does not know of Lena's presence on the island; (3) Ricardo does not know of Lena's double-dealing, that she is using him as part of a scheme to protect Heyst; (4) and Wang, Heyst's servant, believes Lena is betraying his master by secret meetings with Ricardo. Only Lena is in full possession of the truth, and all threads of action emanate from her. Her decisions, then, determine the outcome of the plot, for by now it has been fairly well established that Heyst can and will do nothing.

The shift from Heyst to Lena under different conditions could have been disastrous to the direction of the novel; but here any loss of continuity is not noticed, so subtle and effective are Conrad's devices. This continuity is accomplished through the sustained presentation of character doubles. If, for example, we return to Heyst's relationship to Morrison (Chapter 2 of Part 1), the man with the grandiose business ideas, we find a partnership in which the passive Heyst temporarily saves the penniless Morrison. Although the latter eventually dies a failure, he is infinitely grateful to Heyst, who becomes heir to the Tropical Belt Coal Company. Morrison, now long dead, comes to Lena's mind through Schomberg, who suggests that Heyst killed his partner for gain, hearsay that Lena as Heyst's new partner is prone to believe. In her new situation, she quickly identifies with Morrison and sees the two of them as "representatives of all the past victims of the Great Joke." When Heyst tells of Morrison's being cornered, of his needing help and getting down on his knees to beg, she asks, with herself in mind, " 'You didn't make fun of him for that?' " And then shortly later she says, " 'You saved a man for fun— is that what you mean? Just for fun?' " Heyst immediately disclaims any fun, but he regrets that in a moment of inadvertence he had created for himself a responsibility, feeling that " 'he who forms a tie is lost. The germ of corruption has entered into his soul.' " Heyst's short meeting with Morrison, a relationship that in itself is only of importance in passing, is used by Conrad to generate intense feelings in the more important Heyst-Lena relationship. Through Lena's per- sistent identification with Morrison, one side of her ambivalent feel- ings toward Heyst is presented tangibly and dramatically.[1]

But Conrad worked laterally as well as vertically. The Morrison- Lena-Heyst relationship broadens as Lena is complemented by the predatory Ricardo, and Heyst by the abnormal Jones. Within certain ethical and moral considerations, Lena and Ricardo are evidently dis- similar, but through their particular juxtaposition in the novel, they meet undeniably on psychological grounds. It is Ricardo who recog- nizes what he thinks is a basic similarity when he says to her: " 'You and I are made to understand each other. Born alike, bred alike, I guess. You are not tame. Same here! You have been chucked out into this rotten world of 'ypocrites. Same here!' " Earlier, he had roused her feelings of insecurity by seizing on Heyst's rumored treatment of Morrison, a recurring presentiment to Lena of what she still fears from Heyst. But Lena with her sharper sense of ethics recognizes in Ricardo the same embodiment of evil and vileness that has always attended her; for without Heyst, she realizes, she would be prey for the likes of Ricardo all her life. In one way, then, if only to disprove any further

---

[1] Lena increasingly sees herself as Morrison; for later in the novel she provokes Heyst by repeating Schomberg's words: " 'He was saying that there never were such loving friends to look at as you two; then, when you got all you wanted out of him and got thoroughly tired of him, too, you kicked him out to go home and die.' " By voicing Schomberg's vile lies, Lena is manifesting her own fears; she wants an attachment at the very moment Heyst finds every course of action re- pulsive and every human contact fraught with loss of dignity. For a moment he detests Lena, only to recognize a certain charm that makes her desirable despite his self-imposed wall of separation. Earlier, when he touched her, he had "squeezed her hand angrily"; "squeezed" because she does mean something to him, and "angrily" because his person has been violated—he must take her with all the contaminating circumstances that a human tie imposes, and Heyst can see no escape.

identification with Ricardo, she is spurred to her fierce defense of Heyst, who thus far is the first to show belief in her worth.

The other doubles—Heyst and Jones—are even more subtly complementary to each other. Their superficial similarities—the emphasis on both as gentlemen, for example—are preceded by their sharp psychological identification, more so than perhaps any other related pair in Conrad except Razumov and Haldin. Again, it is Jones, like Ricardo with Lena, who recognizes the similarity; he has said to Heyst: " 'We pursue the same ends . . . only perhaps I pursue them with more openness than you—with more simplicity.' " Though Jones misreads Heyst as a fellow confidence man, he acutely senses a psychological affinity. The same type of reciprocation that existed in *The Secret Agent* between the criminals and police is here reduplicated in the attitude of Jones and Heyst. Each in his way expects a certain given world, in Jones's case to permit him to operate as a confidence man, in Heyst's to allow him detachment without danger of interference. Both presuppose a society which will leave them to their own courses of action. Similarly, each is literally "on his own," insisting on freedom of action, each a rugged individual choosing to act or not to act as personal wishes dictate. Both view the world in a certain light as a shabby affair which is best left alone on its own terms. So Heyst and Jones agree on several common assumptions, as the latter commented above, although they differ evidently on the course of action each chooses for himself.

When they meet they do so as representatives of two distinct cultures which differ in many essentials while overlapping in basic psychologies. Jones's constant physical illness, similar in some ways to Wait's in *The Nigger of the "Narcissus,"* emphasizes his mental perversity; sexually he is incapable of normal intercourse and possibly he disdains all kinds of sexual contact, although the evidence for his being homosexual is strongly suggested. Surely, Jones's illness is of a symbolic nature, manifesting a psychological condition that has festered in society. His illness of mind and body—made visible by his sick body—complements the "sick soul" of Heyst, embodied though it is in a broad and robust frame. Jones's physical weakness is a counterpart of Heyst's incapacity to act, and his sickness of mind a counterpart of Heyst's undeveloped social sense. Each one is less than a fully developed man, and together they suggest many of the human ills of pre-World War I Europe.

Pursuing this scheme of doubles in *Victory*—which like a network of delicate branches spreads throughout the novel—we have seen how Conrad introduced similar psychological types, those of Morrison-Lena, Morrison-Heyst, Lena-Ricardo, and Heyst-Jones. The most important pair of doubles—the pair that finally permitted Conrad to shift the latter part of the novel without disturbing the narrative flow —is of course that of Lena and Heyst. Although Lena feels, while Heyst can only be sincere, she nevertheless willingly effaces herself to gain her goal, which is to find dignity through love. Heyst similarly effaces himself to maintain his dignity, but his goal, psychologically akin to hers, is to lose himself in shadows. Each becomes selfless; each is influenced by society rather than influencing others. Each wants to get out of the world, Lena to prevent further hurts, Heyst to avoid further contact. Each is apart, preferring silence to speech, although paradoxically, Lena's graceful speaking voice is one of her great assets.

If Heyst has godlike characteristics, as one critic claims, and like a mythological god is purified by an expiation ritual, then Lena, too, has a supra-surface role which fits the story of redemption. When Heyst asks Lena her name, she says that she is called Alma, also Magdalen, although she does not know why. As her first name, Alma, implies, she manifests certain soul-like qualities—the soul of Heyst is Lena; and as Magdalen she can be saved by Heyst from whoredom. Lena is the living side of Heyst; through her identification with Morrison, there recurs the same vein of helplessness that drew Heyst to his former patrner. She comes to represent Heyst's concession to society at large; to "save" her he must ask himself new questions and find new answers. By attaching himself to her, he recognizes a hitherto darkened side of his psychological make-up, an aspect continually discouraged in his father's training.

Lena, despite her surface weakness, can act and react in a way impossible for Heyst. Coming as she does already partially connected with Morrison, Ricardo, Heyst himself, and even Jones, she can be accepted in the novel as a powerful figure who acts intuitively on what she knows and feels. Her smoothly-worked assumption of the pivotal role—wherein she is the only one to understand the various aspects of the situation—is, then, a technical as well as human achievement.

Through sustained doubling, Conrad conveyed verbally and formally a unity of structure which marks *Victory* perhaps more than any other of his major novels. In a novel that appeared ten years later, Virginia Woolf's *Mrs. Dalloway* (1925), we find a broad and sustained psychological doubling between the titular character and the mentally disturbed Septimus, a doubling that unifies the book more than any verbalization. Numerous other modern novelists—notably Joyce in *Ulysses*, whose Bloom, Mrs. Bloom, and Stephen, together with several minor characters, overlap and in turn assume qualities of each other—have made wide use of this device, which, although not of course beginning with Conrad, was consciously and deliberately shaped by him into a special technique. Many of Conrad's most effective techniques, including psychological doubling, are no more than assiduous application of principles expressed in the Preface to *The Nigger* and worked out in collaboration with Ford Madox Ford. Trying always to get beyond surface realism, Conrad strove to develop techniques which would broaden his longer works. Verbal irony was not enough—although this element is never far from a Conrad novel—if it were not meshed with a technical apparatus that could be, as he said, "the secret spring of responsive emotions."

A novelist like Conrad, so aware of all the implications of his work, is constantly trying to get beyond mere statement and two-dimensional situations. In his choice of setting in *Victory*, for example, as in *Nostromo*, he was evidently attempting to convey an instance of individual struggle that is none the less universal. The "paradisiacal" island to which Heyst and Lena retreat is something less than Eden and something closer to a symbol of Heyst's own desiccated spirit. What the pair try to hold onto is simply a place to live, a place which in its darker aspects contains an innate ugliness, an innate threat to happiness. From Davidson's point of view, the loneliness and ruined aspect of the island are evident:

> That black jetty, sticking out of the jungle into the empty sea; these roof-ridges of deserted houses peeping dismally above the long grass! Ough! The gigantic and funereal blackboard sign of the Tropical Belt Coal Company, still emerging from a wild growth of bushes like an inscription stuck above a grave figured by the tall heap of unsold coal at the shore end of the wharf, added to the general desolation.

The heap of coal dust, the ghostly rails laid by the company, the dirt of abandoned offices and bungalows all visibly detract from an earthly paradise. Long before Jones and Ricardo have arrived on the island, Conrad's description suggests something different from an Eden which is disturbed by intruders. He suggests that the desolation on the island, mixed as it is with the purely idyllic, is a condition of life, and that even without the predatory violence of Jones and Ricardo, experience in itself is full of threatening shadows.

Arriving at human conclusions through natural description was a mainstay of Conrad's method from *Almayer's Folly* through *The Rover* thirty years later. One remarks Conrad's use of storm symbolism, seen before in *Under Western Eyes*, where he was trying to suggest, however obviously, certain complex emotions through the violence of nature. Frequently his settings are in purpose not unlike the scene on the heath in *King Lear*. In *Victory* itself, as Heyst and Lena go toward dinner with Jones, what is for them literally a last supper, the storm rumbles incessantly, and "pale lightning in waves of cold fire flooded and ran off the island in rapid succession." Similarly, while Jones and Heyst face each other and fence for position, the "muffled thunder resembled the echo of a distant cannonade," and "like the growl of an inarticulate giant muttering fatuously," it is fitting accompaniment for the life and death struggle on the island. Shortly after, the "angry modulation" of the thunder curls its way, ironically, around the framed profile of Heyst's father, a man who had tried to avoid thunder all his life, and who now can only look on severely as his son becomes involved in personal struggle. When Lena's victory is complete and her love has triumphed over death, the thunder ceases to growl, for "the world of material forms shuddered no more under the emerging stars." Admittedly, this type of symbolic accompaniment is superficial; but taken together with the dramatic situation, it realizes the scene. The noise of the thunder is the noise of Heyst's own war, and when it finally rumbles to a halt no one is left to enjoy the clearing skies.

The victory of the title, as Conrad emphasized in the Author's Note, is surely Lena's. Her sacrifice, in this sense like Margaret's in *Faust*, forces Heyst to recognize the inadequacy of his personal philosophy, as Faust himself perceived the enormity of his sins. In his last words to Davidson, Heyst confesses that a man is cursed whose "heart has not learned while young to hope, to love—and to put his trust in life." In short, to follow Stein's advice in *Lord Jim*. The social significance of his words is plain, for Heyst is a living example of Donne's proposition that no man is an island unto himself, and that commitment to humanity must often take precedence over the individual will. For as Heyst attempts expiation through death by fire, the storm fully subsides, Lena's voice is stilled, Ricardo's knife and Jones's gun are useless, and the growls of the ape-like Pedro have been muted. The stage has been cleared; only the knightly Davidson, like Fortinbras, holds the field, and the rest is truly nothing.

As a small-scale *Faust* for the nineteenth and twentieth centuries, *Victory* prophesies that a head-on meeting of the two ages will result in violent destruction for both; but along the way the novel makes clear that moral courage in confronting difficulty is finer than complete withdrawal, and that a satisfactory life for the philosopher, the artist, or even for the man with no pretensions to greatness must include participation and involvement. So Heyst must be chastened into realization, just as Faust had to recognize his transgression before Goethe allowed him to be redeemed.

Its melodramatic and summary ending notwithstanding, *Victory* remains the last of Conrad's major works, a novel that endures dignified and significant. After *Victory*, the surface action of Conrad's novels tended to predominate, as his power of suggestion waned and flickered out; and as he himself recognized, his strength lay in his ability to invest content with what he called the "potentiality of almost infinite suggestion." At his best, he stressed the How of a subject, not the What. After *Victory*, the diligent working out of story detail, the What, predominates, and his fiction is often no more than a careful pastiche of former triumphs. Some of the later work is nevertheless interesting, but the initial creative thrust has passed and the novelist was too old and too tired to begin again. However, in "Heart of Darkness," *Lord Jim, Nostromo, Under Western Eyes,* "The Secret Sharer," and *Victory*, perhaps along with *The Secret Agent* and *Chance*, Conrad added new force to the English novel, a pursuit that he had devoted his life to realize.

Joseph Conrad : SELECTED BIBLIOGRAPHY

CRANKSHAW, EDWARD. *Joseph Conrad: Some Aspects of the Art of the Novel.* London: John Lane, 1936.

DAICHES, DAVID. "Joseph Conrad," *The Novel and the Modern World.* Chicago: University of Chicago Press, 1939.

FORD, FORD MADOX. *Joseph Conrad: A Personal Remembrance.* Boston: Little Brown, 1924.

GORDAN, JOHN DOZIER. *Joseph Conrad: The Making of a Novelist.* Cambridge, Massachusetts: Harvard University Press, 1941.

GUERARD, ALBERT. *Conrad the Novelist.* Cambridge, Massachusetts: Harvard University Press, 1958.

HEWITT, DOUGLAS. *Conrad: A Reassessment.* Cambridge, England: Bowes & Bowes, 1952.

JEAN-AUBRY, G. *Joseph Conrad: Life and Letters,* 2 vols. Garden City: Doubleday, 1927.

LEAVIS, F. R. *The Great Tradition.* London: Chatto & Windus, 1948.

MÉGROZ, R. L. *Conrad's Mind and Method: A Study of Personality in Art.* London: Faber & Faber, 1931.

MOSER, THOMAS. *Joseph Conrad: Achievement and Decline.* Cambridge, Massachusetts: Harvard University Press, 1957.

WILEY, PAUL L. *Conrad's Measure of Man.* Madison: University of Wisconsin Press, 1954.

ZABEL, MORTON DAUWEN. "Joseph Conrad: Chance and Recognition," *Sewanee Review,* liii (Winter 1945), 1–22.

———, ed. *The Portable Conrad.* New York: Viking, 1947.

E. M. Forster xx Life

E. M. Forster stopped writing major novels more than a generation ago without turning, in the years that followed publication of A *Passage to India*, to another creative literary form. Unlike Yeats and Eliot, who largely abandoned lyric poetry for the poetic drama, Forster turned to criticism primarily of other writers, of governments, and of the state of culture. Yet so powerful has been the effect of his few attempts at long fiction—from *Where Angels Fear to Tread* (1905) to *A Passage to India* (1924)—that he occupies an important place even today among the shapers of contemporary fiction. By his example and through his critical direction, writers and students of fiction have been able to see more clearly the elements which combine to form a work of fiction. Such terms as rhythm, pattern, symbol have seemed less nebulous for those who have read *Aspects of the Novel* or *Abinger Harvest*. And though he has at times been slow to recognize the merits of the more flamboyantly experimental like James Joyce, still he has been able to admit his lapses of judgment and to interpret the newcomers to his wide audience.

If Forster did not typify, however, for more than a generation of thinkers, the sensitive liberal mind in a basically insensitive society —if, in other words, he did not live the part which his writings recommend for today's hero: the contemplative, thinking man whose special skills and background of culture demand involvement in the shaping of this world—he might not have carved his literary niche with such finality. But, it may be said, if he were not the man that he is, he might have been a poor novelist, or no novelist at all.

A close contemporary of Virginia Woolf and Joyce, E. M. Forster was born on January 11, 1879, in London. Though his father was a professional man, an architect of reputable standing, and his mother had been brought up in an intellectually oriented middle-class family, he was not spared the unhappiness of a prep school education at Tonbridge—a traumatic experience which colors a great deal of his later writing. A "dayboy" at the fashionable boarding school, Forster found out what it was to fail to "connect," to be at odds with one's society, even in his early teens. Moreover, like Stephen Dedalus at Clongowes, he found that his unathletic frame and his interest in books conspired to increase his alienation from his robust, physically active peers.

The years which Forster subsequently spent at Cambridge were, perhaps by immediate contrast, extraordinarily happy. At last in an atmosphere of quiet study and meditation, able to pick his friends and work at his own speed on his own projects under masters who knew how to bring a young man along intelligently and sensitively, even if the student were a non-conformist, Forster quickly blossomed as a scholar, a writer, and, most important, as a human being. After graduation in 1901, like Milton he decided to see for himself the seat of classical civilization and visited both Greece and Italy, where he sought to absorb the spirit of the Mediterranean area.

In his middle twenties, Forster was at his most productive. Not only did he engage actively in political writing for a time, seeking to appeal to the Liberals for reform, but he also wrote for the *Independent Review* on political subjects. Furthermore, he embodied his enthusiasm for the Mediterranean countries and their culture in stories suggested by Greek mythical themes. In 1905, when he was twenty-six, his first novel was published: *Where Angels Fear to Tread*, a precise, beautifully rounded story, rich in understanding of human nature, spiritual values, and the lure of Italy. Within the next five years appeared all of Forster's significant novels save *A Passage*, so that by the time the author had reached thirty, he had published *The Longest Journey* (1907), the story of his own upbringing and school days; *A Room with a View* (1908), a charming story of the effect of Italy on two women; and *Howards End* (1910), Forster's most ambitious attempt to characterize the malady of modern England and its possible cure. His collection of short stories, *The Celestial Omnibus*, appeared in 1911.

In that same year, Forster paid his first visit to India, and on his return he embodied some of the results of his visit in *A Passage to India*. This book was left unfinished, however, until after its author's second visit to that country in 1921. His most influential novel did not appear, therefore, until 1924, when it received great acclaim mixed with considerable puzzlement. Forster was famous. He was asked to deliver the Clark Lectures at Cambridge in 1927. His comments on fiction were important pronouncements, as were T. S. Eliot's on poetry in the 1930's and 1940's. Yet Forster had not tried to follow up his surprising triumph by further serious attempts in the novel.

The generation which has gone by since *A Passage* was published has helped to put Forster's achievement in perspective. Lacking the complex and intricate artistry of a Proust or a Mann, he is nonetheless a novelist of unusual force. His plots, always simple, direct, and economical, excite the reader's interest and keep his attention. And though in the early years of this century, the ideas behind the plots must have been fresh and startling, so thoroughly have they been made part of the fabric of liberal thought since World War I that they impress today's reader as clichés, no matter how well expressed. As a picture of the intellectual and emotional environment of Forster's younger days, however, his novels remain unparalleled source material.

E. M. Forster xx Works

Though short and slight and quiet, Forster's first novel contains in manner and theme all his later fiction. That it tries to be less than the epic of English folkways—apparently the intent of *Howards End* (1910)—or to operate without the elaborate mystical symbolism of *A Passage to India* (1924), is no reflection on its author. What is unattained as yet in thickness of texture and flamboyance of design is at least compensated for by the directness and simplicity of a young man's vision. For even at the age of twenty-six, Forster had the balance and maturity to understand that a Sawston-like environment must inhibit the deepest (and often the worthiest) human impulses. People nurtured in coldness, hypocrisy, superficiality, and "petty unselfishness," he saw, can hardly reflect man's divinity or even his highest human capabilities.

Forster's plan in *Where Angels Fear to Tread* (1905) is daringly uncomplicated. Take several characters whose mode of life has made them unsatisfactory as fully-functioning human beings. Place them suddenly in a richer, warmer, emotionally more primitive civilization. Record the results, if not with detachment, then with the sympathy that points a moral. The plan had been tried earlier, and with spectacular literary success, by Henry James. Forster gave it the stamp of his own peculiar social and cultural liberalism—and a directness of statement which his predecessor seldom possessed.

The motifs of the book, and of all Forster's fiction, may be seen as a series of antitheses: true communication versus mere suburban small talk; the fundamental love of which men are capable versus the convenient alliances of Sawston society; reality versus a jealously harbored illusion; the forms of civilization (machinery) **versus** the apparently formless currents that connect one human being to another; ancient myths versus their modern application; and the insistence that none of these antitheses is ever fully operative in a world of half tones.

The most recent edition of Forster's novel bears on its front cover pictured fragments of an envelope on which are visible an Italian postmark and a cancelled stamp of that country. So the theme of communication attempted, rejected, and destroyed is given symbolic importance by the illustrator, as it is in more subtle ways by the author. Brought up on such sociological studies as *The Lonely Crowd* and on case histories of psychology, contemporary readers may be prone to disregard Forster's primary motif as trite. His modernity works against him in a sense, for it is hard to think of the novel as a product almost of the 1890's—a time before Leopold Bloom, Lord Jim, and Paul Morel had made loneliness in literature fashionable.

People differ from other animals in their ability to use language. As an intellectual tool, spoken or written, it is of incalculable advantage. Yet, in instances in which the heart and spirit are most involved, it fails us. The words of a prayer are poor counters to express the feelings of the devout toward the object of their worship. Nor can the lover say what his heart feels except in approximate imitation of legends on greeting cards. As inexact and even impotent as words may be in crucial situations, however, they have for Forster a sacredness, representing as they do man's observable link to his fellows. It is precisely this almost religious role which makes Forster reduce his sermon on language, in its simplest terms, to the way people talk, or fail to talk, to one another. Thus, the leisured upper-middle-class citizens of Sawston have elevated small talk to the status of an art. Philip Herriton, his mother, his sister Harriet, and even plain, good Miss Abbott seem never at a loss for words. "Philip talked continually. . . . He did not know that he talked a good deal of nonsense." And Lucy Honeychurch, in *A Room with a View*, is impelled to break her engagement to Cecil when she can no longer put up with his inane prattling—on the surface charming, but empty of understanding. Forster hints at the sacrilege involved in allowing this gift of tongues to be debased by frivolous, insincere, or superficial use.

The theme of communication attains symbolic significance with Lilia's marriage to Gino Carella. The mystery of Italy has brought together the Englishwoman and the unsophisticated Italian. The rich and the poor, the high and the low, the north and the south, the cold and the warm—two very distinct cultures seek, in Forster's phrase, to "connect." Now reference to difficulties with language broadens to encompass universal implications. "Conversation, to give it that name, was carried on in a mixture of English and Italian. Lilia had picked up hardly any of the latter language, and Signor Carella had not yet learnt any of the former." Such awkwardness of communication foreshadows Lilia's social loneliness ("people naturally found a difficulty in getting on with a lady who could not learn their language"), as well as Gino's inability to adjust ("He couldn't or wouldn't understand").

Yet there are two sides to the coin. Slowly the more sensitive of Forster's characters come to know that there is a deeper, more satisfying bond than the spoken or written word—what the tag-line of a popular song approximates in "the language of love." Spiridione tells his friend Gino about this rare kind of communication:

> The person who understands us at first sight, who never irritates us, who never bores, to whom we can pour forth every thought and wish, *not only in speech but in silence*—that is what I mean by *simpatico*. (my italics, except for final word)

Such heightened understanding needs no words. It surmounts barriers of age, of class, of money. With it, Shaw's Liza Doolittle would scarcely have required the professional services of Professor Higgins. George Emerson and Lucy Honeychurch find no need of conversation to achieve ecstatic harmony in *A Room with a View*, though they are surrounded by glib conversationalists who, ironically, never attain to similar deep understanding of their audiences. It surmounts national language barriers (Lucy understands the amorous interplay of the Italian driver and his "sister" better than the articulately verbose lectures on art and love of the Rev. Mr. Eager.).

Harriet Herriton, the petrified woman, uninitiated into the mysteries of the human heart, evaluates her more sensitive countrywoman, Miss Abbott, always with respect to the latter's ability or willingness to communicate. "Couldn't even talk properly," is her complaint when Caroline returns shaken from the afternoon visit to Gino and his baby. And in the next breath Harriet, with typical lack of consistency, wonders "How could a lady speak to such a horrible man?" Forster cannot resist summing up Harriet in terms of her speech. "It was horrible to think of the English of Harriet, whose every word would be as hard, as distinct, and as unfinished as a lump of coal." Considerations of this kind, in fact, lead the author to a paradoxical blessing of "the barrier of language," which often "only lets pass what is good."

Communication among people will become increasingly important to Forster in the novels that follow. The scattered letters and post-cards which Gino sends to Irma to bridge the gap of distance, environment, and culture, will give way to the exchange of letters by the Schlegel sisters in *Howards End*. Finally, the letter from Fielding to Aziz near the end of *A Passage to India*, a letter mischievously or accidentally misinterpreted for the doctor by Mahmoud Ali, plays its part in altering the lives of sender and addressee. But in no later book does Forster deal with the symbolic overtones of communication—spoken, written, psychically transmitted—more clearly and in more detail than in his first novel.

Forster sees, with Matthew Arnold, the irony of "progress." As means for closer connection between man and man have steadily improved, men have grown further apart. Daily newspapers, magazines, telephones, telegraph, radio have erased time and space, but they have been ineffective in improving human relationships. The machinery of government increases with a view toward more stringent control of the citizenry for material benefits. Yet, as Forster is quick to point out, without the machinery of progress, what Lionel Trilling calls the "undeveloped heart" has a better chance to develop more fully, the individual to "connect" more firmly with his fellows. Monteriano is Forster's example. Primitive in "machinery," as in plumbing, its residents know the value of basic human emotions. Philip is pulled into Gino's box at the opera bodily by friendly hands, obviating the need for Sawston's pallid social notepaper and the often insincere "pleasure of a reply." Sawston runs on a well-regulated calendar of events and social duties. Philanthropy is controlled and hygienic. Mrs. Herriton is a precision machine and, as a human being, expendable. Her daughter, off the same assembly line, set in a certain direction and wound up, proceeds to Italy and to baby-snatching with the subtlety of a Univac in action.

Opposing such frightening products of the brave new world, Forster presents disorganized characters like Gino: "He's got a country behind him that's upset people from the beginning of the world." Gino's room is unquestionably "in a shocking mess," unlike the Herriton drawing room, but Forster adds meaningfully that it is "the mess that comes of life, not of desolation." Caroline is rightly appalled as she stares at Gino's baby—a real, flesh-and-blood child to his father—to realize the extent to which the machinery of Sawston living had obscured life itself:

> And this [the baby] was the machine on which she and Mrs. Herriton and Philip and Harriet had for the last month been exercising their various ideals—had determined that in time it should move this way or that way, should accomplish this and not that. It was to be Low Church, it was to be high-principled. . . . Yet now that she saw this baby, lying asleep on a dirty rug, she had a great disposition not to dictate one of them, and to exert no more influence than there may be in a kiss or in the vaguest of the heartfelt prayers.

Miss Abbott's moment of revelation as she looks at the child is the point at which salvation is possible for her, a moment of successful rebellion against the mechanical ministry which Sawston has reared.

The baleful influence of machinery crops up again and again in the novels. The motor car becomes for Forster a symbolic indictment of his time. The most jarring character in A Passage to India is Miss Derek, whose automobile figures in most of the trouble. But the author saves his most elaborate condemnation of mechanical vehicles for Howards End, where he also shows that it is possible in England to reject "machinery" in favor of the full life. We shall examine the motif in that novel later.

Though Forster's style often seems flippant, he deals very seriously with one of his pervasive thematic concerns—love. In this novel, in fact, the author seems by love possessed. He examines maternal affection (Lilia and Mrs. Herriton), spiritual love (Caroline Abbott), sexual love (Lilia and Gino), paternal love (Gino), the absence of love (Philip), and the perversion of love (Harriet). Indeed, the whole quest of the Sawston group in Italy, though they are unaware of it until it is over, is for the love which the ugliness of middle-class suburban life in England has denied them. Harriet fails utterly, too long confirmed in Sawston's sterile hardness of heart. Philip and Caroline, perhaps unhappily for them, are tied to both worlds. At first they represent the sobering, commonsense point of view of Sawston and are, in fact, dispatched to Italy to impose the strength of Philistia's controls upon presumably weaker beings: Caroline to keep the vulgar Lilia from involvement, Philip to repair the damage to respectability when Caroline falters.

Italy works the change, affecting all but the most unregenerate. Lilia mistakes sexual passion for a more enduring emotion and throws her life away: " 'I can stand up against the world now, for I've found

Gino, and this time I marry for love!' " But the demands of Italy can also destroy: Lilia, giving birth to Gino's son (the physical embodiment of the union of north and south), is killed off suddenly in half a line. The Italian stage is left to the apparently unheroic hero and heroine, Philip and Caroline. The rest of the novel portrays their growing awareness of the strength and the personal importance of love.

Philip's problem—like Prufrock's—has always been his inability to participate in life, to give of himself emotionally. Though his first trip to Italy had sharpened his sensitivity to beauty as a panoramic backdrop, it had been unable to shake him from the passive, loveless mold in which Mrs. Herriton had cast him. He concludes that nothing can happen, not knowing that "human love and love of truth sometimes conquer where love of beauty fails." Like Mr. Duffy in James Joyce's "A Painful Case," he brings upon himself the penalty for emotional deprivation: despair and loneliness. The pity is greater for Philip than for Duffy. In Joyce, Mrs. Sinico is dead before the man who has scorned human love realizes the mockery of his egocentric existence. Caroline Abbott, on the other hand, is very much alive for the first time in her life, and it is to her, indeed, that Philip explains his plight:

> I seem fated to pass through the world without colliding with it or moving it—and I'm sure I can't tell you whether the fate's good or evil. I don't die—I don't fall in love. And if other people die or fall in love they always do it when I'm just not there. You are quite right; life to me is just a spectacle, which—thank God, and thank Italy, and thank you—is now more beautiful and heartening than it has ever been before.

But it takes the shock of the baby's death and the suffering of combat with Gino to show him the deep feeling of which even he might be capable. Not only has Miss Abbott arrived in time to save him from death; she symbolizes now his escape from death-in-life. "He would try henceforward to be worthy of the things she had revealed. Quietly, without hysterical prayers or banging of drums, he underwent conversion. He was saved." "Goddess" or priestess, she supervises the communion of Gino and Philip as they drink together the child's milk. In their different ways, both men have come to understanding through love. Their communication is now, though wordless, complete.

To connect with a goddess, however, is a task of a higher order. Though Philip comes to Miss Abbott by "the spiritual path," his awakening senses soon reveal his emotional attachment to the woman behind the figure of the Virgin. Ironically, the awareness is belated. At Sawston "he had known so much about her once. . . . And now he only knew that he loved her." But the former prim candidate for respectable marriage has found in Italy an unattainable god and man of her own: Gino.

Between the opening scene in which Lilia and Caroline entrain for Italy, and the final page on which the English travelers enter the St. Gothard tunnel for the return to Sawston, Italy has done its work. Philip and Caroline have developed: if fulfilment of happiness and love together has eluded them, they at least know what they have missed. They have had what Leonard Bast in *Howards End* calls an "adventure" to sustain them in the colorless years which stretch ahead. Forster is too honest to supply a "happy" ending.

The author's honesty is similarly responsible for his extensive treatment of reality and unreality in this book and elsewhere. In *The Longest Journey* the theme, introduced in the first line, dominates the novel both as philosophical abstraction and in vivid dramatization through the career of Rickie Elliott. In *Where Angels Fear to Tread* it is muted though present throughout.

A man of Forster's intelligence would not deny the necessity of illusion in life to make living bearable. Miss Abbott may dream of a town like Sawston, "a joyless, straggling place, full of people who pretended," but to decry the pretense in the absence of an acceptable substitute is not the author's purpose. The people of Monteriano have their illusions too. When the "famous hot lady of the Apennines" finishes the mad scene from *Lucia:*

> . . . from the back of the stage—she feigned not to see it—there advanced a kind of bamboo clothes-horse, stuck all over with bouquets. It was very ugly, and most of the flowers in it were false. Lucia knew this, and so did the audience; and they all knew that the clothes-horse was a piece of stage property. . . . None the less did it unloose the great deeps. With a scream of amazement and joy she embraced the animal, pulled out one or two practicable blossoms, pressed them to her lips, and flung them into her admirers. They flung them back . . .

But the make-believe of the Italians is harmless, pleasurable, and touched with pulsing life. It does not take the place of living: in artistic proportion, it is part of their healthy life. Forster presents this avowedly sentimental self-deception as somehow beautiful and desirable in the "majestic . . . bad taste of Italy." What he will not brook is the intellectual dishonesty that substitutes the false ideal for the true with deliberate intent to bypass life. If man must have his ideals, let them at least be "honest" illusions to keep him afloat on the stream of existence, not drugs to make sinking painless.

Thus Philip's Baedeker approach to beauty and adventure, like Rickie Elliott's, is punctured by the information that Gino's father is a practicing dentist. Having put his faith in the "romantic" touristy façade of an ancient nation, without once edging below to the vital core beneath, he loses his feeble grip on the place at the first slight distortion of his unreal picture. How false Philip's ideal is, is clear from his pompous speech to Miss Abbott:

> But your real life is your own, and nothing can touch it. There is no power on earth that can prevent your criticizing and despising mediocrity—nothing that can stop you retreating into splendour and beauty—into the thoughts and beliefs that make the real life—the real you.

Nor is Philip moved by Miss Abbott's illuminating reply: "I have never had that experience yet. Surely I and my life must be where I live." Certainly she speaks here for Forster. It is of less importance that her first excursion into "real life" has been ostensibly a fiasco; she has dared to look reality in the face.

If Forster encourages his characters to prefer reality to illusion, he assumes the concomitant duty to be honest with himself. This annoying habit accounts probably for the ambiguity which readers find in his treatment of people and situations. No propagandist for a narrow cause, the author never sees things as black or white. Sawston may be spiritually deadening, but it is clean, polite, and comfortable. Forster is convinced of the superiority of his beloved Italy, though he will not disguise its essential barbarity or its lack of cultivated reticence. While Miss Abbott contemplates saving the baby from the "contagion" of Gino's selfish, violent love, she has to consider the alternative—the dreadfully cold and loveless upbringing of his half-sister, Irma, by the Herritons:

> She was silent. This cruel, vicious fellow knew of strange refinements. The horrible truth, that wicked people are capable of love, stood naked before her, and her moral being was abashed. . . . She was in the presence of something greater than right or wrong.

Forster allows his least intelligent and least appealing character to go through life innocent of any moral ambiguity. Moral judgments come easy to Harriet. As for Italians, "I condemn the whole lot," and she throws in the French for good measure. To the more sensitive Philip, as to his creator, "Things aren't so jolly easy."

In a very short novel, Forster devotes much space to the story of Santa Deodata. Perhaps he concentrates on the legend of Monteriano's patron saint to extend the motif of ambiguity, and, in a way, to bind up the major motifs of the book by affording them the detachment of fable. From a church smelling ambiguously of "incense and garlic," the saint, a remnant of the "Dark Ages," dominates life in modern Monteriano. In her are linked Italy's "sweetness and barbarity." Her career and Philip's have many traces in common: the lack of purposeful activity, the paralysis of effort "in the house of her mother," the resistance of the temptation to taste the joys of this world, and the early spiritual death of the martyr. "In her death as in her life," says Forster, "Santa Deodata did not accomplish much." The next words on the page are spoken by Miss Abbott to Philip: " 'So what are you going to do?' " The problem of love and moral responsibility is implicit too in the saint's history, for she has had to choose between physical action in this world to succor her mother, hurled down the stairs by the devil, and a mortification of the flesh through voluntary paralysis even at a moment when action might save a loved one. The church has sanctified her for sacrificing reality to a religious ideal.

With Forster, as with Joyce, no part of the total work of art is accidental, random, or superfluous. Though economy is the keynote in *Where Angels Fear to Tread*, Forster is impelled to include the story of the saint, and, at the very end, the parallel of the Endymion myth to the Miss Abbott-Gino-Philip story because they provide the necessary backdrop for true perspective. Though Forster will speak at length in future novels of proportion as a basis for modern living, in this novel that quality must be experienced as implicit in the rhythm and the pattern of the fiction.

HOWARDS END

Forster's most ambitious novel is an extension of his liberal philosophy to fiction. This is said not in extenuation of its expository propaganda for a reordering of life: *Howards End* hardly requires apologies. As a novel it attempts—almost successfully—to fix England momentarily under a powerful microscope and to isolate the disease that is sapping the strength of Forster's countrymen. The author's subsequent diagnosis and proposed therapy are no more a superfluous extrusion on the work of art than a physician's prescription would be redundant at the end of his examination.

Though Forster goes into minute details of the malady, it may be summed up briefly as lack of proportion. To put the proposition positively, health will return to England when proportion is restored—proportion in human relations, in social, political, and economic relations, in the equilibrium between thought and action, in the balance of things (machinery) and people, in, finally, the union of the body and the spirit. And if it be alleged that Forster has here served up a large order, made impossible demands on the contemporary world, a line from his "What I Believe" shows the confidence of the author in the immediate availability of the necessary strength: "Not by becoming better, but by ordering and distributing his native goodness, will Man shut up Force into its box, and so gain time to explore the universe and to set his mark upon it worthily."

There is not a "bad" character in the book, whose cast includes a sizeable spectrum of English society, from the vulgar Jacky, a graduate of the streetwalking school, to Mr. Wilcox, rich, eminent, and formerly Jacky's most distinguished client. Even the unattractive Charles, who goes to prison for killing a man, is obviously more sinned against than sinning in his education for life and citizenship. What is awry for all these people is their vision—the ability to see life steady and see it whole. So perceived by rightminded and righthearted human beings, says Forster, it must improve.

For Forster there are a few people who stand above the human struggle, people of whom it can hardly be said that they "see" or "perceive" the truth. The truth for them is felt, is known intuitively, and they exude an influence rather than engage actively in a program of reform. Generally middle-aged, always parents, saintly Mr. Emerson (in *A Room with a View*) is of their group, and Mrs. Moore of *A Passage to India*. In *Howards End* Mrs. Wilcox plays the part, giving way to and blending into Margaret Schlegel after the death of the older woman. These have achieved without conscious effort the proportion which the sages knew. Though their hold on this world may be physically tenuous (Mr. Emerson is a dying man; the two elderly women die long before the novels conclude), they control the living by the strength of their elemental natures. Mrs. Wilcox is part of nature, in fact: pervasive in the past, the present, and the future, she shares the transcendent strength and endurance of the giant tree which stands on the lawn of her country home:

She approached . . . trailing noiselessly over the lawn, and there was actually a wisp of hay in her hands. She seemed to belong not to the young people and their motor, but to the house, and to the tree that overshadowed it. One knew that she worshipped the past, and that the instinctive wisdom the past can alone bestow had descended upon her— that wisdom to which we give the clumsy name of aristocracy. . . .

Her human relationships are instinctive and free from the encumbrances of civilization. She will not say of two people that they break an engagement but only that "they do not love any longer." And as she speaks she stoops down close to the earth "to smell a rose." In her garden she knows the order of nature. With people she senses their thoughts and feelings.

"But Mrs. Wilcox knew."

"Knew what?"

"Everything; though we neither of us told her a word, and had known all along, I think."

"Oh, she must have overheard you."

"I suppose so, but it seemed wonderful. . . ."

With approaching death, her saintliness is emphasized by "the light of the fire, the light from the window, and the light of a candle-lamp, which threw a quivering halo round her hands. . . ." She has a lack of interest in intellectual things and in action generally. "Clever talk alarmed her and withered her delicate imaginings . . . she was a wisp of hay, a flower." To the brittle sophisticates at Margaret Schlegel's luncheon party, Mrs. Wilcox seems, as indeed she is, "out of this world," beyond everyday concerns of ordinary people. Though her funeral occurs only a quarter way through the novel, her spirit infuses the book, and her legacy of her house, Howards End, to Margaret establishes material continuity in the plot.

Margaret Schlegel speaks for Forster in the novel as Mrs. Wilcox cannot. The older woman loses her voice in death, but even if Forster had seen fit to keep her alive as a character, it would have been artistically unthinkable to cast her in the role of propagandist. More a maternal essence than a person, Mrs. Wilcox is fated to "be," not to act. The woman upon whom she moves to confer her mantle of spiritual authority (along with her husband and her beloved house) is, unlike her benefactor, a real person. Mrs. Wilcox chooses wisely, for Margaret is further advanced than her associates toward the total integration which Forster adduces. Where the shadowy Mrs. Wilcox is, without struggle, comfortably settled at the apex of "being," Margaret represents the possibility of "becoming"—the successful aspirant for proportion, an extraordinary human being but still a human being.

The path to understanding for Margaret is rocky. Considerations of class, money, material advancement, a retreat to unreality—all threaten to obscure this pilgrim's progress toward a none too certain goal. Though the epigraph on the title page is "Only connect . . . ," at times Margaret's faith in the efficacy of personal relations is shaken. She and her sister Helen have always assumed the primacy of human contact, of love and friendship in a culture dominated by commerce, but their early experiences with the Wilcox clan bring doubt. Mrs. Wilcox aside, the Wilcoxes represent the modern commercial temperament and, more significantly, the outward, bustling, often inhuman, always insensitive life of affairs which Forster epitomizes in the motif of "telegrams and anger." The surface vigor of this way of life represents the first temptation in Margaret's quest:

> The truth is that there is a great outer life that you [Helen] and I have never touched—a life in which telegrams and anger count. Personal relations, that we think supreme, are not supreme there. There love means marriage settlements, death, death duties. So far I'm clear. But here my difficulty. This outer life, though obviously horrid, often seems the real one—there's grit in it. It does breed character. Do personal relations lead to sloppiness in the end?

Though she is here able to reject this "outer life" for herself, she has not thereby attained proportion. Nor will she find it in the opposite kind of life, temptingly proffered by Helen:

> I mean to love *you* more than ever. Yes, I do. You and I have built up something real, because it is purely spiritual. There's no veil of mystery over us. Unreality and mystery begin as soon as one touches the body. . . . Our bothers are over tangible things—money, husbands, house-hunting. But Heaven will work of itself.

Margaret's answer, and Forster's, is one from which Rickie Elliott might have profited in *The Longest Journey:*

> . . . she felt that there was something a little unbalanced in the mind that so readily shreds the visible. The business man who assumes that this life is everything, and the mystic who asserts that it is nothing, fail, on this side and on that, to hit the truth . . . truth . . . was only to be found by continuous excursions into either realm, and though proportion is the final secret, to espouse it at the outset is to insure sterility.

As the book ends Margaret has come to the knowledge which Mrs. Wilcox intended her to have: "life was a deep, deep river, death a blue sky, life was a house, death a wisp of hay, a flower, a tower, life and death were anything and everything, except this ordered insanity

. . . there were truer relationships beyond the limits that fetter us now." She knows now the necessity for all things in proper balance, and this balance, now attained, is the basis of her "speech" to her husband. "It had to be uttered once in a life, to adjust the lopsidedness of the world." Mr. Wilcox becomes only the symbolic audience, for Margaret, through Forster, goes beyond her husband "to thousands of men like him—[in] a protest against the inner darkness in high places that comes with a commercial age." Her most serious charge against him is that "he had refused to connect."

These flat pronouncements scattered through the book may be worthwhile raw material for a philosophical debate, but there remains the question of their aesthetic projection in the novel.

If the property of Howards End is England itself, as Lionel Trilling convincingly indicates, it passes from Mrs. Wilcox, the great mother and natural aristocrat, to Margaret Schlegel, born of the new aristocracy of culture, refinement, intelligence, money, and liberal democracy. The transference of the house is not accomplished without difficulty, for the Wilcoxes, with business efficiency, make every effort to stave off the fated inheritance by legal trickery. But the power of Mrs. Wilcox is great even in her death: inexorably, affairs arrange themselves so that, by the end of the book, Margaret is wholly mistress of Howards End. The menage which she directs seems symbolic of the future of Forster's England. Mr. Wilcox still lives in the house, but he is a sick man; his power has passed to his wife. Also part of the household is the illegitimate child of Helen Schlegel and Leonard Bast, like Gino's baby in *Where Angels Fear to Tread* the product of two cultures. In the England to come, where every voter will vote Liberal, the depressed civil servant and artisan class will join with the educated and enlightened upper classes to replace the moneyed interests whose trusteeship of the country is without sympathy, love, or even the kind of communication that is more vital than a telegram.

This peculiar household described in the culminating chapters of the novel has not been drawn together through a random whim of the author. Rather there is a careful statement of the motif in the opening pages, followed by a deceptively casual enrichment of the symbolic design. If anything, Forster's offhand manner has meant widespread unawareness of the meticulousness—at times, almost Proustian—of his structural framework.

By calling his story *Howards End*, Forster shows the importance he attaches to the symbol of the country house—natural roots, stability, beauty, the resources of an earlier England. The Schlegel sisters, of Anglo-German stock and representative of the new urban aristocracy based on intellect and leisure, are a step below Mrs. Wilcox in their choice of a place to live. They rent their house in London on lease and, in fact, are to be dispossessed so that their dignified dwelling can be razed to make way for ugly modern flats—the kind which pleases Mr. Wilcox and his children. For Mrs. Wilcox, the notion of destroying a dwelling is traumatic: " 'Howards End was nearly pulled down once. It would have killed me.' "

To reinforce the motif of England as a land of homes as well as a homeland, the ebb and flow of London (and of human) life is presented in terms of real estate development.

> . . . the city herself emblematic of their lives, rose and fell in a continual flux, while her shallows washed more widely against the hills of Surrey and over the fields of Hertfordshire. This famous building had arisen, that was doomed. Today Whitehall had been transformed: it would be the turn of Regent Street tomorrow. And month by month the roads smelt more strongly of petrol, and were more difficult to cross, and human beings heard each other speak with greater difficulty, breathed less of the air, and saw less of the sky. Nature withdrew: the leaves were falling by midsummer; the sun shone through dirt with an admired obscurity.

Verging on Wordsworthian sentimentality here, in other sections of the novel Forster handles the theme with Joycean detachment.

The Schlegels too are forced into canvassing the real estate market for a home, but the mere idea of being uprooted paralyzes them into static indecision. The unfortunate Leonard Bast is set straight by Margaret: " 'You tried to get away from the fogs that are stifling us all—away past books and houses to the truth. You were looking for a real home.' " And though Bast fails "to see the connection," fittingly he dies at Howards End, and his child will eventually call the estate his own home. But this is in the future. In the present, Mr. Wilcox, seeking to enter what is presumably (and legally) his own property, must ask, " 'Who's got the key?' " There is no reply. In the scramble to find a way into ˈHowards End, however, Margaret simply pushes open the door and walks in. It is her lot, as Mrs. Wilcox foresaw, to inherit the earth and the simple, beautiful house and tree that are part of it. What she does with the place, and with England, is apparent from the nature of her household as the novel ends. For keyless Leopold Bloom and Stephen Dedalus, Joyce was to provide no such satisfactory answer in *Ulysses*. Number seven Eccles Street is far from Howards End.

Complementing the motif of home as a national and spiritual organism is Forster's treatment of "machinery." He had considered this theme in *Where Angels Fear to Tread*. In *Howards End* he gives it full development. Agreeing with Matthew Arnold that change, movement, "progress" in themselves may not be desirable, the sensitive characters bemoan the senseless flux and bustle of London. Hurriers, it seems, cannot connect, and speed without consideration of direction is an irresponsible evil. Margaret feels this keenly:

> "I hate this continual flux of London. It is an epitome of us at our worst—eternal formlessness; all the qualities, good, bad, and indifferent, streaming away—streaming, streaming for ever. . . ."

Mr. Wilcox, as a giant of commerce, is guilty of this constant movement for movement's sake. "Henry was always moving, and causing others to move, until the ends of the earth met." His business establishment is based on the rubber industry of the empire. Mechanical movement impinges even upon Mrs. Wilcox who, shortly before her death, is last seen by Margaret rising upward in an elevator: "As the glass doors closed on [Mrs. Wilcox] . . . she had the sense of an imprisonment. . . . A woman of undefinable rarity was going up heavenwards, like a specimen in a bottle. And into what a heaven—a vault as of hell, sooty black, from which soots descended!"

As his pervasive symbol of mechanical movement, Forster chooses the motor car and forces his main characters to take a position for or against the machine. His least sympathetic people are always pro-mechanization. The vulgar and unthinking Charles, more concerned with his automobile than with living creatures, drives at a furious speed without ever seeming to get anywhere. Mrs. Wilcox is early revealed as against this product of modern inventiveness: "She seemed to belong not to the young people and to their motor, but to the house. . . ." Forster describes a scene in which she turns to Charles "who still stood in the throbbing stinking car" and then turns "away from him towards her flowers." Margaret, her spiritual heir, has an even deeper aversion to the motor car and detests driving in one.

A key incident in the novel illustrates the particular significance of this symbol to Forster. Margaret is a passenger in a motor car which runs over and kills a cat. After a sudden stop, Charles takes the wheel and drives on in order to shield the women from unpleasantness while servants attempt to comfort the owner of the animal. Because Margaret feels that her place is at the side of the bereaved girl, she insists that Charles stop the car, but he ignores her frantic entreaties. At last she jumps out of the moving vehicle in desperation. Her action is notable in itself, as an expression of character, but it is also symbolically important. In a civilization run by men of Charles's stamp—a civilization of speed, motion without direction, whose trademark, as Huxley says, is Our Ford who art in Detroit—Margaret alone has the gumption literally to get off the bandwagon even at the risk of personal injury. By her human and humane act, she forces the car to halt, reverses the direction of its occupants, and even brings the rather dense Charles to a temporary reconsideration of his position. Ruminating on her action later on, she "felt their whole journey from London had been unreal. They had no part with the earth and its emotions. They were dust, and a stink, and cosmopolitan chatter, and the girl whose cat had been killed had lived more deeply than they."

Again the objection to the mechanical is that it inhibits contact with elemental, natural things. Determined to prevent the arrangements for Evie's wedding from becoming similarly completely mechanical, Margaret makes a gallant effort to walk to the church rather than to be driven in the motor car to aid in the split-second, mechanical timing of the affair. "Henry treated a marriage like a funeral, item by item, never raising his eyes to the whole." And true enough, the wedding is a prime example of business methods applied to human relationships. Similarly, Margaret is dismayed to see the athletic Charles and his friend frustrated in their desire for a swim because, even surrounding such a natural and uncomplicated sport, the Wilcoxes had allowed a need for machinery to develop—for the key to the bathing shed, the springboard, the servant to carry the bathing suits, and all the rest. Unlike George Emerson, in *A Room with a View*, who regains his youthful vitality through an impromptu swim in a wild brook, the Wilcox children have shut themselves off from nature though they live in so idyllic a spot as Howards End.

Forster is no fuzzy-minded liberal in this novel, complaining about the evils of his world without realizing the complexity of all segments of the social, political, and economic spectrum. In spite of good intentions, human beings may not connect unless they have sufficient money, Forster frankly admits. As Orwell realizes a quarter century later, "the very soul of the world is economic, and . . . the lowest abyss is not the absence of love, but the absence of coin." Bast is pitiful rather than tragic, Forster would say, because he lacks the financial wherewithal to qualify as a hero.

The mere possession of money, however, is insufficient to raise men to heroic status. In Forster's novels, as Lionel Trilling has said, there are few strong men; England depends for its future mainly on the character of its women. Caroline Abbott is a goddess alike to frail Philip and mindless Gino in *Where Angels Fear to Tread*. Even the unsympathetic Mrs. Herriton and Harriet display masculine shrewdness and brutality. In *Howards End* all the principal male characters are immobilized before the end of the book. Charles is in jail, Leonard is dead, Tibby is ineffectual, and Mr. Wilcox is sick. To Margaret and Helen, as to Mrs. Wilcox before them, falls the power to make what they will of Howards End and of England. It is not clear to Forster or to the reader whether they will succeed.

A PASSAGE TO INDIA

Though Forster's two trips to India surely provided him with much of the color and the feeling of the place which his novel reveals, the book is certainly more than a fictional travelogue, a kind of *Inside India*. In the words of Walt Whitman's poem, "Passage to India," Forster's novel is a

Passage to more than India!
Are thy wings plumed indeed for such far flights?
O soul, voyagest thou indeed on voyages like those?

As with Forster's earlier novels, he is primarily concerned with matters of human conduct and especially with the dark places in the human heart which make for unhappiness and confusion not only between individuals but between races and nations:

Passage to you, your shores, ye aged fierce enigmas!
Passage to you, to mastership of you, ye strangling problems!
You, strew'd with the wrecks of skeletons, that, living, never reach'd you.

Perhaps Forster's purpose is the lofty aim ascribed by Whitman to the artist of the future:

Finally shall come the poet worthy that name,
The true son of God shall come singing his songs.

Then not your deeds only O voyagers, O scientists and inventors, shall be justified,

> All these hearts as of fretted children shall be sooth'd,
> All affection shall be fully responded to, the secret shall be told,
> All these separations and gaps shall be taken up and hook'd and link'd
>   together. . . .

Yet even Forster's intelligence and good will have limits which the practical problems of India were calculated to test. For British India seemed to sensitive intellects of the Twenties a crazyquilt, a patchwork of empire. Though England may have made its subject railroads run on time, it had not been able to establish significant rapport with its subject peoples. Forster catches this tragi-comic opera effect in his novel as he first shows how enormous the problem is. Perhaps the only commodity save manpower which India does not lack is a great pantheon of authentic gods. Yet men of Turton's or Ronny Moore's type, no doubt ineffectual in England, would cast themselves and their group in the role of great white gods come to rule the land. As Ronny puts it:

> "We're out here to do justice and keep the peace. Them's my sentiments. India isn't a drawingroom."
> "Your sentiments are those of a god," she [Adela] said quietly. . . .
> Trying to recover his temper, he said, "India likes gods."
> "And Englishmen like posing as gods."
> "There's no point in all this. Here we are, and we're going to stop, and the country's got to put up with us, gods or no gods. . . ."

Characteristically, the Indians refuse to accord these self-appointed deities more than the lip-service of worship. The gap that separates Englishman from Indian is wider than the space between the affluent and the poor, for even the wealthy Nawab Bahadur cannot feel entirely comfortable when he enters the sacred shrine of the lawgivers, the British social club. It is not a matter of the customary gap between the educated and the ignorant either. Even in his respected role as a doctor, Aziz is snubbed by the wives of the English colony with the same contempt they might show the lowest untouchable.

With all his political awareness and liberal astuteness, Forster is concerned with these manifestations of racial and national tension much less as political than as human problems. The crucial years from 1905 to the late Twenties—which included the trauma of the First World War—had if anything reinforced his convictions with respect to the importance of communication and communion among people of varying lands, religions, and social backgrounds. The word "Passage" in his title is highly significant: again the fictional attempt is to "connect," to find the key, the link, between one way of life and another. Nor will it be found in international conferences at the summit. What is needed is no less than the re-evaluation of the place of reason, of feeling, and of the super-rational in the individual psyche.

In *A Passage to India*, Forster's intent is therefore to present not only western civilization in collision with eastern, imperial with colonial, the human heart in conflict with the machinery of government, class, and race, but also a mystical, highly symbolic view of life, death, and human relationship. That he does not succeed entirely is not surprising in view of the great expanse of his canvas.

A degree of ambiguity is essential in symbolic presentation as in the representation of the mystical. For this reason, what precisely Forster has to say in the novel has been debated widely since its publication. The most convincing analysis is presented by Glen O. Allen in a recent article. (See Selected Bibliography.) This critic sees the threefold division of the book—"Mosque," "Caves," and "Temple"—as related respectively to the seasons of spring, summer, and the wet monsoon autumn of India; and to man's emotional nature, his intellect, and his capacity for love. Relating the principal characters to these arbitrary divisions, Allen finds that Forster has equated Dr. Aziz with emotionality, Fielding and Adela Quested with intellect, and Professor Godbole with the capacity to love. The mysterious Mrs. Moore, with her impulse toward emotion and her involvement in things of the intellect, seems equally at home in mosques, caves, or temples. The same critic finds further that the three-part division of the novel adumbrates three attitudes toward life: the path of activity, the path of knowledge, and the path of devotion. It is Forster's triumph, he shows, to weld these diverse paths together through delicate use of symbolic motifs so that they form a total satisfying, if mystifying, pattern of life and art.

In the specific context of the plot, Allen sees India as the formless mass, England and the West as rigid and definitely patterned. Thus, Adela and Mrs. Moore demand an idea of the world that will be reasoned and purposeful. But the Marabar caves show these women that the intellectual response to life is not enough. The awful experience which Adela undergoes in the cave is not subject to the intellect which she brings to bear upon it. It cannot be "understood." The result is her wild accusation of Dr. Aziz, her attempt to manipulate the world that she comprehends when an alien world, beyond reason, reaches out at her in the darkness of the cave. Mrs. Moore, on the other hand, comes close to the condition of the sages. Living in the rarefied atmosphere of one who is detached from the world, she cannot any longer deal sensibly with the values which civilization imposes on those who have not escaped. She may have gained much more, but she loses her practical concern for the things of this life and very naturally and suddenly drifts out of it on a ship westward bound.

The fusion of the three ways of life comes, as Allen sees it, in the water at Mau as all the boats collide. Fielding and Aziz, surrounded by the water of life and fertility, meet. East and West, emotion and intellect, find a common ground as the devotional ritual comes to a climax. Forster still clings to the principle of proportion as the highest human good. As he had insisted many years before, in *Howards End*, the life of bustle and telegrams is, in itself, as futile as the life of love pushed to extremes. But *A Passage to India* expands the canvas and makes use of subtle literary techniques of which Forster seemed incapable in 1910.

Though the demands of symbolic representation in a sense stereotype the principal characters of the novel (Ronny Moore is the stiff-necked British civil servant; Adela is the English tourist in a strange land; and so on), still Forster's knowledge of the way people act is too deep for such superficial sketching. Though Aziz may represent the irrational, emotional element in colonial peoples, he is at the same time a real person in his own right, with all the inconsistencies and contradictions which life implies. Though he literally gives his shirt stud off his collar to a deserving "brother," he is himself capable of the same narrowmindedness and inconsistency as those of another race to whom he kowtows:

> "Slack Hindus—they have no idea of society; I know them very well because of a doctor at the hospital. Such a slack, unpunctual fellow! It is as well you did not go to their house, for it would give you a wrong idea of India. Nothing sanitary. I think for my own part they grew ashamed of their house and that is why they did not send."

Though he is a scientist, a doctor, "his life [is] . . . largely a dream." He reverences a photograph of his dead wife more than any living thing. In a moment of good-hearted posturing, he can declare that "all men are my brothers," but for an imagined slight he shuns Fielding, the one Englishman who has tried to be worthy of his brotherhood. Aziz may be a weak human being, but he is at the same time a strong character. Though unpredictable, he is extremely probable. His name runs the gamut from "A" to "z," as if Forster intended that he should encompass essentially all humanity.

With Mrs. Moore, Forster faced a different task, in the execution of which he has not acquitted himself so successfully. If he worried about the improbable, he would hardly have created the Ruth Wilcox-Mrs. Moore type of character. Psychic goddesses in touch with heavenly bodies as well as with the human soul are disturbing creations. Out of the West comes Mrs. Moore to touch India with the strength of her mystic charm. Her death, and Lilia's, and Ruth Wilcox's, occurring suddenly and shockingly, establish a pattern of artistic impatience. There may be motivation for their ceasing to live, but their removal is artistically jarring. Lionel Trilling may argue that it is the improbable in life to which Forster is pointing, but there are less disruptive ways to do this in literature. The contractual obligation with his audience which a novelist assumes rules out narrative frivolity—or even a pattern of serious improbability—in a mature work. It demands that the fate of a character be determined by the internal requirements of his personality in interaction with the fictional environment. His destruction must not seem to be motivated by convenience or whim, or even by the demands of symbolic resolution.

A kindred shortcoming of many of Forster's novels is his occasional failure to take advantage of the characters which he does not willingly let die. The vivid sketching of the Wilcox clan at the beginning of *Howards End*—so promising as the basis for extended narrative development—becomes more and more pallid as the novel progresses. Charles, Paul, even Mr. Wilcox, retain their exaggerated external attributes much as Daddy Warbucks, in the "Little Orphan Annie" cartoon, keeps his over the years. The result of letting the characters down is that the novel may run down too. Perhaps it is right that dull Charles should be the instrument of Leonard Bast's extinction. But that the weapon should be an ancestral sword and that Bast's fall should bring down upon his head a library of books from which he had sought solace in life is just too pat, too playful for the reader to consider seriously.

Yet Forster's novels are mainly successful in spite of the defects which they sometimes contain. To balance the sense of frivolity and incompleteness which the author encourages by his startling elimination of major characters, there is the utter charm of Forster's narration. He has not surrendered to the vogue of impersonality and detachment. With conservative aplomb, therefore, he brings to bear on the actions of his characters the whimsical, totally honest, totally forthright reflections of an engaging mind. His cultivated sense of humor obtrudes itself to give point to the seriousness of his themes. His awareness of political and social currents is clear, and yet his fiction is free from the propagandizing tendencies which characterize much of the writing of his time. Matthew Arnold's "sweetness and light" emanate from Forster's novels with an intensity seldom matched among modern authors in English.

For his adherence to the conservative virtues which have been adduced here, Forster has had to pay the price of seeming flimsy and even superficial in a literary world dominated by the gigantic literary architecture of Proust, Joyce, Mann, and their imitators. The fact that, unlike Henry James, Forster is content to tell a good story in his own voice with refreshing directness has told against him in academic circles. The fact that his symbolism, though often obscure, is ordinarily not multileveled or, with the exception of *A Passage to India*, esoteric, has caused him to be slighted by critics looking for murky depths to plumb. It is interesting to observe that his support and popularization have come in this country from such men as Lionel Trilling, themselves committed to the study of literature as a sociological or political or general cultural phenomenon. Perhaps the revival which Forster's novels are now undergoing is a sign of changing critical tastes.

E. M. Forster : SELECTED BIBLIOGRAPHY

ALLEN, GLEN O. "Structure, Symbol, and Theme in E. M. Forster's *A Passage to India*," *PMLA*, lxx (December, 1955), 934–954.

DOBREE, BONAMY. *The Lamp and the Lute: Studies in Six Modern Authors.* Oxford: The Clarendon Press, 1929.

FORSTER, E. M. *Abinger Harvest.* New York: Harcourt, Brace, 1956.

———. *Two Cheers for Democracy.* New York: Harcourt, Brace, 1951.

———. *What I Believe.* London: The Hogarth Press, 1939.

HOARE, DOROTHY M. *Some Studies in the Modern Novel.* London: Chatto & Windus, 1938.

JOHNSTONE, J. *The Bloomsbury Group.* London: Secker & Warburg, 1954.

MACAULAY, ROSE. *The Writings of E. M. Forster.* London: The Hogarth Press, 1938.

TRILLING, LIONEL. *E. M. Forster.* Norfolk, Connecticut: New Directions, 1943.

WARNER, REX. *E. M. Forster.* London: Longmans, Green, 1950.

Virginia Woolf xx *Life*

Born on January 25, 1882, Virginia Woolf entered this world only a week before James Joyce and died in 1941, the year of Joyce's death. There, however, the biographical resemblance ends. Certainly there is no analogy between the antecedents of both writers: Joyce the product of a bourgeois Irish home and a family with no pretensions to literary distinction; Mrs. Woolf, on the other hand, the daughter of Leslie Stephen, distinguished editor of the *Cornhill Magazine* who married a Thackeray, was friendly with all the literary figures whose names sparkle in the late-Victorian constellations, and who was the compiler of the illustrious *Dictionary of National Biography*. Virginia and the other three Stephen children could not escape the cultural and intellectual influences of the time and the embryo novelist in particular appeared to thrive on such an upbringing. At least she can report matter-of-factly in later years that when she had finished one of her father's library books and returned it for a new batch, he handed her, and she read with pleasure almost in her infancy, the fifth and sixth volumes of Gibbon's *Decline and Fall*.

Shy in social gatherings and reticent in small talk, Mrs. Woolf alternated early between moods of quiet sadness and energetic vivacity. At least one critic ascribes her moodiness and uncertainty to the early death of her beloved mother (the Mrs. Ramsay of *To the Lighthouse*, in most respects) at a time when she needed her mother badly. It was as though she had been betrayed through the sudden death— a betrayal which led her to be wary of accepting other adults as friends until they had proved themselves. The death of her older sister in childbirth shortly afterward acted to reinforce Mrs. Woolf's suspicion of life as an arbitrary trickster.

With the death of their father and their coming into a considerable inheritance, in 1904 the four Stephen children took a house in Bloomsbury, a literary district which they—especially Virginia—were to make famous as the locale of the highly sophisticated and intellectually brilliant Bloomsbury Group a few years hence. But Mrs. Woolf, whose health had never been robust, suffered a physical and mental breakdown in 1905 which brought her to Europe for convalescence. There, overwhelmed by the beauty and significance of Greece (as E. M. Forster had succumbed to the charm of Italy), she regained her strength only to suffer a setback at the death of her brother Thoby, whose constitution could not withstand the typhoid attack which Greece brought on.

Once more in England, Mrs. Woolf threw herself into her profession, writing reviews and occasional articles, fighting for women's rights, and working on her first novel, *The Voyage Out*, which took seven years to complete. Meanwhile the Bloomsbury Group, though never a formal association, was taking on a fairly definite appearance. Lytton Strachey was in it, and later Roger Fry, Leonard Woolf (to whom Virginia was married in 1912), Clive Bell, Maynard Keynes, and Lady Ottoline Morrell. Much has been written about this famous group which need not be repeated in this brief biographical note. Suffice it to say that without the energy, charm, and intelligence which Mrs. Woolf displayed, an important circle in modern letters might not have existed, much less endured into history.

To those who know the tragic effect of World War II on Virginia Woolf's mind and her nerves, the fact that the holocaust of 1914 destroyed her health will come as no surprise. Nor is it surprising that one who loved London fiercely should have bowed to circumstance by taking a comfortable house at Richmond so that, though near the city, one might enjoy a peaceful room of one's own in which to think and write. Here Mrs. Woolf tried to put together the pieces, with considerable success as her notebooks show. Here too the Woolfs brought a printing press which they had purchased in London—a venture of unusual importance for contemporary letters. The Hogarth Press, as the Woolfs called it, became a center for *avant garde* publications in English. Eclectic in taste and passionately concerned with the printing of worthwhile writing, Leonard and Virginia Woolf published T. S. Eliot and Katherine Mansfield before their reputations had made them safe bets for publishers. Under the Hogarth imprint also appeared several of the early stories of Mrs.

Woolf, as well as critical pamphlets like the oft-quoted "Mr. Bennett and Mrs. Brown" (1924). So successful was the publishing venture that it outgrew the country house and had to be moved to new quarters in London, where it provided a modest income for its owners, though never enough to encourage a feeling of financial security.

Nor did the numerous books which Mrs. Woolf published during her lifetime enable her to live, except for a short time, in anything more than discreet comfort. *The Voyage Out* was published in 1915. *Night and Day* (1920) appeared shortly afterward and was followed by *Monday or Tuesday* (1921), a collection of her occasional pieces. In 1922, *Jacob's Room* came out. Not until *Mrs. Dalloway* (1923) did she hit her stride and speak in the authentic voice which was to make her reputation. This book and *The Common Reader* brought her the fame which her diary often wistfully desires, but also the problems which usually accompany it: unwanted guests, unnecessary letters to answer, visits from literary and pseudo-literary people, invitations to lecture, to dine, to judge, to be displayed at cocktail parties. But it brought her friendship with Vita Sackville-West (Lady Nicolson) and, in that sense, led to the writing of *Orlando* (1928) after *To the Lighthouse* had added to her growing reputation in 1927.

As the last decade of her life approached, Mrs. Woolf wrote furiously, as her diaries show, planning a new book even before the earlier book had been completed, and filling in the brief time between serious efforts with such ambitious projects as *Flush* (1929) simply as a change of pace. Thus, *The Waves* (1931), *The Years* (1937), and *Between the Acts* (1941) were produced before World War II destroyed her will to live and led to her suicide by drowning in the river close to her country home. The final years saw no diminution of effort and drive. She and her husband fought the censor for the right to publish, whether the victim was D. H. Lawrence or an unknown whose manuscript the Hogarth Press had already rejected.

They were years of fighting for the rights of women politically and in the literary world; years of refusal to compromise with principles (she would not accept gifts even from dear friends); and years of agonizing honesty of mind and spirit in the face of physical disasters that were ostensibly destroying much that civilized, cultured man had worked for centuries to establish. No wonder that so sensitive, questioning, insecure a spirit as Virginia Woolf preferred to drift out on the stream which she had so often written about rather than be present at the liquidation of all she loved.

Virginia Woolf xx *Works*

It would be safe to say that the influence of Virginia Woolf on modern letters has been out of all proportion to the number of readers her novels have attracted. Relatively ignored outside of the universities, her quiet works have survived in the noisy and uncongenial world which proved too much for her. Her novels endure though they lack most of the ingredients that publishers consider essential today: brutal realism, detailed exposure of sexual passion, violently frank dialogue, and the sense of material immediacy.

Yet Virginia Woolf is not at all the exotic plant which cursory inspection of her literary wares might indicate. She was neither out of the main stream of life nor of literature, and her suicide during the awful days of Britain's fight with Hitler merely accentuates the concern with which she followed contemporary events. In similar vein, her uncanny judgment in the matter of what to publish at her Hogarth Press speaks well of the good sense which she brought to her professional activities. Her critical tastes are practical, though sensitive, and above all fresh—though eminently tenable. It does not matter that she regarded criticism as an order of creation far beneath the writing of poems and stories: when she spoke as a critic it was not to carp, not to rally a coterie to an esoteric position, but to define clearly and without technical jargon the direction in which she thought worthwhile modern writing should go. Perhaps her creative work has endured at least among literary people—she may be called the "novelist's novelist"—because of the integrity of her own efforts to advance the contemporary novel experimentally along the proper path.

Though Mrs. Woolf was early disturbed over the status quo of her civilization—the place of women in the modern state, for instance —she was not always an experimenter in fiction. Her first novel, *The Voyage Out* (1915) is a wholly conventional book in content and traditional expository style. The interior monologue, later to become Mrs. Woolf's distinguishing technique, has no place in the narrative, and though the Dalloways, Richard and Clarissa, are introduced as peripheral characters, they are mere one-dimensional puppets in comparison to their later expanded state.

But by 1925, ten years later, Mrs. Woolf had evolved a distinctively new style and had broken philosophically and stylistically with her Edwardian predecessors, Wells, Galsworthy, and Bennett, to take her place with the innovators, T. S. Eliot, Joyce, and even Gertrude Stein. In a short essay, "Mr. Bennett and Mrs. Brown," she explains the duty of the newer generation of writers to prevent stifling in the stuffy over-furnished rooms of Edwardian fiction by breaking windows. The first major fruit of this new approach is *Mrs. Dalloway*.

MRS. DALLOWAY

Like Joyce's *Ulysses*, which Mrs. Woolf didn't like but did learn from, this considerably less ambitious novel takes place on one day in the month of June. As in *Ulysses* too, the events and actions which are recorded are trivial and, if the reader ignores the pattern, generally meaningless. A woman in her fifties, married to an inoffensive M.P. and the mother of a gangling seventeen-year-old daughter, plans to give an elaborate dinner party that evening. In preparation, she shops, speaks to the servants about final arrangements, entertains for a few moments a former suitor now elderly and back from India, sews, and ruminates on the meaning of existence.

But for Virginia Woolf, the everyday happenings of practical living are the least of life. In an essay in *The Common Reader*, she explains her position admirably:

> Life is not a series of gig lamps symmetrically arranged; life is a luminous halo, a semi-transparent envelope surrounding us from the beginning of consciousness to the end. Is it not the task of the novelist to convey this varying, this unknown and uncircumscribed spirit, whatever aberration or complexity it may display . . . ?

The projection of this evanescent halo in fiction becomes her problem: the subordination of observable actions to private thoughts and feelings which well up to form the flux of life in the psyche of human beings. Properly executed, this task results in the universalization of Mrs. Dalloway's day in London into all days everywhere for everybody. It results too in the realization that human beings are part of an ever-moving, ever-changing flow of existence, and that, caught up in this stream, they cease to be even discrete individuals, merging their essences instead with those of others in unpredictable amalgamations.

How does Mrs. Woolf accomplish these ambitious ends? First, by utilizing the stream-of-consciousness technique, which provides a verbal and syntactical approximation of the mind in flux, she seizes the initiative from the start. For the mind is capricious, unlikely to sort out in logical arrangement or order of importance the phenomena that count as the world reckons importance, from the items that the mind assigns tenaciously its own peculiar order of significance. Such apparent disorder is caught in descriptions like this one:

> And Richard Dalloway and Hugh Whitbread hesitated at the corner of Conduit Street at the very moment that Millicent Bruton, lying on the sofa, let the thread snap; snored. Contrary winds buffeted at the street corner. They looked in at a shop window; they did not wish to buy or to talk but to part, only with contrary winds buffeting the street corner, with some sort of lapse in the tides of the body, two forces meeting in a swirl, morning and afternoon, they paused. . . . In Norfolk, of which Richard Dalloway was half thinking, a soft warm wind blew back the petals; confused the waters; ruffled the flowering grasses. Haymakers, who had pitched beneath hedges to sleep away the morning toil, parted curtains of green blades; moved trembling globes of cow parsley to see the sky; the blue, the steadfast, the blazing summer sky.
>
> Aware that he was looking at a silver twohandled Jacobean mug, and that Hugh Whitbread admired condescendingly with airs of connoisseurship a Spanish necklace which he thought of asking the price of in case Evelyn might like it—still Richard was torpid; could not think or move. Life had thrown up this wreckage; shop windows full of coloured paste, and one stood stark with the lethargy of the old, stiff with the rigidity of the old, looking in. Evelyn Whitbread might like to buy this Spanish necklace—so she might. Yawn he must. Hugh was going into the shop.

Yet Mrs. Woolf brings order out of the mind's chaos for the reader who traces the total pattern. Possibly less exciting than Joyce's exploitation of Bloom's mind, or of Molly's and Stephen's, the stream that she uses in *Mrs. Dalloway* is simpler to follow and infinitely more poetic and melodious. The attempt is not to be true to the speech or even to the thought groupings of one character or the other. Rather, every stream is verbalized through the author's tongue or mind—all characters are Virginia Woolf—in speech and rhythm of thought as articulate and poetic as their brilliant creator. This can be dangerous in its potentially deadening sameness. There are, after all, no chapter divisions and very few separations of any kind in the three-hundred pages of text. Inexorably, one stream, one manner of speech flows on without a break, imposing a steady rhythm which even the change over from one character's point of view to another's fails to interrupt. In *Ulysses*, Stephen's stream is hard, tough, uneuphonious, intellectual; Bloom's is routine and bumbling; Molly's flabby, mainly unpunctuated, fluid. The personality of each character is underlined by the pattern of his distinctive speech and thought. With Virginia Woolf, though her characterizations are sharp and individual, the prose devoted to the thought and speech of each is the author's pattern, consistent, unwavering. Thus, Mrs. Dalloway—cool, snobbish, upper-class, may be represented in the same quiet accents as Peter Walsh, a failure—passionate, broken, insecure—as these excerpts testify:

He had escaped! was utterly free—as happens in the downfall of habit when the mind, like an unguarded flame, bows and bends and seems about to blow from its holding. I haven't felt so young for years! thought Peter, escaping (only of course for an hour or so) from being precisely what he was, and feeling like a child who runs out of doors, and sees, as he runs, his old nurse waving at the wrong window. But she's extraordinarily attractive, he thought, as, walking across Trafalgar Square in the direction of the Haymarket, came a young woman who, as she passed Gordon's statue, seemed, Peter Walsh thought (susceptible as he was), to shed veil after veil, until she became the very woman he had always had in mind; young, but stately; merry, but discreet; black, but enchanting.

"Who can—what can," asked Mrs. Dalloway (thinking it was outrageous to be interrupted at eleven o'clock on the morning of the day she was giving a party), hearing a step on the stairs. She heard a hand upon the door. She made to hide her dress, like a virgin protecting chastity, respecting privacy. Now the brass knob slipped. Now the door opened, and in came—for a single second she could not remember what he was called! so surprised she was to see him, so glad, so shy, so utterly taken aback to have Peter Walsh come to her unexpectedly in the morning! (She had not read his letter.)

The process of universalization is aided by Mrs. Woolf's unerring ability to provide both a past and a future for her characters as part of their immediate interior monologues. As David Daiches has so ably shown (see Bibliography), the added dimension afforded by allowing the persons of the novel to move back and forth in time to encompass an entire life in a few seconds of thought enriches not only the personality of the characters but, in greater measure, the philosophical depth of the book. There is nothing new about this device of the flashback or the glimpse into the future: what is noteworthy is Mrs. Woolf's smooth manipulation of time so that the transitions seem effortless and inevitable, as here:

> And Lady Bruton went ponderously, majestically, up to her room, lay, one arm extended, on the sofa. She sighed, she snored, not that she was asleep, only drowsy and heavy, drowsy and heavy, like a field of clover in the sunshine this hot June day, with the bees going round and about and the yellow butterflies. Always she went back to those fields down in Devonshire, where she had jumped the brooks on Patty, her pony, with Mortimer and Tom, her brothers. And there were the dogs; there were the rats; there were her father and mother on the lawn. . . .

Part of the effectiveness of Mrs. Woolf's manipulation of time as it affects the lives of her characters comes from her frequent confrontation of "real" clock time with the "unreal" sense of past and future—infinitely stretchable, now so far away in fancy, now so close when the mood demands. So Peter Walsh speaks "to himself rhythmically, in time with the flow of the sound, the direct downright sound of Big Ben striking the half-hour. (The leaden circles dissolved in the air.)" Later on, as Dr. Holmes examines Septimus Smith, "it was precisely twelve o'clock; twelve by Big Ben." For Richard Dalloway, "Big Ben was beginning to strike, first the warning, musical; then the hour, irrevocable." Upon each major character, clock time impinges menacingly while the time that counts, above and beyond mere chronological measurement, takes possession of his being.

Clock time is neutral, impersonal, implacable; it affects alike all who have physical existence. Using a device later adopted by motion pictures, Mrs. Woolf occasionally will stop the novel to fix her characters in a moment of this clock-time as they pursue disparate aims simultaneously. Thus, summaries like this are given:

> It was precisely twelve o'clock; twelve by Big Ben; whose stroke was wafted over the northern part of London; blent with that of other clocks, mixed in a thin ethereal way with the clouds and wisps of smoke, and died up there among the seagulls—twelve o'clock struck as Clarissa

Dalloway laid her green dress on her bed, and the Warren Smiths walked down Harley Street. Twelve was the hour of their appointment. Probably, Rezia thought, that was Sir William Bradshaw's house with the grey motor car in front of it. The leaden circles dissolved in the air.

Similarly, Virginia Woolf plays with space. Her dissimilar characters, dispersed in London's maze of streets and din of activity, are held by the common sights which they see as well as by the simultaneity of the time at which they see them. So, the sky writer, advertising toffee in the air above London, is observed by Mrs. Coates, Mrs. Bletchley, and Mr. Bowley in one place, by the Septimus Smiths in another. It hovers above Peter Walsh as he wanders through the streets. Mrs. Woolf calls the aeroplane "a concentration":

Away and away the aeroplane shot, till it was nothing but a bright spark; an aspiration; a concentration; a symbol . . . of man's soul; of his determination . . . to get outside his body, beyond his house, by means of thought, Einstein, speculation, mathematics, the Mendelian theory—away the aeroplane shot.

Such devices have the double effect of creating a "small world," in which the actors on the stage are all related by seeing and hearing the same sights and sounds. On the other hand, the oneness of the human beings involved, in terms of their simultaneous response to common stimuli, acts to expand the one-day, one-place, one-cast-of-characters arrangement to cover all people at all times in all places. In the same way, the unlikely coincidences involved in the crossing paths, the "accidental meetings" of the characters wandering about London on this June day, stress the closeness of the environment as well as the wide sweep of human interaction, of people relating to people.

What does Virginia Woolf have to say in *Mrs. Dalloway*? There is no political or social or religious "message." Perhaps the author hints at her purpose in the thoughts of Peter Walsh:

The compensation of growing old, Peter Walsh thought, coming out of Regent's Park, and holding his hat in hand, was simply this; that the passions remain as strong as ever, but one has gained—at last!—the power which adds the supreme flavour to existence,—the power of taking hold of experience, of turning it round, slowly, in the light.

The experience which Mrs. Woolf takes hold of is basically the reality of life and death—the significance, in a word, of the flow of consciousness on which human beings are borne from birth to death. The persistence of imagery of waves attests to the importance she assigned to this flow. Writing of Lady Bruton's nearness to death, the author says of her:

. . . she . . . felt often as she stood hesitating one moment on the threshold of her drawing-room, an exquisite suspense, such as might stay a diver before plunging while the sea darkens and brightens beneath him, and the waves which threaten to break, but only gently split their surface, roll and conceal and encrust as they just turn over the weeds with pearl.

Peter Walsh sums up the motif:

For this is the truth about our soul, he thought, our self, who fish-like inhabits deep seas and plies among obscurities threading her way between the boles of giant weeds, over sun-flickered spaces and on and on into gloom, cold, deep, inscrutable; suddenly she shoots to the surface and sports on the wind-wrinkled waves. . . .

It is no accident that Mrs. Woolf some years later centered a whole book around the theme which in *Mrs. Dalloway* is hardly more than a shadowy pattern.

No one phrase appropriately sums up the meaning of *Mrs. Dalloway*. Insights turn up on every page to heighten the reader's appreciation of human nature, of the English system, of parties, and of the thought pattern of psychotics. But if a pervasive concern had to be attributed to the author of the novel, it might be called universal love. As in Forster's novels, each of the central characters is delineated with respect to his place on the scale of love.

Clarissa Dalloway herself holds the center of the stage, not for any intensity in her love of others but as the focus of their own warmth. Even her maid basks in the sunlight of a kind word from her mistress. Richard, her phlegmatic husband, considers his good fortune in being married to Clarissa. The unstable suitor whom she has spurned years before returns with the same intensity of feeling for her as had once inflamed him. Almost everyone loves Mrs. Dalloway. Though Clarissa is cool, snobbish, and superficial in social relationships, her ability as a catalyst in producing satisfactory emotional reactions in other people becomes her chief concern. With Forster's characters, she emanates the admonition, "Only connect," without being able herself to attain the ultimate connection. She suffers from heart disease—and not only in a physical sense. Meaningfully, she conceives her role as a creative one: to bring other people into combination:

. . . what did it mean to her, this thing she called life? Oh, it was very queer. Here was So-and-so in South Kensington; some one up in Bayswater; and somebody else, say, in Mayfair. And she felt quite continuously a sense of their existence; and she felt what a waste; and she felt what a pity; and she felt if only they could be brought together; so she did it. And it was an offering; to combine, to create; but to whom?

The whole affair toward which the book tends is the symbolic party at the end at which the principal characters meet in time and space. Long away from the center of the stage, Sally Seton and Peter Walsh choose the party to re-enter Mrs. Dalloway's orbit. The old and the young, Lady Bruton and Elizabeth, make their way through the crowded drawing-room. The high and the low—domestics and the Prime Minister—pay homage to Mrs. Dalloway's gifts as hostess. Appropriately too, Sir William Bradshaw, the chief external link between the world of the Dalloways and the world of the Septimus Smiths, makes his appearance to verbalize the connection.

Of all the main characters, only Septimus Smith, dead by his own hand, is missing from a party to which he would not in life have been invited. His absence would seem significant, for he alone has had visions of Evans, a Christ-like figure killed in the war. He alone has verbalized the message of "Universal love."

Now for his writings; how the dead sing behind rhododendron bushes; odes to Time; conversations with Shakespeare; Evans, Evans, Evans—his messages from the dead; do not cut down trees; tell the Prime Minister. Universal love: the meaning of the world. Burn them! he cried.

And he alone has been found wanting by the practical, worldly men of London, the Holmeses and the Bradshaws, who have sought first to suppress his message and his person in a lunatic asylum and then have driven him, frantic, to suicide. Mrs. Woolf grimly identifies Smith's persecutors as human nature.

Septimus Smith is, however, very much present at the party, for he is Clarissa Dalloway's other self: the irrational, withdrawn, tormented side of the serene, outgoing heroine. Even if Mrs. Woolf had not revealed her intention in a preface, the clues to the Dalloway-Smith connection would not have been hard to find. At times, Clarissa feels in one sense terribly isolated from the people around her:

. . . But she said, sitting on the bus going up Shaftesbury Avenue, she felt herself everywhere; not "here, here, here"; and she tapped the back of the seat; but everywhere. She waved her hand, going up Shaftesbury Avenue. She was all that. So that to know her, or any one, one must seek out the people who completed them; even the places. Odd affinities she had with people she had never spoken to, some woman in the street, some man behind a counter. . . . she believed . . . that since our apparitions, the part of us which appears, are so momentary compared with the other, the unseen part of us, which spreads wide, the unseen might survive, be recovered somehow attached to this person or that, or even haunting certain places after death . . . perhaps—perhaps.

That Mrs. Woolf brooded over the difficulty of reconciling universal love with barbed wire, deep feeling with brittle party talk, is clear from the frequency and the intensity with which she intrudes the idea of death as a concomitant of love and of communication:

> Death was defiance. Death was an attempt to communicate; people feeling the impossibility of reaching the centre which, mystically, evaded them; closeness drew apart; rapture faded, one was alone. There was an embrace in death.

Conscious, in the midst of her social triumph, of her own basic failure to communicate what matters, Mrs. Dalloway has her private vision of death. As she looks across the street and sees in the window an old woman preparing for bed, as she thinks of the death of Septimus, Clarissa is, of course, seeing her own impending death. The irony of her lifelong ambition to bring people together is that, in a sense, connection is much deeper than meeting at parties. Everyone is everyone else. Even Miss Kilman, whose name and raincoat all combine to suggest sterility, repression, and death—even Miss Kilman has kinship with Mrs. Dalloway when the final account is rendered.

TO THE LIGHTHOUSE

"What is the meaning of life?" Lily Briscoe wonders as she contemplates her unfinished painting on its easel. This is the question to which Virginia Woolf had addressed herself in *Mrs. Dalloway* with perhaps inconclusive results. In *To the Lighthouse*, she returns to it with a singlemindedness of approach which controls rigidly the nebulous, filmy texture of existence.

The segment of life which Mrs. Woolf selects for fictional analysis is no raw sample. Severely delimited and brought into sharp focus, its events are highly organized into an obvious artistic pattern. The novel has a three-part division. In the first section, "The Window," a trip to the nearby lighthouse is planned by Mrs. Ramsay for her young son James in spite of the practical admonitions of other grownups—notably of Mr. Ramsay—that the weather will not permit the excursion. The journey is not made. The short interlude called "Time Passes," which makes up part two, describes the passage of time during which the actors of the piece grow older and the house on the seashore ages, free from the habitation of its owners. Mrs. Ramsay dies, two of her children lose their lives, and time holds sway. The long final section sees the trip to the lighthouse successfully undertaken many years later by Mr. Ramsay and two of his children, and the pattern of life completed on canvas by Lily Briscoe, who, as artist and creator, is the rightful heir to Mrs. Ramsay. As the book ends, she can say, with the reader, "I have had my vision."

From the abortive early attempt to the final disembarkation at the lighthouse, the stark tower with its bright shafts of light is the dominant symbol—punctuating the darkness, offering security to seafarers, dreams of mystery to children, and the certainty of its recurring rhythms to all who exist in time. But the meaning of this central symbol, isolated and immutable in a sea of flux, eludes full comprehension. That it has something to do with Mrs. Ramsay is clear from the start:

> Often she found herself sitting and looking, until she became the thing she looked at—that light, for example. And it would lift up on it some little phrase or other which had been lying in her mind . . .

> She praised herself in praising the light, without vanity, for she was stern, she was searching, she was beautiful like that light. It was odd, she thought, how if one was alone, one leant to inanimate things; trees, streams, flowers; felt they expressed one; felt they became one; felt they knew one, in a sense were one. . . .

David Daiches calls it "a symbol of the individual who is at once a unique being and a part of the flux of history. To reach the lighthouse is, in a sense, to make contact with a truth outside oneself, to surrender the uniqueness of one's ego to an impersonal reality." (See Bibliography, on page 149.) Only when the lighthouse is reached, he points out, do personal grudges disappear, compassion and understanding emerge, and egotism give way to impersonality.

In Mrs. Ramsay, Virginia Woolf has created another Clarissa Dalloway—though with a difference. Beautiful, absolute mistress of her domestic environment, a symbol of motherhood surrounded by her eight children, this woman dominates every character in the novel. Like her earlier counterpart, Mrs. Ramsay is less concerned with intellect than with intuition: "She did in her heart infinitely prefer boobies to clever men who wrote dissertations." She herself reads little. Like Clarissa, her aim in life is to gather people together ("She asked too many people to stay"), to marry them off (she exults in arranging the

marriage of Minta to Paul Rayley, and she tries to pair William
Bankes with Lily Briscoe). Even her main hobby, knitting, allows her
to create, to join threads, and to form a pattern with skillful fingers,
while her mind roams free. Nor does her influence end with her death.
As though to die is simply to enter a new phase of flux, Mrs. Ramsay,
killed off meaninglessly in a parenthetical sentence, is vividly alive in
the minds of her husband and of Lily Briscoe. Like Mrs. Wilcox of
Howards End, her spirit is the controlling factor in the last section of
the novel.

It is Lily, however, acting for the authoress herself, who takes up
the reins on earth for Mrs. Ramsay, as Margaret Schlegel does for
Ruth Wilcox. Lily's canvas is Mrs. Woolf's view of reality, and Lily's
final vision on the last page of the book *is To the Lighthouse* itself.
Lily's canvas is the embodiment of Mrs. Woolf's wish to make "life
stand still here," to "make of the moment something permanent." If
life is flux, then the capturing and fixing of reality—its shape and
texture—is for the artist the supreme activity and, even for Mrs. Ramsay, utterly desirable. Thinking of her dead hostess, Lily muses:

> In the midst of chaos there was shape; this eternal passing and flowing
> . . . was struck into stability. Life stand still here, Mrs. Ramsay said.
> "Mrs. Ramsay! Mrs. Ramsay!" She repeated. She owed it all to her.

To the Lighthouse is also a study of human relationships. As Mrs.
Dalloway seeks in partygiving a link with the stream of life, so Mrs.
Ramsay gathers a party of houseguests whose interrelationships with
her family and with one another help to suggest, if not to define, the
meaning of life. Forster's problem of how to "connect" is Mrs.
Woolf's as well.

> Sitting on the floor with her [Lily's] arms round Mrs. Ramsay's knees,
> close as she could get, smiling to think that Mrs. Ramsay would never
> know the reason of that pressure, she imagined how in the chambers of
> the mind and heart of the woman who was, physically, touching her,
> were stood, like the treasures in the tombs of kings, tablets bearing
> sacred inscriptions, which if one could spell them out, would teach one
> everything, but they would never be offered openly, never made public.
> What art was there, known to love or cunning, by which one pressed
> through into those secret chambers? What device for becoming, like
> waters poured into one jar, inextricably the same, one with the object
> one adored? Could the body achieve, or the mind, subtly mingling in
> the intricate passages of the brain? or the heart? Could loving, as people
> called it, make her and Mrs. Ramsay one? for it was not knowledge but
> unity that she desired, not inscriptions on tablets, nothing that could

be written in any language known to men, but intimacy itself, which is knowledge, she had thought, leaning her head on Mrs. Ramsay's knee.

But in Mrs. Woolf the connection is not political or social or economic or even familial. The problem for her is to separate the human being from the sea of flux—to capture the essence of individuality in an intuitive moment. This is hardest of all, for what she asks by implication is that essence. The senses are not always reliable in ferreting it out: to one's eyes on a certain day, the image of Mr. and Mrs. Ramsay watching their child at play is nothing more than that; at another moment, the image, fraught with significance, becomes deeply symbolic, Lily Briscoe's ears hear arrogance in the harsh accents of Charles Tansley's voice while in reality he shrinks inwardly with an acute inferiority complex.

Nor will intellectual attainments fit one for the task of extracting the essence of human experience. Mr. Ramsay, whose name counts in the history of contemporary philosophy, may frighten his children, but he becomes himself a child before his wife's intuitive knowledge of his psychic needs. The scholarly chats in which he and Charles Tansley engage are tolerated by Mrs. Ramsay because she has the wisdom to see that they are merely a species of baby talk when measured against the sum total of meaningful experience.

Mrs. Woolf allows the remnants of the Ramsay clan to reach the lighthouse only after travail, war, death, and an accumulation of human wisdom—rather than at the start of the book—to show that such experience is necessary to the attainment of the balance that comes with impersonality. This is the reason, perhaps, that Mrs. Woolf associates Mrs. Ramsay so frequently with the lonely tower. The cynosure of all eyes, a welcome sight to all travelers in flux, both Mrs. Ramsay and her lighthouse are generally distant and unapproachable. They give direction to the human beings who steer by their light (Paul Rayley watches Mrs. Ramsay's eyes for signs of approval in his wooing of Minta Doyle, though Mrs. Ramsay has never spoken to him about her interest in the match). Even her husband, though he can find repose in her motherly sympathy, is far from understanding his wife in life. Only after many years of suffering and maturing can sullen James Ramsay, who has harbored violent oedipal thoughts of murdering his father, find release from personal antagonism as he and his chastened father tie up at the lighthouse. In bringing the quest for self-knowledge to a successful culmination when the tower is reached, the author points symbolically to Mrs. Ramsay as the principle of impersonal involvement—as strong a force in death as in life.

Mrs. Woolf deals with life and death in and out of time even more imaginatively than in *Mrs. Dalloway.* In the twenty-five page interlude entitled "Time Passes," normal, traditional relationships of human beings to nature in fiction are reversed. The fate of the protagonists is subordinated in narration to the vagaries of climate and the passage of time. Thus:

The nights now are full of wind and destruction; the trees plunge and bend and their leaves fly helter skelter until the lawn is plastered with them and they lie packed in gutters and choke rain pipes and scatter damp paths. Also the sea tosses itself and breaks itself, and should any sleeper fancying that he might find on the beach an answer to his doubts, a sharer of his solitude, throw off his bedclothes and go down by himself to walk on the sand, no image with semblance of serving and divine promptitude comes readily to hand bringing the night to order and making the world reflect the compass of the soul. The hand dwindles in his hand; the voice bellows in his ear. Almost it would appear that it is useless in such confusion to ask the night those questions as to what, and why, and wherefore, which tempt the sleeper from his bed to seek an answer.

[Mr. Ramsay, stumbling along a passage one dark morning, stretched his arms out, but Mrs. Ramsay having died rather suddenly the night before, his arms, though stretched out, remained empty.] (brackets are Mrs. Woolf's)

And:

Moreover, softened and acquiescent, the spring with her bees humming and gnats dancing threw her cloak about her, veiled her eyes, averted her head, and among passing shadows and flights of small rain seemed to have taken upon her a knowledge of the sorrows of mankind.

[Prue Ramsay died that summer in some illness connected with childbirth, which was indeed a tragedy, people said, everything, they said, had promised so well.]

And now in the heat of summer the wind sent its spies about the house again. . . .

As it does in actuality but in very few fictional representations of reality, the sweep of flux is allowed to dominate the discrete individual segments of human experience which occasionally impinge.

Space, too, is carefully delineated by the author. Deliberately, she avoids specific identification (except to set the scene in the Hebrides) so that the bare rocks, the water, and the lighthouse may share the classical symbolic associations of Anywhere. The body of water which leads to the lighthouse—being the sea of flux, the river of consciousness—must be nameless, for it is life itself.

The cast of characters, too, though identified as individuals, are discernible as types. Old Mr. Carmichael, useless to his wife, dependent on charity for simple pleasures like tobacco, ostensibly lazy and unproductive, surprises everyone by succeeding at lyric poetry. Mr. Bankes, the scientific mind in action, preferring solitary perfection to immersion in the stream of human involvement, refuses Mrs. Ramsay's silent offer of marriage to Lily Briscoe. (That his name is Bankes may be meaningful in the sense that he rejects the offer to immerse in life.) Nor can the name Lily, conferred on the spinsterish artist who acts as surrogate for the late Mrs. Ramsay, be ignored as indicating the pure beauty, the flowering whiteness appropriate to weddings and funerals. In Mr. and Mrs. Ramsay, finally, Mrs. Woolf weds intellect and intuition, but shows clearly that there is no real equality in the match. Whatever the world may think, it is Mrs. Ramsay's intuition that controls the union. After her death, her husband's rudderless intellect blunders tellingly until he is reunited with her spirit in the arrival at the lighthouse.

THE WAVES

For the one who had dealt exhaustively in fiction with the stream of life as it impinged on the consciousness, now of Mrs. Dalloway, now of Mrs. Ramsay, the logical next step would be a study of identity. What is this thing in human beings upon which the disorderly rush of external flux can impinge? Is it the same in all human beings? Can one retain one's identity, hemmed in on all sides by the insistent "machine" which seeks to break it down? Are all identities really one as, in *The Waves*, "all deaths are one death"? And, finally, does the individual identity remain constant in time and space?

Mrs. Woolf presents to the reader six formal and distinct identities —characters whose changing fortunes she will set down during the course of the novel. She calls them Bernard, Neville, Louis, Susan, Rhoda, and Jinny. Though much more space is devoted to the three men, all six characters emerge as clearly delineated personalities with easily remembered, distinguishing traits. Lonely Bernard, who thinks in terms of literary phrases and seeks the answers to questions of life and death, probably acts as a partial surrogate for the author. The shy poet, Neville, needing acceptance but courting rejection, is sympathetic in his attempts to relate to the others. To Louis, life means material success in a shipping firm, and identity is a matter of signing letters which he has dictated. The three women are treated more cursorily. They seem, in fact, to be meaningful only as their relationship with the men around them is significant. Susan connects with earth and produces crops and children. Jinny encourages barren sexual promiscuity. Rhoda finds release in loving Percival and, after his death, in being mistress to Louis.

The interaction among these six characters is the basis of Mrs. Woolf's narrative—the device which keeps the novel from being a philosophical treatise. In a formal way, each of the six comes to the center of the stage to deliver a silent soliloquy, then moves off to be replaced by one of the others. The reader learns thus how they appear to themselves, how they think they appear to others, and, as speaker gives way to speaker, how one actually impinges upon the next. Almost scientifically, and in the best tradition of experimental control, Mrs. Woolf introduces the shadowy figure of Percival, a schoolfellow of the other six, who dies in India in his middle twenties. He has no speaking part of his own and lives only in the minds and memories of the six. A control figure, because of his apartness, what he means to each of them is a measure more of their personality than of his own. He becomes the touchstone, the marker from whose fixed position the reader measures the depth, height, and distance of the participating actors. Percival does not matter; the reactions to him of the rest are all-important.

The theme of overriding importance is the struggle for individual identity against the vast, noisy, ever-encroaching outer world. It takes a traumatic experience, says Mrs. Woolf, to stop the enormous machine even for a few minutes. Bernard receives two almost simultaneous jolts—the birth of his son and the news of Percival's death. Yet even then he is unable entirely to shut out of his consciousness the external world:

> This then is the world that Percival sees no longer. Let me look. The butcher delivers meat next door; two old men stumble along the pavement; sparrows alight. The machine then works; I note the rhythm, the throb, but as a thing in which I have no part, since he sees it no longer. (He lies pale and bandaged in some room.) Now then is my chance to find out what is of great importance, and I must be careful, and tell no

lies. About him my feeling was: he sat there in the centre. Now I go to that spot no longer. The place is empty.
But almost immediately:

Yet already signals begin, beckonings, attempts to lure me back. Curiosity is knocked out only for a short time. One cannot live outside the machine for more perhaps than half an hour. Bodies, I note, already begin to look ordinary; but what is behind them differs—the perspective. Behind that newspaper placard is the hospital; the long room with black men pulling ropes; and then they bury him. Yet since it says a famous actress has been divorced, I ask instantly, Which? Yet I cannot take out my penny; I cannot buy a paper; I cannot suffer interruption yet,

I ask if I shall never see you again.   But for how long? Things will become too difficult to explain: there will be new things; already my son. . . . The sequence returns; one thing leads to another—the usual order.

Later, in the magnificent reunion dinner scene at Hampton Court, the shock of discovering old age in one's youthful friends leads to a temporary deep silence which almost dissolves identity and defeats the encroaching stream:

"But listen," said Louis, "to the world moving through abysses of infinite space. It roars; the lighted strip of history is past and our Kings and Queens; we are gone; our civilization; the Nile; and all life. Our separate drops are dissolved; we are extinct, lost in the abysses of time, in the darkness."

"Silence falls; silence falls," said Bernard. "But now listen; tick, tick; hoot, hoot; the world has hailed us back to it. I heard for one moment the howling winds of darkness as we passed beyond life. Then tick tick (the clock); then hoot, hoot (the cars). We are landed; we are on shore; we are sitting, six of us, at a table.

Each of the six attempts to achieve identity in his own way. Louis's method is simplest and perhaps least satisfying:

"I have signed my name," said Louis, "already twenty times. I, and again I, and again I. Clear, firm, unequivocal, there it stands, my name. Clear-cut and unequivocal am I too. Yet a vast inheritance of experience is packed in me. I have lived thousands of years. I am like a worm that has eaten its way through the wood of a very old oak beam. But now I am compact; now I am gathered together this fine morning.

That he fails is implicit in his inability to achieve total integration of his personality. Not even affluence and business success bring satisfaction: though he sends luxury liners to ply the sea routes of the world, he cannot leave the sordid slums to which he has become accustomed or throw off the inferiority complex developed in child-hood. To reiterate his "I"-ness on paper is not to escape ambiguity.

Neville seeks identity through poetry, but in personal relationships he is less successful. Mrs. Woolf notes that even after his fame has spread, he carries credentials in his pocket as if he must prove his special qualifications by an identification card.

For the three women, assertion of identity is attempted through a relationship with a man. In Susan's case the partner is less important than the result of the partnership: children, fertile land, the evolution of natural processes. Jinny reverses the order of importance Identity is achieved in the hunt for a partner. Attraction of the male takes precedence over any meaningful outcome. And Rhoda, in between both extremes, longs for love first with Percival, then with Louis, and needs always to identify with the male of the moment.

Bernard is the most complex of the lot, for his is the job of com-menting for the author on the interplay of forces. Even as a school-boy he has assumed that he will one day be a novelist:

> When I am grown up I shall carry a notebook—a fat book with many pages, methodically lettered. I shall enter my phrases. . . . The tree "shades the window with green fingers." That will be useful. But alas! I am so soon distracted—by a hair like twisted candy, by Celia's Prayer Book, ivory covered. Louis can contemplate nature, unwinking, by the hour. Soon I fail, unless talked to. "The lake of my mind, unbroken by oars, heaves placidly and soon sinks into an oily somnolence." That will be useful.

He insists that in all of his acquaintances there is "a story" for the telling, though occasionally he is unable to finish one that he begins to tell. Unathletic and moody at school, he is "shaded with innumer-able perplexities" and cannot concentrate on games for long. Like Lily Briscoe, he aims for a balanced work of art: "I must open the little trap-door and let out these linked phrases in which I run to-gether whatever happens, so that instead of incoherence there is per-ceived a wandering thread, lightly joining one thing to another." As an illustration of Bernard's method, Mrs. Woolf, in what seems a rare moment of irony, has him build up as a fictional hero a man whom he encounters briefly in a railway carriage. Going purely by externals, he proceeds in identical fashion with Arnold Bennett as Mrs. Woolf imagines that author would create Mrs. Brown—also in a railway carriage (see Bibliography).

The more intense Neville resents Bernard's easy intimacy with casual strangers, his fluent speech and ease in storytelling. It is only because Bernard can live a life of separateness that he is, thinks Neville, able to be casually concerned with everything. If he felt strongly about any one person, his ease of manner would alter. But "we are all phrases in Bernard's story, things he writes down in his notebook under A or under B. . . . He does not need us." Bernard disagrees with Neville's unspoken estimate of him:

> What am I? I ask. This? No, I am that. Especially now, when I have left a room, and people talking, and the stone flags ring out with my solitary footsteps, and I behold the moon rising, sublimely, indifferently, over the ancient chapel—then it becomes clear that I am not one and simple, but complex and many. Bernard, in public, bubbles; in private, is secretive. That is what they do not understand, for they are now undoubtedly discussing me, saying I escape them, am evasive. They do not understand that I have to effect different transitions; have to cover the entrances and exits of several different men who alternately act their parts as Bernard.

He perceives moreover that it is impossible for any binding external evaluation to be fully meaningful, since identity is a complex and changing entity: "I am Bernard; I am Byron; I am this, that and the other. They darken the air and enrich me, as of old. . . . For I am more selves than Neville thinks. We are not simple as our friends would have us to meet their needs."

In the final long section of *The Waves*, Bernard is allowed to sum up "the meaning of my life." Old age has taught him that no "stories" are completely true, and that fine phrases and neat designs of life are suspect. Like Mrs. Woolf, he begins "to seek some design more in accordance with those moments of humiliation and triumph that come now and then undeniably." He discovers that the world impinges upon each newborn child in a different way: "Louis was disgusted by the nature of human flesh; Rhoda by our cruelty; Susan could not share; Neville wanted order; Jinny love; and so on."

Bernard reports too that even the terms of his own separate identity have been altered from time to time by the effect on his psyche of his reading.

> For I changed and changed; was Hamlet, was Shelley, was the hero, whose name I now forget, of a novel by Dostoevsky; was for a whole term, incredibly, Napoleon; but was Byron chiefly. For many weeks at a time it was my part to stride into rooms and fling gloves and coat on the back of chairs, scowling slightly.

Such inroads on the elemental "I," though important in shaping the identity, do not obscure it permanently: "from some completed experience I had emerged."

I rose and walked away—I, I, I; not Byron, Shelley, Dostoevsky, but I, Bernard. I even repeated my own name once or twice. I went swinging my stick, into a shop, and bought—not that I love music—a picture of Beethoven in a silver frame. Not that I love music, but because the whole of life, its masters . . . then appeared in long ranks of magnificent human beings behind me; and I was the inheritor; I, the continuer; I, the person miraculously appointed to carry it on.

Having toyed with one of the themes of *Orlando*, Bernard now considers the pervasive motif of *Monday or Tuesday*:

The crystal, the globe of life as one calls it, far from being hard and cold to the touch, has walls of thinnest air. If I press them all will burst. . . . Faces recur, faces and faces—they press their beauty to the walls of my bubble. . . . How impossible to order them rightly; to detach one separately, or to give the effect of the whole. . . .

Nevertheless, life is pleasant, life is tolerable. Tuesday follows Monday; then comes Wednesday. The mind grows rings. . . . How fast the stream flows from January to December! We are swept on by the torrent of things grown so familiar that they cast no shadow. We float, we float. . . .

Though he has tried to pierce beneath the wall which each person erects to hide himself from the gaze of others, in the end he finds such probing unnecessary, for he concludes that his life is in reality the life of his associates, his identity their identity. Bernard goes even further than this in musing that in the combination of all six friends would be found "the complete human being" whom we have failed to be. But soon he doubts again that anything is certain—even the "fixity of tables." He asks: "Who am I?" "I have been talking of Bernard, Neville, Jinny, Susan, Rhoda and Louis. Am I all of them? Am I one and distinct? I do not know." Even with Rhoda and Percival dead, there is as much oneness with them as with the living. As his own death approaches, he finds silence better than literary phrases, prefers solitude to involvement in the noises of the world.

The Waves is a triumph of technique. Planned to achieve almost geometrical balance and order, the book must appear also to be a faithful literary rendering of formless flux. To contain the inherent untidiness of environmental chaos, Mrs. Woolf blocks out the book as an elaborately contrived series of orderly designs. She sets up first an equation between the macrocosm and the microcosm. The rising of the sun, its passage through the sky and its descent as night falls, on the one hand, is equated to the childhood, adolescence, maturity, and old age of the six characters who play their parts in the novel. In long italicized passages preceding each chapter of narrative, the journey of the sun, as seen from the shore, is described in sentences of heightened prose:

The sun had not yet risen. The sea was indistinguishable from the sky, except that the sea was slightly creased as if a cloth had wrinkles in it. Gradually as the sky whitened a dark line lay on the horizon dividing the sea from the sky and the grey cloth became barred with thick strokes moving, one after another, beneath the surface, following each other, pursuing each other, perpetually.

As they neared the shore each bar rose, heaped itself, broke and swept a thin veil of white water across the sand. The wave paused, and then drew out again, sighing like a sleeper whose breath comes and goes unconsciously. Gradually the dark bar on the horizon became clear as if the sediment in an old wine-bottle had sunk and left the glass green. Behind it, too, the sky cleared as if the white sediment there had sunk, or as if the arm of a woman couched beneath the horizon had raised a lamp and flat bars of white, green and yellow spread across the sky like the blades of a fan.

Just as the onward march of the sun brings subtle alterations in the view—the color of the horizon changes, the water becomes more or less deep and intense in hue—so there are corresponding shifts of relationship among the six actors as their lives advance toward eventual death. Yet, just as the phenomena of sunrise and sunset are ever new but ever predictable and basically unvarying, so the end of each of the characters may be found in his beginnings.

Mrs. Woolf tries, even numerically, to maintain balance by entrusting the working out of her novel to six characters—three men and three women. Nor does she allow these people to interact in accordance with the normal laws of fictional exposition. They must instead appear, each separately, as though in the spotlight, on an otherwise darkened stage, to deliver a soliloquy to the reader. What each says will involve the others in content, but it will be presented in detached isolation. When the protagonists are children, the monologues are generally short, stressing the sensuous and the immediate. Thus the first series of speeches, wooden in method of presentation, goes like this:

'I see a ring,' said Bernard, 'hanging above me. It quivers and hangs in a loop of light.'

'I see a slab of pale yellow,' said Susan, 'spreading away until it meets a purple stripe.'

'I hear a sound,' said Rhoda, 'cheep, chirp; cheep, chirp; going up and down.'

'I see a globe,' said Neville, 'hanging down in a drop against the enormous flanks of some hill.'

'I see a crimson tassel,' said Jinny, 'twisted with gold threads.

'I hear something stamping,' said Louis. 'A great beast's foot is chained. It stamps, and stamps, and stamps.'

As the children grow intellectually and emotionally, the monologues increase in length and complexity—often approaching philosophical dissertations. And in the long final chapter narrated by Bernard, who emerges as Mrs. Woolf's principal instrument of expression and the embodiment of all the other characters combined, the method is carried to its logical conclusion.

The difficulties in which Mrs. Woolf involves herself by experimenting with such a technique are considerable. Only an artist of unusual talents would oppose the current of taste for realism, for naturalness of dialogue and action, and for dramatic interaction of the fictional characters. The reunion of the actors in a restaurant at Hampton Court is a remarkable example of the problems which Mrs. Woolf faced. She is limited to a maximum of six separate streams—six monologues which must stand without authorial comment. These, presented consecutively, must render vividly and with simultaneous effect the atmosphere of the celebration. Not only must the author show what each guest at the gathering is thinking and doing but also the reaction in the others to what is thought and done. The interplay of identities is complex.

Bernard notices the group at the door of the inn:

Now Rhoda sees me, but she pretends, with her horror of the shock of meeting, that I am a stranger. Now Neville turns. Suddenly, raising my hand, saluting Neville I cry, "I too have pressed flowers between the pages of Shakespeare's sonnets," and am churned up. My little boat bobs unsteadily upon the chopped and tossing waves. There is no panacea (let me note) against the shock of meeting.

It is uncomfortable too, joining ragged edges, raw edges; only gradually, as we shuffle and trample into the Inn, taking coats and hats off, does meeting become agreeable. . . .

What compensates for the loss of naturalness and ease is the sheer intensity of Mrs. Woolf's insight into the meaning of life. She has the courage to eschew the easy way: rather, on the elaborately artificial framework which she prescribes in *The Waves,* she carves a delicate and fragile view of existence.

Virginia Woolf : SELECTED BIBLIOGRAPHY

BENNETT, JOAN. *Virginia Woolf: Her Art as a Novelist.* New York: Harcourt, Brace, 1945.

BLACKSTONE, BERNARD. *Virginia Woolf: A Commentary.* London: The Hogarth Press, 1949.

CHAMBERS, R. L. *The Novels of Virginia Woolf.* Edinburgh: Oliver and Boyd, 1947.

DAICHES, DAVID, *The Novel and the Modern World.* Chicago: The University of Chicago Press, 1939.

———. *Virginia Woolf.* Norfolk, Connecticut: New Directions, 1942.

FORSTER, E. M. *Virginia Woolf.* Cambridge. Cambridge University Press, 1942.

HAFLEY, JAMES. *The Glass Roof: Virginia Woolf as Novelist.* Berkeley: The University of California Press, 1954.

HOLTBY, WINIFRED. *Virginia Woolf.* London: Wishart and Co., 1932.

PIPPETT, AILEEN. *The Moth and the Star: A Biography of Virginia Woolf.* Boston: Little, Brown, 1953.

WOOLF, VIRGINIA. *Mr. Bennett and Mrs. Brown.* London: The Hogarth Press, 1924.

———. *A Room of One's Own.* New York: The Fountain Press, 1929.

———. *A Writer's Diary,* ed. Leonard Woolf. New York: Harcourt, Brace, 1953.

D. H. Lawrence xx Life

In *Sons and Lovers*, Lawrence reproduces in the guise of Paul Morel the general circumstances of his own birth and childhood in the Nottingham coalfield district of England. Born in 1885, the fourth child of an illiterate coal miner and a genteel schoolteacher, Lawrence almost from the first had a sensitive nature and interests which set him apart from his brothers and sisters. Unlike Forster, Conrad, Huxley, and Virginia Woolf, who grew up in an intellectual atmosphere, Lawrence did not gain much help even from his sympathetic mother, who was limited, we recognize, by the provinciality of her surroundings. Nevertheless, Lawrence showed an early talent in writing (as Paul Morel in painting) and after clerking in a Nottingham surgical manufacturing company, entered Eastwood as a pupil-teacher, then going on to Nottingham University College for two years and qualifying as a teacher in 1908.

After four years of teaching, with several stories and poems and two novels (*The White Peacock*, 1911; *The Trespasser*, 1912) behind him, Lawrence ran off to Germany with Frieda von Richthoven, the wife of his French teacher, and herself the mother of three children and a daughter of the aristocratic Richthovens of Germany. His mother's death shortly before had freed Lawrence from any further ties with England, and he left England to begin the extensive traveling with Frieda that would continue until his death in 1930. From this time, Lawrence returned to England only intermittently, except for the war years, as his travels took him to nearly all the corners of the world, from Italy, France, and Germany to Australia, Mexico, and finally New Mexico, where, now married, he and Frieda settled.

During the First World War, Lawrence was a conscientious objector, although his health, already weakened by incipient tuberculosis, would not permit his acceptance by the army. In 1915, he tried to encourage a small group of followers, including Aldous Huxley, Bertrand Russell, Mark Gertler, Michael Arlen, and Dorothy Brett, to set up a utopian colony in Florida that would, with the phoenix as its symbol, regenerate the world. The idea fell through when Bertrand Russell became disenchanted with Lawrence, who, now bearded and Messiah-like, was full of improbable schemes for the individual's rebirth through what he called "blood-consciousness." These ideas work themselves out in Birkin's speeches in *Women in Love* (1920) and in the dramatic situations of that novel and its predecessor, *The Rainbow* (1915), as well as in most of Lawrence's other fiction. Throughout the war years, Lawrence remained in England a virtual prisoner of the government which suspected him, among other things, of being a troublemaker and a German spy.

When the war ended, Lawrence and Frieda began a new series of frenzied travels, from Italy to Sicily, then on to Germany, back to Italy, then to Ceylon, Australia, New Mexico, Los Angeles, New Orleans, and finally to Mexico. A trip to Russia was also planned, but it became impossible to undertake. In 1923, Lawrence returned to England, still retaining his idea of *Rananim*, the Florida utopia he had earlier planned. Then the travels started all over again: United States (New Mexico), Mexico, England again, Italy in general, Capri, Florence, Baden, London, Italy, Austria, Switzerland, France, London, Bavaria, and finally to a sanitarium at Vence, France, where Lawrence died from tuberculosis.

These frenetic years of constant upset are also the ones that contain Lawrence's deepening sense of mission and the development of his unique way of conveying his messianic principles. Tremendously prolific, a year rarely passed during these extensive travels when he failed to publish three or four volumes of poems, articles, novels, and assorted essays. Everything Lawrence saw, felt, and touched became part of his system to regenerate mankind through making it aware of the "lower half of consciousness," that part which the mind could not reach. Lawrence was imbued with a view of the world in which man as he had thus far developed was less than human, in which man, like the phoenix, would first have to die before he could be reborn from his own ashes. In a phoenix-like rebirth, Lawrence found a suitable image for the message that penetrated into nearly everything he wrote. Even his travel books and his works of literary criticism are laden with his insistence on regeneration.

Becoming at times more a polemicist than an artist, Lawrence had constant trouble with the English authorities over the censorship of his novels and paintings. A later volume of poetry, called *Pansies*, was seized in the mails, *The Rainbow* and *Lady Chatterley's Lover* could not appear as written, and a painting exhibition he held in London was raided by Scotland Yard and the paintings confiscated. None of these authoritarian actions dissuaded Lawrence, whose only reaction was to show greater fierceness and dogmatism. For a time, he flirted with right-wing groups in England, particularly with Rolf Gardner, a type like Webley in Huxley's *Point Counter Point*. Less a fascist than a believer in balance between mind and body, Lawrence was drawn to nearly any group that showed distaste for man's present state and promised to lead the way to rebirth in the future.

In addition to more than two dozen volumes of short stories, poems, essays on life and literature, and travel material, Lawrence's novels include: *The White Peacock* (1911), *The Trespasser* (1912), *Sons and Lovers* (1913), *The Rainbow* (1915), *Women in Love* (1920), *The Lost Girl* (1920), *Aaron's Rod* (1922), *The Boy in the Bush* (1924, with M. L. Skinner), *The Plumed Serpent* (1926), *Lady Chatterley's Lover* (1928), *The Escaped Cock* (1929, retitled *The Man Who Died*). Several of his important prose writings are collected in *Phoenix* (1936), and his letters, edited by Aldous Huxley (1932), are especially revealing. For the student of American literature, his *Studies in Classic American Literature* (1923) demonstrates his genius for throwing new light on old subjects. For the reader interested in the relationships between Lawrence's fiction and psychology, his *Psychoanalysis and the Unconscious* (1921) and *Fantasia of the Unconscious* (1922) are significant. His other important works include: *Reflections on the Death of a Porcupine* (1925), "Pornography and Obscenity" (1929), "A Propos of Lady Chatterley's Lover" (1930), *Apocalypse* (1931), and a separate collection of his letters to Bertrand Russell (1948).

More than any other of his contemporaries, Lawrence took battle with the middle-class spirit in life and literature. His constant struggles with authority, with friends, with critics, and with himself and Frieda are indicative of a nature that was never at ease. Lawrence's endless travels and need to touch more of life reveal his search for something that ever eluded him. Too much an idealist to settle for what life could give him and too much a perfectionist to accept the partial embodiment of his ideal, Lawrence hoped to find in the Mexicans, Etruscans, and Sicilians something that the modern Englishman, the epitome of "civilized man," could not offer. To make his point, he exaggerated greatly, but, nevertheless, the descriptive power of his nervous prose and the incisive quality of his probing mind, with its ability to cut away inessentials at a stroke, constitute his unique contribution to the English novel.

D. H. Lawrence xx Works–General

In a significant passage about the individual and his responsibilities in his spiritual autobiography, *If It Die* . . . , André Gide suggested a point of view strikingly similar to D. H. Lawrence's central beliefs:

> I now admitted only individual moralities, with imperatives that were sometimes opposed. I was convinced that everyone—or at least every one of the elect—had a part to play in the world which was his very own and unlike any others; so that every effort to submit to a common rule became in my eyes treachery; yes, treachery; and I likened it to the sin against the Holy Ghost "which shall not be forgiven," the sin by which the individual loses his exact, irreplaceable significance, the "savour" which cannot be given back to him.

Lawrence himself had written that the "goal of life is the coming to perfection of each single individual"; and again, the "final aim is not to *know*, but to *be*." Lawrence's quest, from the unsureness of *The White Peacock* to the decisiveness of *The Man Who Died*, was first to determine the nature of the individual and then to inspire him to flower. Everything else, he felt, is eventually unimportant—place, nature, objects, possessions, all meaningless in themselves, are only relevant in helping man to define himself.

Each individual, however, in coming to life must somehow "connect" with others; his unconscious, Lawrence wrote in his attack upon Freudian psychology, *Psychoanalysis and the Unconscious*, needs an external universe in order to evolve its own individual psyche. Accordingly, there must not be abstraction or idealization of self, but concreteness, specificity; and there must always be another individual to effect a relationship—what Lawrence called a polarity. We grow, he emphasized, by means of a polarized flux, through an ever-moving and changing connection with other selves.

In effecting this connection, mind is non-creative and non-construc-tive. It is, he says, the "dead end" product; so too the word. Mental consciousness is not a goal, but a cul-de-sac; it is solely a *means* of adjusting ourselves to the external universe, and merely gives "appli-ances" toward our coming to "spontaneous-creative fullness of being." The mind, he repeats, "as author and director of life is anathema." Therefore, in reading Lawrence's novels, one must be aware of several ways in which he replaces strict mental consciousness—in the ash-tree of *Sons and Lovers*, the cathedrals and arches of *The Rainbow*, the snow and African sculptures of *Women in Love*, the escaped cock of *The Man Who Died*. These phenomena contain life of their own, and first juxtaposed to a character and then, in turn, to the whole novel, they suggest a world more profound and powerful than mental consciousness could yield. They provide mysterious but magnetic pulls from the subconscious and unconscious, the areas in which Lawrence felt man really lives and the regions that must be polarized for the individual to realize stability. The extent to which an indi-vidual can polarize his "primal unconscious" with that of another, is the degree to which he realizes his "man-ness" and activates his very being. Real love, for Lawrence, can result only from polarization in which one's consciousness enters into flux with another's, and contact is made on all planes of being.

Lawrence, obviously, was not talking about anything startlingly new. E. M. Forster years before him had also been anxious to de-emphasize mental consciousness as a source of power—his long line of "feeling" women characters is merely one example of this attempt. Lawrence, however, surpasses Forster and others of similar intentions in the variety and depth of his work, in the intensity he brought to bear upon both character and situation, in his ability to evoke the mysterious core of things and to provide a realm of incantation where discursiveness would have been ineffective. Thus, the great scene of wild horses which enclose and trap Ursula at the end of *The Rainbow*, or the one in which Gudrun dances before the cows in *Women in Love*, or another in which Birkin pitches stones into the moon-bright lake while Ursula looks on, in the same novel.

By the time he wrote these novels, Lawrence was no longer inter-ested in the externalities of man, but only in his essence. He was try-ing, as Catherine Carswell, one of his friends, wrote, to get beneath into the life stream itself. Accordingly, he was not concerned with his characters' lives in the objective world. He *was* interested, however, in the inner world of their emotional and spiritual lives; and when Lawrence becomes somewhat tenuous, as he often does, we recognize that he is forcing an "internal life" upon a recalcitrant character whose tendencies are almost entirely external. Therefore, the sameness of many of Lawrence's characters, the lack of differentiation and identifiable individuality, for all of them on occasion are Lawrence rather than themselves.

In his early work before *The Rainbow* (1915), nevertheless, Lawrence was very close to the direct reality of his own experiences, and in *The White Peacock* (1911) and *Sons and Lovers* (1913), he was still rooted in everyday reality. This does not mean that the early novels necessarily lack the magic of the later work, but that the characters live recognizably, neither all spirituality nor unconsciousness. The desires of Paul Morel are very much of this world, although his relationship with Miriam is tinged with the positive and negative polarities that Lawrence was later to develop more fully. These two early novels, in fact, written while Lawrence was in his mid-twenties, offer an excellent guide to his later *Rainbow-Women in Love* period when he assumed the mantle of prophet and Messiah for the twentieth century.

The White Peacock is a slight novel, Hardyesque in its pastoral element, yet, none the less, full of Lawrence's typical characters and situations. The prototypes for his sensitive intellectuals, sensual gamekeepers, and emasculated aristocrats are all suggested here. Already, we see the Lawrence who was to do more than any one of his contemporaries to slam the door on the Victorian age and to clear away an atmosphere of moral stuffiness and sexual hypocrisy. Where Lawrence tried intentionally to shock or to raise sexual relationships to a type of spiritual mystique, one must recognize the hundred-years silence on such matters that he, almost single-handedly, tried to combat.

SONS AND LOVERS

In his first novel, Lawrence was caught between the magical world that would eventually be his main subject matter and the demands of the naturalistic novel with its emphasis on cause and effect, on cataloguing stimuli and responses. George Saxton, like the woodsman Annable, foreshadows Lawrence's later game-keepers and grooms, the type who remains, despite the pressures of civilization, in some secret communion with life itself. After his marriage to the prosaic Peg, Saxton drifts away from her world of home and children into a sanctuary of his own, in which drink increasingly alienates him from his family. His decline, although differently motivated, is akin to Walter Morel's in *Sons and Lovers*, who is, we must remember, as much ruined by his marriage as Mrs. Morel. The stress on drink, brutal language, and physical violence suggests the naturalistic style that Lawrence was not to forsake until *The Rainbow* in 1915. But while these elements were still strong in his work, certain individual themes were already emerging in embryo form. Here we find suggestions of Lawrence's attitude toward women both as mothers and as lovers, a foreshadowing of Mrs. Morel, Miriam, and Clara Dawes in *Sons and Lovers*. Lettie Beardsall, the sister of the narrator, is, in her way, a forerunner of Gudrun and Ursula of *The Rainbow*, although, unlike them, she indulges her natural desire for security. Her relationship in marriage to Leslie Tempest has affinities with that of Lady Chatterley and her husband, the woman of feeling married to the rich man of business. Already suggested are Lawrence's characteristic motifs: the need for sexual fire, the rejuvenation through orgasm, the necessity of the natural life and the primitive in man, the excoriation of modern life, particularly everything denoted by science and technology, the necessity of a man and woman meeting in a completely polarized relationship—all these are present in Lawrence's youthful first novel.

Before making any claims of originality for *Sons and Lovers*, one must come to terms with its traditional elements, which, in large, determine the essential structure of the novel. Lawrence's novel is in the familiar pattern of the *Bildungsroman*, the novel of development, which traces the growth of a hero from childhood through later conflict. In this group, we find *Tom Jones*, *David Copperfield*, Goethe's *Wilhelm Meister* (the prototype of the development or apprenticeship-to-life novel of the nineteenth century), *The Way of All Flesh*, *Pendennis*, *The Ordeal of Richard Feverel*, and several others. *Sons and Lovers* also has kinship with the *Künstlerroman*, the novel that traces the growth, specifically, of an artist and the artistic conscience as it attempts to come to terms with the world. In this group, we also find *A Portrait of the Artist as a Young Man*, which was to be published shortly after Lawrence's novel. The chief characteristics of both the *Bildungsroman* and the *Künstlerroman* are a certain episodic construction in which only the ever-present hero, as worker,

student, lover, or artist, holds together the various scenes. The looseness of construction in all but *A Portrait*, in which Joyce gained tightness through the repetition of motifs rather than using chronological
sequences, was almost a necessity, for the author had to bring his hero
from birth through several conflicts into manhood and then on into
love, marriage, family, or artistic success, or a combination of all. As
long as the author relied on chronology, the episodic form was un-
avoidable, and the Victorian apprenticeship novel is representative
of the type. Actually, the nineteenth-century three-decker novel lent
itself most advantageously to this kind of presentation, with its twenty
or so monthly magazine instalments and the frequent necessity for the
author to pad or string out his material to fulfil requirements of
length. Often, extraneous characters would be brought in merely to
fill out a sequence that fell short of the required wordage or that
ended too soon to afford suspense for the next instalment.

Lawrence, however, claimed form for *Sons and Lovers*. In a remark-
ably frank letter to Edward Garnett, his editor, he outlined his intentions in the novel:

> . . . And I want to defend it quick. I wrote it again, pruning it and
> shaping it and filling it in. I tell you it has got form—*form:* haven't I
> made it patiently, out of sweat as well as blood. It follows this idea: a
> woman of character and refinement goes into the lower class, and has
> no satisfaction in her own life. She has had a passion for her husband,
> so the children are born of passion, and have heaps of vitality. But as
> her sons grow up she selects them as lovers—first the eldest, then the
> second. These sons are *urged* into life by their reciprocal love of their
> mother—urged on and on. But when they come to manhood, they can't
> love, because their mother is the strongest power in their lives, and holds
> them. It's rather like Goethe and his mother and Frau von Stein and
> Christiana—As soon as the young men come into contact with women,
> there's a split. William gives his sex to a fribble, and his mother holds
> his soul. But the split kills him, because he doesn't know where he is.
> The next son gets a woman who fights for his soul—fights his mother.
> The son loves the mother—all the sons hate and are jealous of the
> father. The battle goes on between the mother and the girl, with the
> son as object. The mother gradually proves stronger, because of the tie
> of blood. The son decides to leave his soul in his mother's hands, and,
> like his elder brother, go for passion. He gets passion. Then the split
> begins to tell again. But, almost unconsciously, the mother realises what
> is the matter, and begins to die. The son casts off his mistress, attends
> to his mother dying. He is left in the end naked of everything, with **the
> drift towards death.**

Lawrence evidently tried to achieve form through imposing several closely-knit motifs on an elongated chronological sequence, what Conrad had tried to do in the episodic *Lord Jim*. A great many years in Paul Morel's life are touched upon, but usually in terms of certain relationships which expand and contract, rather than change, with the passage of years. Thus, in one series of motifs, we have Mrs. Morel as center, and around her are grouped, in time, Walter Morel as young man and then as broken husband, her oldest son, William, then Paul, and, at times, her other children, Annie and Arthur. In another, Paul is center, relating to, in turn, his mother, Miriam, and Clara Dawes. The two central characters are constantly in conflict until Mrs. Morel's death, while the others meet and criss-cross throughout the novel: Mrs. Morel and Miriam, Mrs. Morel and Clara, Miriam and Clara, and so on. The edges of the novel are carefully protected against extraneous characters, for except for Miriam's family and Clara's husband, Baxter, Lawrence makes no attempt to extend the novel further in depth or breadth.

Going beyond mere connections between the characters, Lawrence cast over each an idea, so that when Clara Dawes and Miriam, for example, come together with Paul in the center, they do so as the meeting of two ideas, as well as two people. Similarly, Paul's parents have extension value beyond their singularly unhappy situation. If we compare the Morels with another finely drawn pair of parents, the Gants in Thomas Wolfe's *Look Homeward, Angel*, we immediately recognize the difference in Lawrence's intentions. The Gants are superb as characters; they *live* fully amidst their eccentricities and idiosyncrasies. In fact, these very qualities give them distinction and individuality, indeed make them live as particular people. Contrariwise, the Morels are always more typed than particular, more the semi-educated "aristocratic" woman with the semi-articulate "peasant" husband than people whose specific characteristics remain in our minds. What we do remember about Mrs. Morel is her moral tightness, a Puritanical strain that kills life; what we remember about Walter Morel is his easy-going sensuality, his physical being and black limbs. Our memory, then, is more of a typed contrast than of distinctive qualities. The war between the parents is a war between, on one hand, culture and, on the other, half-culture, a war between mental consciousness and primitive animalism, a war between Spirit (intellect) and Soul (body), as Lawrence later defined these terms.

Likewise, the relationships between Mrs. Morel and Paul and between Paul and Miriam are also full of typed reactions. That is, Lawrence has removed the individual need, the individual reaction, the individual frustration and conflict to a more universal need and conflict. As yet, in *Sons and Lovers*, he is still concerned with certain particulars, perhaps because the novel is so clearly autobiographical; but by the time of *The Rainbow* and *Women in Love*, with autobiography behind him, Lawrence was ready to suggest only universal situations, and his characters are no longer within a realistic world. Cast over all is Lawrence's idea of life, his idea of reality. It is at this point that a novelist becomes a poet in its generic sense, a maker and creator, a seer and prophet. This tendency, not so apparent in *The White Peacock*, is already suggested in *Sons and Lovers*. The gospel of the twentieth century according to Lawrence is centered in the age-old conflict between mother, son, and potential daughter-in-law.

It is fitting that Lawrence should have attempted to universalize his material around Freud's concept of the Oedipus complex, a condition universal in the history of culture. Along these lines, in his Foreword to *Sons and Lovers*, cast in a Biblically pompous language, Lawrence, among other remarks, said:

> But the man who is the go-between from Woman to Production is the lover of that woman. And if that Woman be his mother, then is he her lover in part only; he carries for her, but is never received into her for his confirmation and renewal, and so wastes himself away in the flesh. The old son-lover was Oedipus. The name of the new one is legion. And if a son-lover take a wife, then is she not his wife, she is only his bed. And his life will be torn in twain, and his wife in her despair shall hope for sons, that she may have her lover in her hour.

Here we have the entire import of the conflict in the novel. Paul is a son-lover unable to bring to his "wife" wholeness, and she in turn will remain unfulfilled until she becomes a mother-lover, and so on. Lawrence, who violently opposed Freud and his "scientism," for reasons noted below, found in the Oedipus complex a type of universal interpretation that provided both continuity with the past and a means to comment upon the present. In brief, Paul's union with his mother both fulfills and emasculates him, both completes him and leaves him unfinished.

Working outward from the Oedipus complex itself, Lawrence was able to give shape to several general themes: in Mrs. Morel, we find the intellectually superior, physically soulless female whose sexual responses become increasingly more frigid. Opposite her is the sensual miner, Morel, close to the earth in occupation and spirit, open in his responses to life, fond of singing, dancing, and drinking; a man slowly crushed to a non-entity by his wife's spirituality and withdrawal from his kind of reality. A possible domestic hero, he slowly disappears from the novel as Mrs. Morel possesses her sons in turn.

Morel, early in the novel, is described as "soft, non-intellectual, warm, a kind of gambolling" creature; later, as: ". . . there was a slight shrinking, a diminishing in his assurance. Physically even, he shrank, and his fine full presence waned. He never grew in the least stout, so that, as he sank from his erect, assertive bearing, his physique seemed to contract along with his pride and moral strength." Yet, Mrs. Morel continues to strive with him. Too much a Puritan—part of her inheritance—and too full of her high moral sense to love, Morel, she tries to remake him through continual opposition and ridicule. Driven to fierceness by her realization that she had once loved this man, she bullies him with Puritanical strictures. She drives him to drunkenness, lying, cowardice, and then castigates him for sinning. Discontented with what Morel is and anxious to have him change, she destroys him while trying to ennoble him. In making Morel into a complete outsider—a shadowy householder who emerges from the mines only to disappear into the bars—she of course scars her own feelings; but she, unlike him, retains her worth. As Lawrence writes: "She also had the children."

As to Morel himself—whom Lawrence reveals only from the outside or from Mrs. Morel's point of view—we see the man reacting in the sole way he can, becoming a bully, a freak, a spiritual stone, and by so doing only aggravating the sterile relationship. Too much himself to accede to his wife's demands, he resists until, finally, his manhood breaks to pieces. Left alone, he has nothing to turn to; inwardly, he is empty of values, and, outwardly, his physical part, the flesh, has been denied. Just as Paul, after his mother's death, is to become a "Derelict" (as Lawrence titled the final chapter), so Morel is already adrift in Mrs. Morel's wake. "Morel made the meal alone, brutally. He ate and drank more noisily than he had need. No one spoke to him. The family life withdrew, shrank away, and became hushed as he entered. But he cared no longer about his alienation." His only answer is to meet Mrs. Morel's gentility with his exaggerated vulgarity. Lawrence's very prose in the above passage is cruel in its brief frankness, in its description of a man now more animal than human.

So Morel is effaced—one part of the Oedipus situation has been fulfilled. The husband no longer rules the household: Lawrence emphasizes that Morel dominates only the hearth, the sole part of the home still sanctified for the male, while the rest of the social activity proceeds smoothly without him. Frustrated by her marriage, Mrs. Morel turns to her sons and gains husband-substitutes, though only one at a time, for her high moral sense dictates monogamy. Once she "seizes" William, the split in the family is irremediable, merely to be intensified as Paul succeeds to William's place. For his part, William finds himself involved in a frantic attachment to Lily, whose slipshod manner strikingly recalls Morel's own; yet William, tied as he is to Mrs. Morel, is unable to avoid an obviously poor match based solely on sexual infatuation. Disrespecting Lily as much as Mrs. Morel does Morel, William mocks his fiancée before his mother, and by so doing demonstrates that the latter is his true lover and that Lily will provide only temporary sexual satisfaction. Recognizing this, Mrs. Morel warns him against marrying the girl—" 'Nothing,' " she says, " 'is as bad as a marriage that's a hopeless failure' "—but William has already been destroyed by his mother's influence. Split into parts, he cannot leave Lily because of her physical appeal, or Mrs. Morel because "he was accustomed to having all his thoughts sifted through his mother's mind." Thus William as a unified person is destroyed; divided into pieces, he drives himself into a life whose substance he can neither order nor even understand. Destroyed young by his mother, William, suitably, dies under her care.

Shortly after William's death, Paul falls ill with pneumonia, and when he recovers, Mrs. Morel has captured his spirit, making him the successor to his older brother in her affections. In turn, Paul's illness saves Mrs. Morel by taking her mind off William. With the consummation of the new marriage, Part One of *Sons and Lovers* ends, to begin, in Part Two, with Miriam, who also, as Paul sees her, has the motherly instincts to possess him. Love, Lawrence recognized, was a prime requisite of life, but love means attachment, while life, real life, can take place only in the individual. Therefore, the conflict, inherent in all meaningful activity, between love and life. Lawrence wrote that the "central law of all organic life is that each organism is intrinsically isolate and single in itself." Yet the individual, he tells us again, can be fulfilled only through contact, specifically between a man and woman who must preserve the "intrinsic otherness of each participant." The love of both Mrs. Morel and Miriam, as Lawrence presents them, denies this "otherness," and therefore their love forfeits the elements of a true feeling which would build, while theirs destroys and debilitates. Love *is* necessary, but too much love can cause death or strangulation. Thus the necessity of polarization, of real balance.

When Paul comes to Miriam, he is, of course, off balance. As long as his mother dominates him, he is unable to come to terms with Miriam, or, in fact, with any woman, except for physical necessity, and therefore his unsatisfactory relationship with Clara Dawes. Lawrence repeatedly warned, as if answering his puritanical critics, that the flesh was only holy if the spirit (intellect) were holy. The one without the other—Paul had only flesh in Clara Dawes—is as futile as spirit alone. The two together will bring out the god-hero in man, will dignify him, will enable him to flower in himself.

When Paul is with Miriam, he lacks completely this sense of fulfilment that he expects from life. He suggests what life should mean to him when he describes one of his sketches to Miriam; she had remarked that one sketch in particular seemed so true, and he answered:

It's because—it's because there is scarcely any shadow in it; it's more shimmery, as if I'd painted the shimmery protoplasm in the leaves and everywhere, and not the stiffness of the shape. That seems dead to me. Only this shimmeriness is the real living. The shape is a dead crust. The shimmer is inside really.

This "shimmer" Paul quests for in painting and life, and while he wins first prizes in the former, he finds little satisfaction in the other.

Unable to flower in himself, Paul can find no salvation in a single person. He is himself a flower plucked, not cultivated in its natural surroundings. Therefore, his rage at Miriam's attitude toward flowers, and Lawrence's insistence on Mrs. Morel's garden and love of flowers. Both, however, and particularly Miriam, love flowers not in themselves but as possessions, as beauty which they can control. In an essay on "Nottingham and the Mining Countryside," in *Phoenix*, Lawrence wrote of this connection:

Now the love of flowers is a very misleading thing. Most women love flowers as possessions and as trimmings. They can't look at a flower, and wonder a moment, and pass on. If they see a flower that arrests their attention, they must at once pick it, pluck it. Possession! A possession! Something added on to *me!* And most of this so-called love of flowers today is merely this reaching out of possession and egoism: something I've *got*; something that embellishes *me*.

Thus, Paul turns to Miriam as she crouches and kisses the flowers, and angrily asks why she always clutches things and pulls the heart out of them. " 'You wheedle the soul out of things . . . I would never wheedle—at any rate, I'd go straight.' " In a later scene, as Paul becomes the center of a silent conflict between Miriam and Clara, he also pulls out flowers in bunches, and when the latter asks him what right he has to do so, he answers that there are plenty for him to pluck and that their beauty pleases him. Here, he does not wheedle, he "goes straight"—Miriam will be his sacrifice, will be deflowered because he needs part of her. Then he turns to Clara and almost for the first time notices her breasts swinging in her blouse, her graceful arching back, her proud neck, her overall desirable figure.

Here, in one brief scene, is Paul's situation, caught as he is between his sense and his senses, between the influence of his mother and the real pangs of his own desire. Later, near the end of the novel, when Paul returns to Miriam, he realizes that marriage with her is still impossible, although it is also the only solution for both of them. As they go out, supposedly to part forever, he gives her flowers, dripping out of the jar, and she takes them, as she would have taken Paul himself, snipped off from his past and now drifting away into the dark.

According to the original of Miriam, one Jessica Chambers, whom Lawrence knew in his youth, Lawrence was so tied to his mother that he could not be normal with another woman. In her book on Lawrence, E.T., as she signed herself, claimed that his mother was both a parent and a lover; so that he constantly split his interest in women into spiritual (Miriam) and physical (Clara) attachments. In Miriam, he saw his mother and was unable to find sexual satisfaction, while after he married another woman (Frieda von Richthoven) for sex, E.T. claimed, Lawrence wanted to continue seeing her for the intellectual interests they shared. Accordingly, E.T. feels that Lawrence completely falsifies Miriam; he could not give of himself, and in order to put his mother on a pedestal, he presented a caricature of their real relationship. She remarks that it was impossible to tell Lawrence this, so attached was he to his mother; and so *he* came to Miriam as to a mother, making any sexual relationship psychologically impossible for him. In the book, Clara Dawes provides a sexual outlet, unobtained by Lawrence in real life until his marriage to Frieda, already the mother of three children by a previous marriage. So far has Lawrence falsified, E.T. stresses, that no one would recognize that Miriam wanted a physical *and* spiritual relationship while he tried to make it entirely spiritual.

For psychological reasons, Lawrence legitimately made several changes in his affair with E.T.; however, the real point is not whether he changed the original relationship, but what significance he attached to the changes. Lawrence found in the disintegration of Paul a peculiar symbol of modern man, of all men who are unable to achieve a balance between sex and purpose in life. Assert one at the expense of the other, he repeated, and you fall either into collapse or sterility. "You have got to base your great purposive activity upon the intense sexual fulfillment of all your individuals. That was how Egypt endured. But you have got to keep your sexual fulfillment even then subordinate, just subordinate to the great passion of purpose: subordinate by a hair's breadth only: but still, by that hair's breadth, subordinate." Those words from *Fantasia of the Unconscious* (1922) underscore Lawrence's insistent belief in the individual Holy Ghost, the voice of the self in its wholeness, which makes balance and proportion possible. In terms of Paul, purpose in life is fulfilled—first prizes in painting contests and supervisory position in his factory—yet he remains sterile, a typical twentieth-century man Lawrence later labeled him. His mother, by spiritualizing sex, has made it meaningful only as love, family, babies, not simply as a means of fulfilment in which man proves his maleness and woman her femaleness.

Not, however, until *Lady Chatterley's Lover* (1928) did Lawrence dramatize the relationship solely in terms of fulfilment, with the rest of the world held in abeyance. In that novel, the force that reconciles the flesh and spirit is a moral force; therefore, sexual promiscuity, false sentiment, sheer sensationalism were, according to Lawrence, the real immoralities in a world that denied honest feeling. For Lawrence, sex must never be a game, a drama, a mere show of will, or a sign of power. Consequently, the charges against Lawrence that he was immoral—his difficulties with the censor over *The Rainbow* and *Lady Chatterley's Lover*, for example—are particularly nonsensical once one recognizes the strong puritanical strain in Lawrence that demands individual fulfilment in every coming together of male and female. Thus, as a social power, sex puts the individual into balance with his society. How close, one perceives, Lawrence comes to Freud despite his running argument with the latter!

Consequently, Paul's sterility, his inability to function as an integrated man, is the sterility of an industrialized society that necessarily cleaves men into pieces. In *Point Counter Point*, Huxley, speaking through Mark Rampion, reconstructs one of Lawrence's answers to this society. Rampion offers what he considers the solution to man's need to work as an idiot for eight out of every twenty-four hours:

> " 'Do the job, then, idiotically and mechanically, and spend your leisure hours in being a real complete man or woman, as the case may be. Don't mix the two lives together; keep the bulkheads watertight between them. The genuine human life in your leisure hours is the real thing. The other's just a dirty job that's got to be done. And never forget that it *is* dirty and, except in so far as it keeps you fed and society intact, utterly unimportant, utterly irrelevant to the real human life. Don't be deceived by the canting rogues who talk of the sanctity of labour and the Christian service that business men do their fellows. It's all lies. Your work's just a nasty, dirty job. . . . Make the effort of being human.' . . . In the meantime . . . we must shovel the garbage and bear the smell stoically, and in the intervals try to lead the real human life."

Lawrence, in Rampion's words, was trying to keep man as whole as the world would permit. He therefore categorically opposed the spiritualizing of work (an emphatic denial of Morris's and Ruskin's argument), the application of Christian ideals to the physical make-up of man, the splitting up, in brief, of man's total response. He tried to keep the "shimmer" of life that Paul explained above as the *thisness* of his paintings. But, paradoxically, Paul's sense of shimmer, his revelation of the undercurrent of life, is activated only in his art; in life he is a mere husk, with the center split open and the pieces cast away.

Recognizing that Paul has lost control of himself, we can better understand Lawrence's words at the end of the novel that he is "naked of everything, with the drift towards death." Paul's beating by Baxter Dawes is merely one more step toward what he calls the "tangled sort of hole, rather dark and dreary" into which he is falling, with "no road anywhere" out. After the beating, he is physically smashed and his old world smashed as well—now even Clara is behind him, Miriam is a stranger, and his mother is to die shortly after. With her death, he "felt as if his life were being destroyed, piece by piece, within him." The horror of watching her die, the pain of her slow decline and wasting away, the fact that he abets her death—all these are part of Paul's martyrdom to past indulgence, as is the aid he tenders Baxter Dawes in the hospital. Each incident cuts into his spirit, each diminishes him further. The result is a Paul completely dead inside, cast off as a derelict, heading into the town, which, despite its "gold phosphorescence," can hold no life for him.

After creating Paul Morel, Lawrence turned from realistic characterization to another plane of creation in which an ideal character has emerged, as it were, from the ashes of Paul's burned-out spirit. This regenerated figure takes the form of Birkin in *Women in Love*, Mellors in *Lady Chatterley's Lover*, the Christ in *The Man Who Died*. The rebirth implicit in these works was further symbolized by Lawrence's choice of the phoenix to represent the regenerated soul rising from the fire of its former body. So Birkin, Mellors, and Christ rise from the sordidness of their surroundings and become fully "souled" integrated beings. Like the phoenix, they re-emerge after destruction, and unlike Paul, they drift toward life, toward a revitalized existence. This was the only direction Lawrence could take after *Sons and Lovers*, for to continue in the same vein would mean further negation. Through Birkin and Ursula Brangwen, he returned to life.

In *Sons and Lovers*, once we get beyond the social tragedy implicit in the Morels' way of life—the antagonism between body and spirit, between work and culture, between passion and religiosity—we can discern the small touches that make Lawrence not only a brilliant social critic but also a nearly great artist. Several of the touches revealed in *Sons and Lovers* appear later in expanded form, and as Lawrence is often more effective in parts than in entirety, these delicate strokes reveal the best of his craftsmanship. Perhaps because of his great concern with parts, Lawrence failed to create tragic wholes which fulfil as, say, some of Conrad's major novels. While individual parts contain a tragic vision, the whole always seems to contain, one critic has commented, a retreat into the idyllic in which the full human implications are never completely realized. This is less true of *Sons and Lovers* than of many others of Lawrence's novels, but even here some of the potentially terrifying conflicts vanish because of inconsistencies or changes of tone, or are dissipated through a gratuitous emphasis on minor details.

As Mark Schorer has pointed out, Lawrence never wrote what we may call perfect works of art. *Sons and Lovers* itself is marred by Lawrence's inability to project sufficiently beyond himself and to allow Paul a life beyond the author's. For example, Lawrence presents the mother sympathetically, while the father, despite Lawrence's attitude, gains the reader's empathy; further, Paul's dilemma makes him into a cruel person who would perhaps be less attractive to women than Lawrence forces him to be; also, Miriam seems to the reader somewhat different in the novel from what Lawrence would have her to be—Paul, more than *she*, wants to suck life dry. These and other inconsistencies often hurt the book as a whole, creating doctrine where dramatic conflict should exist, and discursiveness where human tension is called for. Therefore, the individual scene or image frequently shows Lawrence at his best; for through a seemingly minor detail, he could, as in his paintings and sketches, suggest the whole without destroying it.

To illustrate: Paul constantly feels a sense of impending doom, as if destiny were ready to strike and smash his hopes and plans. He has the typical fears of a tubercular (Lawrence stresses his weak lungs) who lives under the pall of possible illness and long inactivity; he is, as it were, more aware than the average person of the dark elements of life, living as he does close to impending death. Part of the demonic mystery which Paul is aware of centers around a huge old ash-tree in front of the Morel house. As a child, Paul identified the shrieking of the ash-tree during a storm with the discord in the house, the wind whistling through its vast limbs suggesting the snarling shouts and waving arms of his drunken father, its shrieks and cries the fist of Morel pounding the kitchen table. "There was," Lawrence writes, "a feeling of horror, a kind of bristling in the darkness, and a sense of blood. They [Paul and Annie] lay with their hearts in the grip of an intense anguish. The wind came through the tree fiercer and fiercer. All the cords of the great harp hummed, whistled, and shrieked. And then came the horror of the sudden silence, silence everywhere, outside and downstairs. What was it? Was it a silence of blood? What had he [Morel] done?"

Later, in the chapter called "Death in the Family," when William is dead and the body to be brought home for burial, Paul goes to the bay window and looks out. "The ash-tree stood monstrous and black in front of the wide darkness." Here, as earlier, the tree suggests a dark interior, paralleling the grubby mining life of Morel, but with Paul the interior is a state of mind more than a physical fact. The tree, like the mine, becomes the other side—the dark side—of life, of which the flowers, garden, Willey Farm are the light side. Everything connected with Paul's father is dark—the image of the tree reappears only in context with Morel; conversely, everything connected with his mother is light. In the passage above, Paul, after staring at the tree, turns away from its ominous darkness. "It was a faintly luminous night. Paul went back to his mother." There then follows a scene with glittering candles and bright gleams, until Paul peers again into the darkness of the street and sees his father struggling with William's coffin. Right after this, Paul succumbs to pneumonia, "when all the cells in the boy seem in intense irritability to be breaking down and consciousness makes a last flare of struggle, like madness." The blackness which Paul had always felt now claims him. When he recovers, he is his mother's son-lover, and his destiny has been determined—William's fate will be his.

After Paul's beating by Baxter Dawes—once again struggle comes for him in the darkness, with the glare from the houses far in the distance—he is nursed back to health by Mrs. Morel, drawn by her out of the darkness into a light world that will, ironically, cripple him as much as the struggle with Baxter in the dark. Then, at the end of the novel, Paul, now a derelict, drifts through the darkness of doubt and indecision, "one tiny upright speck of flesh, less than an ear of wheat lost in the field," drifts toward the lights of the city which, deceptively, offers light to one now internally defeated.

What started with the darkness of the ash-tree is now the darkness of Paul's interior being. Unable to burst forth like the spectral colors of the flowers he loves, Paul retreats into the dull colors of his fears. Paul's indecision in the presence of light and his fear of the dark are complemented by his love of the bowed Norman arches which "meant the dogged leaping forward of the persistent human soul"; he accuses Miriam of preferring the Gothic arch, which in its perpendicular lines "leapt up at heaven and touched the ecstasy and lost itself in the divine." He points the distinction: "Himself," he said, "was Norman, Miriam was Gothic." The religiosity that he attacks Miriam for casting over everything is the same feeling he is drawn to and repulsed by in his mother. By praising the horizontal, the Norman, as opposed to the vertical, the Gothic, Paul tries to reject his mother's and Miriam's spirituality which reaches up high into the light of heaven, while also trying to retain, almost unwittingly, the earthy darkness and secularity of his father. The latter's qualities, Lawrence indicates, could make him a complete person—Paul should literally embrace the dark—but the boy's tragedy is that these qualities appear in a man he has been conditioned to despise.

Through the lights and darks of natural phenomena and through Paul's choice of objects to worship, Lawrence was able, in parts, to create tensions and give a thick texture to the novel. When we recognize that Paul's ambivalence toward light and dark is, in miniature, the core of his major problem, we can better understand what Lawrence meant when he told Garnett that the novel had form. In its parts, *Sons and Lovers* is closely organized and thought out. Certain scenes contain Lawrence's characteristic ability to intensify a situation in an almost casual image. The scene, for instance, with the burned bread (Chapter 8), in which Miriam becomes, as it were, the forgotten loaf in the oven, exemplifies Lawrence's power of suggestion. Or again, the scenes with the flowers, particularly the one in which Clara communes with flowers while Miriam must pluck them (Chapter 9), scenes which evoke the very heart of things Lawrence understood intimately. In bringing out physical qualities—particularly of natural phenomena—he seemed to sense exactly what made things live. In some ways an expressionist like Van Gogh, Lawrence had powers of intensity similar to the Dutch painter's. In the hands of both, houses, as it were, move, fields flow, flowers grow, trees wave—objects seem to have an existence of their own. When Lawrence turned to people, however, this ability is not so evident, and when he wrote *The Rainbow*, he no longer even attempted to define his characters realistically.

Following Stein's advice to Marlow in *Lord Jim*, in which he maintains the paradox that meaningful life results from one's immersion in the very things that ultimately will destroy him, Lawrence leaves Paul at the end of *Sons and Lovers* stumbling into a future which will eventually bring death. To heed Stein's warning is something that Lord Jim, Decoud, and Heyst in Conrad's novels never learned while still able to help themselves, and this lack of recognition nullified their desires for a positive existence. It is a lesson that Paul evidently has learned, particularly from his experience with Baxter Dawes, but such is the contradictory nature of the world, Lawrence suggests, that Paul, in any case, will be destroyed; until, like the phoenix, he will rise up in triumph from his own ashes. Perhaps a passage, particularly relevant here, that Lawrence wrote in his long and perceptive study of Thomas Hardy shortly after the publication of *Sons and Lovers*, sums up his attitude toward Paul. Lawrence said:

> He who would save his life must lose it. But why should he go on and waste it? Certainly let him cast it upon the waters. Whence and how and whither it will return is no matter in terms of values. But like a poppy that has come to bud, when he reaches the shore, when he has traversed his known and come to the beach to meet the unknown, he must strip himself naked and plunge in, and pass out: if he dare. And the rest of his life he will be a stirring at the unknown, cast out upon the waters. But if he dare not plunge in, if he dare not take off his clothes and give himself naked to the flood, then let him prowl in rotten safety,

weeping for pity of those he imagines worse off than himself. He dare not weep aloud for his own cowardice. And weep he must. So he will find him objects of pity.

THE RAINBOW AND WOMEN IN LOVE: LAWRENCE AS MESSIAH

At the end of 1913, Lawrence, writing to Edward Garnett, remarked that he would send to him the first half of *The Sisters*, which he would prefer to call *The Wedding Ring*: "It is very different from *Sons and Lovers*: written in another language almost. I shall be sorry if you don't like it, but am prepared. I shan't write in the same manner as *Sons and Lovers* again, I think—in that hard, violent style full of sensations and presentation. You must see what you think of the new style." In another letter, he claims that "it is really something new in the art of the novel. . . ." Later, in June, 1914, again to Garnett, he draws a comparison between himself and the Italian futurists, a group whose violent theories were making a stir in literary circles. Lawrence's remarks are particularly relevant to *The Rainbow*:

> But when I read Marinetti—"the profound intuitions of life added one to the other, word by word, according to their illogical conception, will give us the general lines of an intuitive physiology of matter"—I see something of what I am after. I translate him clumsily, and his Italian is obfuscated—and I don't care about physiology of matter—but somehow—that which is physic—non-human, in humanity, is more interesting to me than the old-fashioned human element—which causes one to conceive a character in a certain moral scheme and make him consistent. . . . You musn't look in my novel for the old stable ego of the character. There is another ego, according to whose action the individual is unrecognizable, and passes through, as it were, allotropic states which it needs a deeper sense than any we've been used to exercise, to discover are states of the same single radically-unchanged element. . . . You must not say my novel is shaky—it is not perfect, because I am not expert in what I want to do. But it is the real thing, say what you like. And I shall get my reception, if not now, then before long.

The novel which started as *The Sisters*, then passed through a stage when it was called *The Wedding Ring*, also *Noah's Ark*, was split into the books that became *The Rainbow* (1915) and *Women in Love*, the latter written in 1916 but not published until 1920. Having recognized that the style of *Sons and Lovers* could not possibly exhaust what he wanted to say, that, in fact, the style would work counter to his material, Lawrence consciously tried to create a new style both individual and expressive. He remarked: "I am going through a transitive stage myself. . . . I write with everything vague —plenty of fire underneath, but, like bulbs in the ground, only shadowy flowers that must be beaten and sustained, for another spring. . . . But I must write to live, and it must produce its flowers, and if they be frail or shadowy, they will be all right if they are true to their hour." When *The Rainbow* was ordered withdrawn by the authorities only two months after its publication—ostensibly for the scene in which the pregnant Anna Brangwen dances naked in her room—Lawrence recast some of his remaining material for *Women in Love* and withheld publication until 1920.

These two novels taken together—Lawrence considered the second as a potential sequel to *The Rainbow*—indicate Lawrence's major direction and demonstrate nearly every vice and virtue of his mature style. Although embittered by the suppression of *The Rainbow*, he continued in the same vein of the latter half of the novel, foreshadowing *The Plumed Serpent*, *Lady Chatterley's Lover*, *The Man Who Died*, and several of his major short stories. The "rightness" of the Ursula-Birkin relationship and the "wrongness" of the one between Gudrun and Gerald Crich reappear in somewhat different form in the Connie-Mellors, Connie-Clifford relationship of *Lady Chatterley's Lover*, in Kate-Cipriano of *The Plumed Serpent*, in the relationship between Alvina Houghton and Cicio in *The Lost Girl*, in Somers and his wife in *Kangaroo*. In addition, at this time, Lawrence had found the method whereby he could compare the liveness and verve, the inner being, of animals with the empty husks of modern industrialized man. Here, he suggested the horse St. Mawr, the escaped cock in *The Man Who Died*, the plant and animal life of his later poetry.

Only suggestions of Lawrence's new style are conveyed in the first half or so of *The Rainbow*. The novel begins in a conventional enough way—somewhat in the pastoral tradition of George Eliot and Thomas Hardy, though including, of course, Lawrence's intensification of interior life—and appears in the first two hundred pages to be proceeding as a typical family novel then so prevalent on the continent. In its cataloguing of generations, in its emphasis on family genetics, it is close to the tradition of Mann's *Buddenbrooks*, with which Lawrence was familiar, or any of those long family novels that the Danes, Norwegians, and French were producing. *The Rainbow* however, only begins this way; about midway through it changes considerably in style, and the careful reader will see departures even before that. Perhaps one of the very difficulties the reader has in a later Lawrence novel stems from his shifts from one type of narrative to another, from one key to a second and a third, from Naturalism to Symbolism, or vice versa. As Graham Hough points out, for the sake of the symbolic value, Lawrence often makes us believe what is impossible naturalistically, and thus seems to leave the realm of the possible.

Both of these trends—Naturalism and Symbolism—are visible in *Sons and Lovers*, although the former predominates, heightened though it is by Lawrence's use of symbols. In that novel, however, the symbols are evident and traditional, symbols as every novelist has used them, without the peculiar evocative and musical value the twentieth-century novelist has placed upon them. Not until Conrad's novels do we find a characteristic modern mode of Symbolism in the English novel. Moreover, it is not unusual that the young Lawrence, influenced as he was by Thomas Hardy—his long essay on Hardy was written at about the same time as *The Rainbow*—should be aroused by the naturalistic elements in Hardy, whose own ideas about destiny could easily be fitted into a naturalistic framework. In Lawrence's peculiar handling of the generations of Brangwens in *The Rainbow*, as in his handling of the Morels in *Sons and Lovers*, the emphasis is on heredity, physical and otherwise, and this quality is also a part of the traditional chronicle novel, from Mann's *Buddenbrooks* to Galsworthy's *Forsyte Saga*. Also working in Lawrence, however, were the symbolist ideas of Baudelaire, Verlaine, Rimbaud, and Mallarmé, whose overall influence can be found in several scenes in *The Rainbow* and *Women in Love*: in the former, Ursula and the moon, Ursula and the horses, Will Brangwen and his cathedrals; in *Women in Love*, the chapters called "Moony," "Rabbit," "The Industrial Magnate," and others.

Not only in individual scenes was Lawrence strongly influenced by the French symbolists but also in the structure of the whole. *Women in Love*, the result of Lawrence's new style, is more insistent on a general tone and rhythm than on a traditional narrative. Each scene is organized somewhat like the movements of a vast symphony in which various motifs will be counterpointed, the scenes being connected by relationships always beneath the regular narrative line. The novel often seems disjointed, often merely a succession of separate scenes which have a loosely-held relevance to the main issues. But to read *Women in Love* this way is to read it with assumptions carried over from the realistic or naturalistic novel in which the direct narrative is the connecting force. Lawrence's novel, and parts of *The Rainbow*, demands a different kind of reading, in its way the type of reading that must also be given to *Ulysses* and certain of Virginia Woolf's novels. Cognizant of different values, one finds, as Mark Schorer has termed it, a "pattern of psychic relationships," an undertone more in the sub-surface of the novel than in the story line. The novel's coherence must be found in terms of rhythms (musical or dance-like, as in the symbolists), nuances of feeling, varied reactions and interactions of characters, common symbols, and so on. The pulse of *Women in Love* is revealed in the unstated, what an abstract painter tries to convey through color rather than through pictorial representation, what an atonalist attempts to present through an infinite counterpointing of seemingly unrelated notes rather than through a long melodic line. No more do we have the length of a Brahms theme or the steady and even thrust of a George Eliot narrative. What Conrad started in the "breakup," Lawrence, perhaps without consciously seeing any "new" qualities in Conrad, has continued. The looseness, then, of *Women in Love* and *The Rainbow* is only an apparent looseness; the novels, actually, contain a strict development, one that proceeds, however, according to its own dictates and not to an established style.

"According to its own dictates" is also one way of describing the chief trait of a Lawrence character, who must, if he wishes to fulfil himself, establish connection with another person who can complete him. In his quest for completion—a quest that is different for each individual—there is of necessity a great deal of chance. Because a relationship must be examined in its entirety before being continued or rejected, Lawrence was horrified at promiscuity, sexual or otherwise, in which only *part*, not the *whole*, of the person is involved. Solely by a complex relation with others—one that involves body, spirit, mind, and certain mystical elements of identification—can one be sure that that relationship is right or wrong. In marriage, this creative relationship can be achieved apart from producing children; the creative part saturates the relationship, as Anna and Will are drawn to each other even if at times in hate, or Birkin finds Ursula magnetic even as he smashes her moon-image in the pond, or Tom Brangwen finds a certain completion with the alien Lydia Lensky *because* she is foreign.

because she is dark and unrevealing. Even Paul Morel, in *Sons and Lovers*, recognizes that his parents had once had something, now of course smashed; and even as he hates his father, he can look with admiration on the now broken miner for once having temporarily fulfilled another person.

The necessity of this trial-and-error process in choosing a partner to complete oneself accounts in Lawrence's novels for frequent sequences of counterpointing and paralleling characters. In *The Rainbow*, there are, first, the Brangwens, then Ursula and Skrebensky; in *Women in Love*, Ursula and Birkin, then Ursula and Hermione, also Hermione and Birkin, then Gerald and Birkin, Gerald and Gudrun, Gudrun and Loerke, and completing the circle, Gudrun and Ursula. Each character of the sextet has his personal significance, and each relationship its own meaning; furthermore, Lawrence plays off the character against the relationship, contrasting the internal person in isolated consciousness with the external person involved in a particular situation. Ursula, for example, is not the same alone with Birkin as with Birkin-and-Hermione, and not the same alone with Gudrun as with Birkin-and-Gerald-and-Gudrun. Moreover, opposed to her is a counter-person, say, Gerald, and to each relationship a counter relationship overlapping the preceding one while also moving the narrative forward. This overlapping, particularly noticeable in *The Rainbow* with its succeeding generations of Brangwens, at first seems like needless repetition; but within the novel it is suggestive less of artistic inadequacy than of a way of conveying density and thickness, a way, so to speak, of stressing *Brangwen-ness*.

In *The Rainbow*, the repetition recurs in the attempt of every generation of Brangwens to attain polarities, in which each person could, as Lawrence once wrote of the later Etruscans, "draw life into himself, out of the wandering huge vitalities of the world," a world in which every man and natural object has a distinct and peculiar consciousness. From this point of view, the first paragraph of the novel is one of those brilliant intuitions which contain, in small, everything that will follow. Fable-like, the novel begins:

> The Brangwens had lived for generations in the Marsh Farm, in the meadows where the Erewash twisted sluggishly through alder trees, separating Derbyshire from Nottinghamshire. Two miles away, a church-tower stood on a hill, the houses of the little country town climbing assiduously up to it. Whenever one of the Brangwens in the field lifted his head from his work, he saw the church-tower at Ilkeston in the

empty sky. So that as he turned again to the horizontal land, he was aware of something standing above him and beyond him in the distance.

And if we add to that a passage a little further on, we have the incipient conflict almost fully suggested:

She [the Brangwen woman] faced outwards to where men moved dominant and creative, having turned their back on the pulsing heat of creation, and with this behind them, were set out to discover what was beyond, to enlarge their own scope and range and freedom; whereas the Brangwen men faced inwards to the teeming life of creation, which poured unresolved in their veins.

The key words in the first passage are "church-tower," "above him and beyond him in the distance"; in the second, "outward," "scope and range and freedom," "inward," "unresolved." These words recur in different contexts with endless repetition throughout *The Rainbow*, and they help define, in large part, the Brangwens and the Skrebenskys, both the older and younger generations. They also extend through *Women in Love*, foreshadowing the yearnings of Birkin toward a perfect union, the inability of Gerald to identify with something meaningful, and the search of Ursula and Gudrun for love beyond the physical and sensual.

Tom Brangwen in *The Rainbow* finds certain satisfaction in Lydia Lensky, the Polish exile in England, especially because of her darkness which completes his own inner desolation. She is unknown, always the foreigner in both manner and speech, while he is a foreigner to himself; turning inward he can find only blackness, the same blackness that his son-in-law, Will, seeks in his beloved cathedrals. This blackness, like a curtain covering something they feel they should see for survival, is at the core of the Brangwens; it creates their constant yearnings and precludes material achievement from resolving into self-satisfaction. Lydia's unknownness is, then, a complement to Tom's own; her underground existence in a strange Poland with a strange husband gives her a mystery similar to that Tom feels within himself; and while the relationship between them is not completely realized, they reach an understanding somewhere beyond the physical, in an area that Lawrence was beginning to explore almost for the first time in English fiction: "He [Tom] did not understand her foreign nature, half German, half Polish, nor her foreign speech. But he knew her, he knew her meaning, without understanding. What she said, what she spoke, this was a blind gesture on her part, he saluted her, was with her."

Tom's identification with the blond pixie, Anna, the child of Lydia's marriage to a Polish revolutionary intellectual, suggests that in his desire to comprehend the darknesses of his own soul, he must come to terms with things he can never fully understand; and in this striving, he recognizes there is life. In a particularly magical scene, with the driving rain outside and Lydia in the house straining in child-birth, Tom removes the screaming Anna to the cow-shed; there he finds the warm, snuffing animals in a great silence that suggests the mysterious cycle of life and death and complements all the dark yearnings he has ever experienced. This scene connects the hu-man and animal cycle and as well allows Lawrence a transitional passage to Anna, who now comes to assume the center of the novel. Tom Brangwen has completed his cycle, and except for his death in the flood, where, unlike Noah, he perishes, his role in the narrative is reduced to that of a figurehead.

As Anna grows up, the Brangwens become a family with a law to themselves, separated, isolated, a "small republic set in invisible bounds." Brangwen turns inward to the "teeming life of creation" which remains still unresolved in his blood, while Lydia has her for-eign memories which satisfy her yearnings for a world beyond. With the appearance of Will Brangwen, Tom's nephew, the initial situa-tion between Tom and Lydia is intensified and carried further in the young man's relationship to Anna; then *their* relationship in turn is carried still further in the affair of Ursula and Skrebensky; and, finally, out of all, the most effective union occurs in *Women in Love* between Ursula and Birkin, who are the only ones to attain to the condition of the rainbow.

The rainbow of the first novel, which Ursula sees as a vision of the living God within her after the episode with Skrebensky has become a memory, is a symbol of fulfilment, attainment, and achievement beyond the sensual and fleshy, beyond the recognizable borders of a seemingly satisfactory physical relationship. The quest for the rain-bow is, in several ways, opposed to the dominant image of the novel: that of churches and arches, particularly Gothic arches. If we return to *Sons and Lovers*, in a passage quoted above, Paul compares his quest for Norman arches—the "dogged leaping forward of the per-sistent human soul"—with Miriam's quest for the Gothic arch, which in its perpendicular grace signifies her desire for the spiritual and divine. In *The Rainbow*, Ursula's vision of the bent arch, with its fulfilment within life, is the Norman arch of Paul; and Will Brangwen, with his Gothic cathedrals, becomes a spiritual brother of Miriam.

The rainbow stands for the realization of those things that the modern world ordinarily frustrates. Giving evidence of an inner life that is beyond consciousness, the rainbow suggests a more dangerous path, a possible disaster; for to follow the rainbow is to reject all society in one's quest for individual satisfaction. Devotion to the Gothic arch, contrariwise, means a kind of safety—it allows a foothold in both worlds, the spiritual and sensual—but its very balance must lead to dissatisfaction. Thus, Will Brangwen is unable to find himself: the cathedrals become an escape rather than a way of life. He cannot integrate the scoffing fleshy Anna with the dark mystique, the yearning vaults, of his churches. He *flees* to the church; he embraces the *opposite* of what might have fulfilled him. In achieving a sort of personal balance, in substituting mystery for personal failure, he still must live at least half frustrated. Yet Will, with his cathedrals, like Skrebensky with his sense of duty and patriotism, and Gerald, with his devotion to his coal mines, can never achieve the vision of the rainbow. He can find spiritual release in his cathedrals' womb-like vastness and darkness, he can gain a certain satisfaction from his crafts; he can even connect in sensual pleasure with Anna; but he can never achieve "Soul," that co-ordination of spirit and body which makes possible integration and fulfilment. Something in his perceptions or responses is lacking, and by attempting to obtain vicarious satisfaction beyond the natural world he tries to defy the possible; for Lawrence believed that matter, spirit, and soul are all of the natural world, and one must achieve integration here on earth by reconciling the opposites of spirit and matter without recourse to any supernatural reality.

Ursula, however, has powers of perception which go beyond Will's. As an analogy, in Proust's *The Remembrance of Things Past*, the haunting strains of Vinteuil's sonata, like the rainbow and arches in Lawrence's novel, become a kind of testing ground or frame of reference to measure the sensitivity of several of the characters. Swann, like Will Brangwen in this respect, is reminded of his love for Odette by the thematic recurrences of the sonata. The music carries, for him, the memory of love. For Marcel, on the other hand, as with Ursula, the music transcends earthly or sensual love to connote a vision of art and creativity. Marcel, in brief, transcends Swann's perceptions, just as Ursula exceeds Will's. The rainbow, here, is creative, is equated with a kind of art; churches, conversely, are an extension of the sensual, and therefore must, eventually, be found inadequate. That Will, Skrebensky, and Gerald Crich can never, so to speak, get beyond the church is an indication of their failings as modern men and their unsuitability for either Ursula or Gudrun. Only Birkin can go beyond, and while his quest is truly of worth, his attempt to verbalize his experience is ludicrous, as Ursula perceives, until she too "feels" in him a polarity she had never before recognized.

The force that reconciles flesh and spirit and that makes Soul possible is an outcome of the integration Lawrence called by many names: crown, rainbow, rose, Holy Ghost; further, it can be illustrated by one's reaction to flowers, to industrialization, to personal contact, to personal freedom, to horses, to the sun, the moon, and so on. For man to realize his Holy Ghost, he must first destroy his false conventions, especially those related to money and possessions, and "re-establish the living organic connections with the cosmos, the sun and earth, with mankind and nation and family. Start with the sun," Lawrence stressed, "and the rest will slowly, slowly happen." It is this desire to re-establish affinity with the Unknown that explains Anna's naked dance while pregnant, a dance that celebrates her fertility and her relationship with the sun that brings life. Her dance is one of exultation, a ritualistic performance in which her dedication is to powers that ripen corn, bring rain, provide warmth—that, in short, make growth possible.

This line of communication that Anna is able to establish with the gods of creativity is sufficient justification for her life: she is content with marriage, child-bearing, the slow, sensual passage of time. The look of bliss on her face, so infuriating to Ursula, suggests that her circuit of happiness has been closed, that intrusion is impossible. Her very fixity of purpose, then, explains her mockery of Will's love of churches and his search for the infinite. In the central chapter of *The Rainbow*, toward which the entire book moves as to the tip of a Gothic arch, and from which the rest of the narrative declines until the rainbow on earth is achieved, Anna is first awed by Lincoln Cathedral and then angered by it. While Will feels release, she senses confinement—the leaping stone closes her in and makes her feel there is no beyond. Will wants completion, but she, a true Brangwen woman, looks further to a connection with something the arch can never attain. In her frustration, she remarks the "wicked, odd little faces carved in stone" which mock man's illusion that the church is absolute. For her, they jeer at Will's desire to believe; their separate wills, like hers, are frozen in defiant amusement. With this realization, Anna divides herself still further from Will and gets free of the cathedral-idea. Will's anguish is complete; his only release is to retreat to the organ, and while he plays the swelling music, Lawrence comments that to Anna, the "baby was a complete bliss and fulfilment."

Will is a modern victim of the condition Lawrence had attacked in *Apocalypse*, his explication of the *Book of Revelation* of John of Patmos, published posthumously in 1932. Lawrence claimed that the Apocalyptic Gospel epitomizes the glorification of the weak as against the splendors and richness of the strong who are to be eliminated, and it is precisely this document, he continues, which dominates in present-day religion. *Apocalypse* appeals to the poor (in spirit) because it attends to their glorification; by "poor," Lawrence means those collective souls who have no aristocratic singleness and aloneness—thus, he defines Will Brangwen, who must look up and not inward; Winifred Inger, with whom Ursula has a short and unsatisfactory lesbian affair; Tom Brangwen, her homosexual uncle, whose addiction to mining machinery suggests his paucity of soul; Skrebensky, whose dedication to the army reveals his need for external identity. All these inadequate figures are exalted by the *Book of Revelation* which denies personal power and replaces it with authority, the weak substitute for natural rights. *Apocalypse*, Lawrence says further, is the Judas Iscariot of the Bible. Fear of being outshone makes the mass of poor bring down the leader—as Gerald Crich must resist Birkin, then Gudrun, finally Loerke. And *Apocalypse* supports the authority of each mass-man to be a little ruler, a little Christ. This supererogation of power, Lawrence feels, destroys any live communication between people; those with this sense of authority deny either mind or body, without whose balance perversion results. People who negate one quality at the expense of the other cut off the chance of outward flow toward an absolute and perfect union. Thus the conflicts between Will and Anna, Ursula and Skrebensky, Birkin and Hermione, Gudrun and Gerald, and so on throughout Lawrence's characters.

As Ursula is unwilling to settle for less than a complete relationship, it is not unusual that she feels she should be seized by a Son of God, one of those who make off with mortal women and immortalize them; only then, like the phoenix, can she be resurrected into wholeness, joy, and fulfilment. Only a God, Ursula realizes, can save her.

and the Voices she hears add credence to her hope. Each setback almost destroys her—her life at home, her experiences as a teacher, the affairs with Winifred and Skrebensky—but each makes her recognize further that a normal mortal man is insufficient, is a mechanical trap for her budding ideals.

Nevertheless, Ursula's "God" might have lowly origins and small pretensions. For example: the atmosphere on the barge which Ursula and Skrebensky board (Chapter 11) is indicative of a delicately balanced relationship that only Ursula can feel and react to. While she is aware of an electric quality between the bargeman and his wife, Skrebensky reflects condescendingly that the woman once must have been a servant. Comparing the two men, Ursula recognizes that the bargeman gave her a pleasant warm feeling, whereas Skrebensky ". . . had created a deadness round her, a sterility, as if the world were ashes." On his part, Skrebensky envies the bargeman's ability to communicate with Ursula, body and soul, in a way that he, Skrebensky, could never do. Only the physical part of him reacts; the rest is dead, sterile, as Ursula fully realizes when she favors the bargeman.

From this carefully placed scene, Lawrence moves into one of darkness, a funereal blackness, in which the only significant light is the moon. Functioning as a kind of moon goddess, Ursula by seeking consummation with the light of the moon asserts the triumph of the female. In the darkness, Skrebensky complies heroically with her wishes, but senses death in her attempt to transcend his sensuality. Under the piercing lunar light, his inadequacies become obvious; a mere mortal unable to make contact with the moon, he is incapable of satisfying one who is reanimated by its beams. Later, on a black night under a brilliant moon, Ursula crushes Skrebensky's body to the ground in an embrace that drains away his manhood and leaves him bewildered by her power. With her, he fears the darkness, for he senses that she can perceive clearly a presence that he can barely discern; and since the darkness contains mysteries that only a "complete" person can penetrate, Ursula exults while Skrebensky dreads.

As a person interested in the good of the greatest number and dedicated to the defense of his country, Skrebensky is not interested in individuals, only in forces and vague ideas. He is monistic, committed to power by itself, or action by itself, or physical satisfaction by itself. Ursula, however, as a moon goddess who can penetrate the darkness, contains the duality of light and dark that Lawrence felt was necessary for completion, what earlier was identified as the coalition of spirit and flesh to create Soul. Only when the seed of light (the moon) joins with darkness (one's vital self) can Ursula be fulfilled, and only Birkin in *Women in Love* is capable of effecting this combination in her. He, unlike Skrebensky with his transitory interests, aims at the absolute, without which Lawrence claimed man is nothing; man must, he stressed, break through to a new heaven as the chicken breaks his shell and bursts out.

Obviously, by this time, Lawrence's characters have begun to take on non-realistic qualities in which symbolic elements often supersede human personality. Ursula, in the episodes with Skrebensky, becomes a mythical character whose sympathies extend beyond the confines of the recognizable world. Anna herself, no longer a sarcastic and bickering individual, is now the great Mother, fulfilled in her breeding, a being complete in herself. "Brangwen," Lawrence writes, "continued in a kind of rich drowse of physical heat, in connection with his wife. They were neither of them quite personal, quite defined as individuals, so much were they pervaded by the physical heat of breeding and rearing their young." Ursula's Uncle Tom, in turn, has become a symbol of mechanical man who seems to gain satisfaction solely from the life-sucking qualities of the pit, who worships the abstraction of the machine as a substitute for a vital self; and therefore Winifred Unger seems to Ursula to be a perfect mate for him. "There, there, in the machine, in service of the machine, was she [Winifred] free from the clog and degradation of human feeling. There, in the monstrous mechanism that held all matter, living or dead, in its service, did she achieve her consummation and her perfect unison, her immortality."

In abstracting his characters, Lawrence increasingly identified and defined them as forces rather than people. Ursula's association with the moon, for example, is merely one way of emphasizing her otherness. Her aloofness and her repulsion by average people further define her removal of self from day to day life and indicate her need to come to terms with her own nature in some mysterious connection. Yet, Lawrence was fully aware of his direction and of the need to maintain at least a semblance of reality. Recognizing that his characters were becoming almost unearthly in their functions as symbols, Lawrence moved them back into real conflicts, epitomized by Ursula's experience in the Brinsley Street School. In every novel of apprenticeship—and *The Rainbow* shares characteristics of this genre as well as of the family-chronicle novel—there is one large conflict, a type of ordeal —perhaps a remnant of the perilous quest of the chivalric romance—

which the hero(ine) must successfully sustain in order to survive and triumph. So, in *The Rainbow*, Ursula has to come through an ordeal which tests her every ideal and which, simultaneously, shows her exactly how the world expects her to behave. Once she has gained full knowledge of what the world *is*, then rejection, if it is to come, can be sure and final.

Ursula conceives of teaching as *creative*, as a means of reaching individual needs through compassion and understanding and as a way of treating each child as unique in himself. She expects teaching to provide freedom, specifically freedom from the kind of prison her home has become. "She dreamed how she would make the little, ugly children love her. She would be so personal. Teachers were always so hard and impersonal. There was no vivid relationship. She would make everything personal and vivid, she would give herself, she would give, give, give all her great stores of wealth to her children, she would make them *so* happy, and they would prefer her to any teacher on the face of the earth." Teaching, also, would provide a release for Ursula's ego, a justification of her own need for warmth and understanding.

Ursula's experience in the school provides, then, a brutal contrast between her ideal and what reality offers. She looks for freedom and finds another prison; she searches for release and meets frustration. The only way she can survive as a teacher, she sadly recognizes, is to destroy all feeling, to appeal to mass understanding in which uniqueness has no place, to bully and whip the class into a hostile and complaining group of children with whom human communication becomes impossible. Her desire for personality is turned into the embracement of impersonal numbers. Ursula finds herself in a quest not for a vivid relationship but for simple survival in a world that would destroy her if she relented. As soon as she realizes that only the abuse of authority and power commands respect, that only the abnegation of personal self allows one to achieve a calculable result, that only mass treatment leads to the imparting of certain knowledge, then she succeeds in a nightmarish world whose frustrations exceed her morbid existence at home. She recognizes, in her awakening to the real world, that until she pursues the troublemakers she herself will be pursued. And she knows that her punishment of the Williams boy is merely one event in a series that will break her spirit; for the Williams case, she now foresees, will be repeated continuously, and the scene with Mrs. Williams, who is both forcefully abject and servilely arrogant.

is one she can expect to recur. With this knowledge, she seizes each opportunity to cane the boys into submission and obedience: she becomes a successful teacher.

But she had paid a great price out of her own soul, to do this [Lawrence wrote]. It seemed as if a great flame had gone through her and burnt her sensitive tissue. She who shrank from the thought of physical suffering in any form, had been forced to fight and beat with a cane and rouse all her instincts to hurt. . . . She would rather bear all their insults and insolences a thousand times than reduce herself and them to this. . . . Yet it had to be so. She did not want to do it. Yet she had to. Oh why, why had she leagued herself to this evil system where she must brutalise herself to live? . . . The children had forced her to the beatings. No, she did not pity them. She had come to them full of kindness and love, and they would have torn her to pieces.

Ursula becomes hard and independent under this ordeal; she matures by forcing herself into routines that her whole person tells her she must despise, although she never fully surrenders herself to the demands that reality makes upon her. Therefore, when she leaves St. Philip's to go to college in London, she has somehow been completed; the Ursula who now meets Skrebensky upon his return from India is quite different from the teen-age girl infatuated with her cousin. In her temporary disillusionment, she realizes that her fight is to be a continual one against a mechanistic universe that would turn her, as it turned Winifred, her Uncle Tom, and her father, into an inadequate puppet. Even after she enters college in London, her teaching experience makes it impossible for her to accept what is to her "a sham workshop," a "sham store," a "sham warehouse, with a single motive of material gain . . . a flunkey to the god of material success." Here, too, she sees evidence of a mechanical universe, a denial of the self in its oneness with the infinite.

This feeling of the cheated emotions inevitably carries over into her relationship with Skrebensky, who with his "assumed self" denies, like the others, the "dark, fertile beings that exist in the potential darkness." Since he can never realize (literally, "make real") the infinite within her, he can engage only the lesser part of her, her active body. The routine of the college becomes, as it were, the routine of Skrebensky, for neither proves satisfactory. In her refusal to marry him, she denies him the right to reject part of herself in a lifetime union. And he receives her decision with the recognition that he cannot fulfil her, that their denials of each other are somehow equated. While Ursula, in her nakedness and in the sexual act, is trying to recall lost mysteries, to create a *ritual* of physical union—as Birkin, in turn, tries to do in *Women in Love*—Skrebensky is willing to settle for existing feelings, and thus denies the possibility of an infinite beyond. Lacking darkness, he lacks, in the final sense, virility. He would, in turn, succumb to the feminine principle, for the Ursula-Moon would be too strong for him to resist. His escape, actually, is a form of salvation from eventual destruction, and their mutual release of each other is, in effect, an escape from prison for both.

After the realism of the school episode and the semi-realistic mysticism of Ursula's affair with Skrebensky, Lawrence moves into a scene that in its visionary symbolism tries to approximate a state of hallucination that borders on the real. Although Ursula, when she finds herself pregnant, seriously considers giving up her quest for some "fantastic fulfilment" by marrying Skrebensky and submitting to her fate, she plans her future as a sort of doom which it is pointless to resist. The conflict has by now exhausted her, driven her to desperation, and in this condition she slips out one day to walk in the rain-soaked woods. The romping wild horses that bear down upon her and cut off her retreat are the visionary reality of her conflict taking physical form. The huge, heavily-breathing horses, superb in their incandescent physicality, create a sensual atmosphere at sharp conflict with her present barrenness of spirit. The horses return again and again, trapping her amidst their crashing bodies and cruel hooves, full of the living God that she has decided to reject by accepting her lover. As the bodies flash by her, she is ever aware of the "urgent, massive fire that was locked within these flanks." When she finally escapes over the hedge, the vision has become the only reality for her, is, in effect, reality, and in her ensuing illness she miscarries, thus losing her last contact with Skrebensky. Now *he* seems the hallucination, a person who had not become fully real. "In the end he had failed and broken down."

With Skrebensky solely a memory filling the void of the past, his cablegram announcing his marriage can stir in her only anger and contempt, mixed as it is with her total repudiation of the former relationship. Then, amidst the ruins of her own desolation and frustration, she sees over the corruption of the mining town the iridescent colors of a rainbow forming in the distance. And in its arch, she sees a possible future perfection for herself and the world; she looks ahead to some earthly Messiah, and in *Women in Love*, which completes *The Rainbow*, she meets him in the form of Birkin.

Shortly after he finished *The Rainbow* in its final form, Lawrence in remarks to Bertrand Russell threw a great deal of light on the new novel that he was beginning, *Women in Love.* Lawrence wrote:

I have been reading Frazer's *Golden Bough* and *Totemism and Exogamy.* Now I am convinced of what I believed when I was about twenty [now thirty]—that there is another seat of consciousness which exists in us independently of the ordinary mental consciousness, which depends on the eye as its source or connector. There is the blood-consciousness with the sexual connection holding the same relation as the eye, in seeing, holds to the mental consciousness. One lives, knows, and has one's being in the blood, without any reference to nerves and brain. This is one half of life, belonging to the darkness. And the tragedy of this our life and of your life, is that the mental and nerve consciousness exerts a tyranny over the blood-consciousness and that your will has gone completely over to the mental consciousness, and is engaged in the destruction of your blood-being or blood-consciousness, the final liberating of the one, which is only death in result.

These words indicate in brief what Birkin says at great length in *Women in Love,* and they constitute Lawrence's unique insight into the type of mind—here Russell's—that would reject feeling in favor of intellect. To put feeling back into a mechanical world, Lawrence had to over-emphasize the "lower half" of man's consciousness as against his mental and nerve consciousness. Therefore, Lawrence's relentless attack on Gerald Crich and Hermione Roddice, and, therefore, the paradox that Birkin is nearly always seen as a *failure* whose words and actions border on the ludicrous. He *is* ridiculous because he is unable to express in suitable words what his "blood-consciousness" tells him is true, and his dogged earnestness will not allow his message to lie fallow. Birkin *must* attack, as if pursued by a Fury that makes him forfeit peace. Even Ursula, who comes closest to understanding him, finds him alternately absurd and selfish. When he asks, for example, for a strange conjunction with her in which he cannot see her, she laughs at him: " 'I'm sorry I can't oblige you by being invisible.' " Yet Ursula understands Birkin's need for duality—for the part that can be submerged to another and the part that must remain forever inviolate in the individual.

Birkin's kind of spirituality should not be confused with that of Hermione Roddice, for she intellectualizes what Birkin wants to leave as a bodily function. Lacking a "robust self," she has no "natural sufficiency," and in this respect she is in the line of Laurentian characters who worship a false divinity: Miriam Leivers, Will Brangwen,

Gerald Crich. This type of divinity worship, by being an act of will or ego which destroys passion, makes them deny all inner mystery. Hermione realizes that Birkin's creed destroys everything she needs to believe, and when she tries to crush his head with a paperweight, she is attempting to smash out of existence the only person who understands her deficiency. Her Will makes her alternately despise and love this external attacker who recognizes that she is unable to flower within; and by crushing what is, cancer-like, eating her alive, she tries to gain freedom from her personal Fury. Birkin, in turn, can only recover from her attack through communion with flowers, whose responsiveness is directed to his feelings, untinged by the deadly nerves. Naked, in a kind of natural Paradise where good and evil are unknown, Birkin knows where he belongs: "This was his place, his marriage place. The world was extraneous."

Women in Love is a necessary sequel to *The Rainbow*, for although the later novel is complete in itself, the earlier is inconclusive when taken alone. Both the ideas and characters of *The Rainbow* need extension: its world is too singular, its profile too self-contained. In *Women in Love*, Lawrence created several new dimensions by introducing not only Birkin but as well Gerald Crich, Hermione Roddice, and the artist, Loerke, while also bringing Ursula's sister, Gudrun, into prominence. In addition, several scenes in *Women in Love* by reflecting on earlier passages explain and enlarge their significance. Surely, Lawrence recognized the necessity of a sequel when he wrote on the last page of *The Rainbow* manuscript: "End of Volume I."

In Gerald Crich, Lawrence introduced a wholly new type of person into his fiction, a character who in the Victorian novel was often the hero or near hero, the "advantageous suitor" in a potentially "good marriage." Lawrence took this stock figure, transformed him into a hollow commercial husk of a man, and came out with Gerald, Clifford Chatterley, Rico (*St. Mawr*), and the dozens of incomplete humans who appear in his short stories. In opposition to this type of person, Lawrence placed a Birkin, a Mellors, or, in several instances, an animal, usually a horse. Thus horses appear in key scenes in both *The Rainbow* and in *Women in Love*. In the latter, the arrogant but insecure Gerald, instinctively recognizing that his new Arabian mare must be mastered before he, Gerald, can triumph, systematically makes his horse's will conform to his own. Accordingly, the horse must have its will crushed by subjecting it to the noise and vibrations of the industrial world: a freight train, whose efficiency is Gerald's real master. The horse is spurred bloody before it will become a part of Gerald's system, and yet it must; for he can tolerate no opposing will and has to ride the horse, as later Gudrun, toward destruction in his singleness of purpose. His attitude toward the mare foreshadows his scenes with Gudrun and Loerke; in both, as in the animal, he senses a quality that will nullify him unless his own will prevails. In effect, this is what happens: Gerald is finally destroyed because he wearies in his constant struggle against a world of opposing wills.

Watching Gerald spur the horse unmercifully, Gudrun and Ursula react in completely different ways. Gudrun experiences in the sadistic scene a type of sexuality that originally attracts her to Gerald; he rides the mare with a persistence and tenaciousness that recommend him as a potential lover. As the horse suffers pain and humiliation, she senses sensuality: "And then on the very wound the bright spurs came down, pressing relentlessly. The world reeled and passed into nothingness for Gudrun, she could not know any more." Gudrun wants to be possessed and Gerald's combination of sadism and hardness of purpose draws her toward him, as much as it revolts Ursula, who better than her sister understands Gerald's egoism from the outset.

Not fortuitously, Ursula agrees only in part with Birkin's remarks to Gerald that every horse has two wills: one that desires complete subjection, and the other that wants to be free and wild. Gerald of course denies the horse's freedom, and, conversely, Ursula asks why even half a horse should want to put itself in human power. Birkin's answer suggests his reply when later she inquires what he really expects from a love relationship. There is, he says, the highest love-impulse in which you must "resign your will to the higher being." In this area of resignation, two pure beings, paradoxically each remaining free and yet united, would balance each other "like two poles of one force, like two angels, or two demons." Gerald obviously can never achieve the balance; and Gudrun, after searching for it once she has exhausted the range of his sadism, soon rejects him for Loerke, who at least can make art out of selfish possessiveness. Ursula herself in time comes to understand what Birkin means, although the resignation part continues to rankle her; while Hermione, by ceasing to listen, cuts herself off completely, as she realizes, from Birkin's world of sympathetic polarities. Her world of animality, Birkin tells her, begins and ends in her head. "Passion and the intimate," he says, "—you want them hard enough, but through your head, in your consciousness." Not by chance, then, Hermione insanely smashes Birkin on the head.

If horses indicate one major line of comparison in *Women in Love*, then statues also work as recurring images, forming, so to speak, a spine to certain relationships in the novel. Quite early, when Gerald visits Birkin's London flat, he is upset by the "obscene" foetus-like Negro statues around the rooms, particularly by one of a pregnant naked woman bearing down on the ends of a board to help her in child-birth. "He [Gerald] hated the sheer African thing," for it touches him in areas where he has no defense, exactly as he is both fascinated and revolted by the naked figures of the house guests indifferently walking through the apartment. Gerald, in his blondness, is a man of the north, a man of snow and ice—"He was one of these strange white wonderful demons from the north, fulfilled in the destructive frost mystery."—and therefore the African statues with their thousands of years of purely sensual, warm knowledge are antipathetic to his ideas of efficient manliness.

Birkin himself makes the comparison between the statues' sensuality and Gerald's coldness when in the "Moony" chapter he recognizes that these Africans had passed through every stage of phallic knowledge and had gone beyond into areas where great mysteries are to be unsealed. Whereas the African had penetrated into mindlessness through the teeming creativeness of the sun, the northerner had only the vast abstraction of ice and snow with which to fulfil himself. Birkin fears not only for Gerald—"Was he a messenger, an omen of the universal dissolution into whiteness and snow?"—but also for himself. What could he do to deny the disintegrative forces of the Africans, whose sun would destroy him? Birkin answers with the only possible working solution for a northerner:

> There was another way, the way of freedom. There was the paradisal entry into pure, single being, the individual soul taking precedence over love and desire for union, stronger than any pangs of emotion, a lovely state of free proud singleness, which accepted the obligation of the permanent connection with others, and with the other, submits to the yoke and leash of love, but never forfeits its own proud individual singleness, even while it loves and yields.

Birkin does not waver in his belief even when he might lose Ursula because of his doctrinairism. Therefore, the statues rarely affect him as strongly as they do Gerald, nor do they become a significant part of his life. But the statues keep recurring to Gerald—we remember that Gudrun does small African-like miniatures, pieces from the primeval past—until the problem of statues in the scene with Loerke sets him off to destroy everyone in his way and finally himself. That scene in the mountain hostel between the quartet of lovers and Loerke brings together all the main plots and sub-plots of the novel in which Loerke's cold statue becomes a central symbol of destruction, an image of complete annihilation. But to understand all the nuances of this key passage, one must first return to an earlier chapter, called "The Industrial Magnate," which holds together the first half of the novel as this one the latter part.

Mr. Crich, Gerald's father, like Gould in *Nostromo*, confuses moral idea with self interest and makes the welfare of his coal mine(r)s his *idée fixe*. Obsessed with his mines, he finds identity only in work which is morally as well as economically satisfying to him. "He wanted his industry," Lawrence writes, "to run on love." Not unnaturally, his heart is broken when he finds love is not enough, bread is also necessary. Conscience-stricken, he finds himself on the wrong side when the miners strike, and while rejecting their objectives he feeds them from his own pocket. The men are really willing to be machines in exchange for more pay, but Mr. Crich wants them to be men and insists that the machine should not change them.

Gerald, on the other hand, realizes that these men are, in essence, already machines, the thing to do is to make them more efficient and smoother running. Accordingly, what Mr. Crich has hitherto met with love and do-goodism, Gerald will encounter with facts. His obsession is, likewise, with the mines, but not as a moral idea. As morality was the key to Mr. Crich, so efficiency—"perfect instruments in perfect organisation"—explains Gerald's aims. "It was this inhuman principle in the mechanism he wanted to construct that inspired Gerald with an almost religious exaltation. He, the man, could interpose a perfect, changeless, god-like medium between himself and the Matter he had to subjugate." Between his will and the great Matter of the earth, there rested the Machine which would give him the incarnate power to prevail. His lifework becomes, then, the imposition of his perfect system upon the collective will of men. As a man of will, Gerald does not, of course, stop at the mines: he must impose himself and destroy resistance in every way. By the time Gerald has modernized the mines, his father's old-fashioned benevolent capitalism has been forgotten, and Gerald's world is already accepted, not despite its destructiveness but because of it. His perfect system of getting the maximum work from a minimum number of men through the use of machinery gives his workers identification with a kind of cosmic order. In that connection they find the type of limited freedom they can under-stand. Mechanical themselves, they strive to smash their souls in Gerald's great mechanical purpose.

Only Gerald is dissatisfied. The mines no longer interest him once the system is perfected. Beneath the outward order, there still re-mains the dark mystery of the mine in himself, the fears that seem a birthright of the Brangwens. Gerald feels as isolated as Cain, indeed he is a kind of Cain, having accidentally shot his brother when they were children. There hangs a doom over him—his sister had drowned while he was in charge of the bathing-party, and he himself always feels the premonition of death. The dark fears implicit in the statues, in the family deaths, in his own insufficiency and lack of substantial self, in his need to prove his mastery—all these become focused in his hate for Loerke, the German sculptor, whose remarks and sneering tones probe places Gerald had hitherto tried, unsuccessfully, to forget.

In the Volsung-Nibelung myth, the central northern mythology, Loki (Loerke) is the Evil One, one who lurks; Gudrun, the name of Siegfried's wife in the Edda, plays a destructive role in the saga of the Nibelungs; and Gerald signifies, in Teutonic, a spear-bearer. Loki is described as a small underworld creature, one who brings disturbance into the party's complacency. Lawrence, while not directly equating his characters to those in the Scandinavian saga, perhaps wanted to give an heroic dimension to this "Battle of the Gods" high up in the snow-covered mountains and, therefore, the mythical references. In addition, Loki-Loerke causes death in both the myth and in the novel, although, of course, differently in each. By making Loerke an artist, Lawrence stresses his "other-world" characteristics, and by suggesting his Jewishness separates him from the typical Christian middle-class, at the same time allowing his character to reject a society essentially not his.

Almost every aspect of Loerke will challenge Gerald's assumptions and defenses, and certain of his attitudes also affront Birkin and Ursula, although except for Ursula's intermittent comments they re-main essentially aloof in themselves. Only Gudrun is sympathetic to Loerke, and through her accord with him her divergence from Ursula is fully revealed; for Gudrun accepts a view of art and life that more or less denies everything Ursula and Birkin stand for. Loerke claims that his frieze for a granite factory in Cologne—a representation of * peasant and artisan fair scene—will interpret industry as art once interpreted religion. It will glorify work, motion, the machine; by beautifying the factory, it will beautify work. So revealed, Loerke's independence of mind and his understanding of the "rock-bottom of all life" immediately impress Gudrun as well as Ursula. His very poverty gives him a "pure unconnected will, stoical and momentaneous," while his social and physical inferiority in a world of gentlemen constitutes his attraction for the sisters.

Birkin shrewdly recognizes his appeal as that of a criminal type toward whom women rush both in pity and repulsion. He remarks that Loerke is completely corrupt, a person who hates the ideal and who, therefore, must crush it for everyone else. As an underworld character—Birkin calls him a wizard rat who explores sewers—Loerke is too far from Gerald's and Birkin's experience for any communication to exist, even for Birkin, with his Bohemian friends. Loerke is in earnest, while Birkin's Bohemians are soft and malleable and marked by promiscuity. Furthermore, Loerke's statuette of a young naked girl on a great naked horse can only outrage them; and although Gudrun understands the work, *they* cannot possibly do so. Loerke explains that the horse is his *conception* of a horse, part of an art form, and not to be confused with a real horse. The work of art, he explains haughtily to Ursula, has nothing to do with anything else; it is itself or nothing. Art and life, he underlines, should not be confused—"they are two different and distinct planes of existence. . . ." The latter is relative, while the former is absolute. Ursula, however, persists in confusing them and merely gains his mocking disapproval, as well as Gerald's, who understands nothing but feels that she is being obtrusive. Gerald then attempts assertive comment, only to make himself a laughing-stock. He talks about life and rejects art; while they discuss art and deny life. Gerald's frustration becomes murderous. By ridiculing his literalness, they deny him; and he soon senses that Gudrun and Loerke are part of the underworld which has always tormented him, part of the enemy world which, Cain-like, he must always wander, alienated and alone.

In this scene—whose complexities and cross-currents create a situation that is at once cruel and lyrical—each character is exposed and diminished as Lawrence probes his weaknesses. Lawrence is using here a series of paradoxes to create a miniature world in which all strivings based on ego are frustrated or rendered ludicrous: Loerke must deny life to create art; Gerald must face the dark that will eventually doom him; Gudrun must turn furiously on her sister, whose views she had hitherto generally shared, in order to assert her own individuality; Ursula, even while defending Lawrence's own point of view in his remarks on Cézanne, must make a fool of herself in a situation that means re-living her disastrous school experience; and Birkin himself is revealed as limited, almost provincial. not at all the man of broad potentiality Lawrence had presented earlier. Birkin, we see, understands merely those he can easily circumvent, chiefly disciples; whereas Loerke is no fool and provides no "give." Although Birkin and Ursula, we realize, cannot possibly accept Loerke's deadening of soul, we also sense their vulgarity and admire Loerke's pluck. He has, at least, the spunk of the devil in opposing pompous virtue. And despite his satanism, we do want him to deny Gerald's bourgeois literalness and Birkin's insularity; further, we see that Ursula *is* wrong in identifying, without additional qualification, the artist with his art; we see, also, that Gudrun will back the force she feels the stronger while respecting spontaneity of creation, and that Loerke in derogating spontaneity *is* inhuman, *is* sadistic perhaps beyond the demands of his art. In this world of life and art, everyone is tarnished, everyone is incomplete; Lawrence suggests that there are no heroes or heroines, and that Birkin and Ursula, who are the best he has to offer, are only a small part of a complicated world.

After this confrontation, the novel, like its characters, spreads out; all else is anti-climactic. Gerald's near throttling of Gudrun and his beating of Loerke are almost afterthoughts. He has already seen his death when he recognizes that Gudrun identifies with Loerke; pushed out by a scrawny, possibly Jewish, somewhat homosexual, perhaps hermaphroditic artist-type, Gerald must go to his pre-determined frozen death: the northerner meets an icy entombment. By now, Ursula and Birkin are away, and only Gudrun and Loerke remain to work out their plans to frustrate the Geralds of this world. All major feelings have been defined except for the curious relationship between Birkin and Gerald.

Birkin accepts the classical idea of friendship in which a man is fulfilled only by relating to another man, and a woman as the child-bearing mate is unfit for companionship on a higher plane. No matter how complete Birkin's union with Ursula may be, there is still something left over; he tells her, " 'You are enough for me, as far as a woman is concerned. You are all women to me. But I wanted a man friend, as eternal as you and I are eternal.' " He adds: " 'Having you,

I can live all my life without anybody else, any other sheer intimacy. But to make it complete, really happy, I wanted eternal union with a man too; another kind of love. . . .' "

Ursula thinks this a perversity, but Birkin is far from homosexual in his desires. Even if sexual contact with a male is in his mind, it is incidental to his real purpose: the need for touch with each species, man and woman, the need for connection with every one of life's kind. The famous gladiatorial scene in which Birkin and Gerald wrestle naked—this chapter parallels a later one called "Woman to Woman," in which Ursula and Hermione also "wrestle"—fulfills both, especially Birkin, who has just been rejected by Ursula; for it allows the men to destroy each other while also establishing an electric current between them. Their struggle "to the death" conveys life and meaning, just as earlier, Birkin's stoning of the water to destroy Ursula served to attract her and bring her to life, the moon on the water, Ursula on the bank. Their mindless wrestling, intent and rapturous, allows the play of blood, intuition, and physical intelligence. It denies all women; it negates marriage; it especially nullifies Hermione.

This contact, Birkin recognizes, is a part of human relationships, and it provides a type of sexual completeness that no woman, obviously, could give. When these men seize each other, Lawrence suggests, the contact releases sources of energy that otherwise would be wasted. And their swearing a *Blutbruderschaft*, a blood-brotherhood, is their way of keeping open the flow of energy which makes possible a personal union in which the individual self is still free. The choice of word, *Blutbruderschaft*, not to be confused with its later use in fascist countries, is fitting indeed for Birkin, for he believes that in the blood there is a conscience, an intuitive knowledge, through which we can test instantly whether or not we do well. We may live, Lawrence tells us, by what the blood says, and rather than having chaos, we shall have increasing order. As one critic wrote of this aspect of Lawrence-Birkin: "Each man's church should be inside himself, his own daily life the liturgy, his pulsing blood the sacrament." Through their blood relationship, Gerald and Birkin take, in effect, religious vows, but Gerald, as a fated man, holds himself back and swears only halfheartedly. Birkin, ironically, has not gained a whole man for a friend, and at the end of the novel, as Ursula perhaps ruefully suggests, he mourns somebody who never came so close to understanding him as she does.

What Birkin seeks in connecting with another man, Ursula finds in the moon, and Gudrun in her Dalcroze variations before the cows. Lawrence realized that to suggest these unearthly communions, he had to find valid objective correlatives to dramatize Birkin's doctrines and the sisters' feelings, or else the novel would be completely cerebral and defeat its own purpose. The particulars of the scenes are, admittedly, often ridiculous—the image of Gudrun stamping voluptuously, breasts lifted and throat exposed, before the hypnotized cows excites laughter rather than deep feeling, although the scene as a rhythmic sequence is strongly conveyed and does work effectively in the total plan of the narrative. Again, the particulars of the "Moony" chapter, the title itself, are ludicrous—Birkin becomes like a petulant boy scaling stones into the pond after having been chided. As a literal representation, the scene must fail, for, literally, the main character has lost all dignity, particularly as his moon-girl, the one he is attempting to destroy, watches him incredulously—"Ursula wanted to laugh loudly and hysterically, hearing his isolated voice speaking out. It was so ridiculous." His curses against Cybele and Syria Dea (goddesses of the earth, fertility) add to her amusement, which then turns to horror when she realizes it is her image he is endeavoring to split apart. Nevertheless, this scene out of a Rider Haggard novel does have figurative significance. If it is taken as symbolic, along with Gudrun's dance and Birkin's wrestling, if, in fact, Birkin himself is taken symbolically, then the risible elements decrease and the novel gains in meaning.

Mentioned earlier was Lawrence's tendency to mix naturalistic and symbolical elements together or in alternating sequences, a practice that creates difficulties in the interpreting of individual scenes. Most of *Women in Love* should be taken figuratively, for only there has the novel significance; but the reader, unprepared for Lawrence's radical departures after the first two chapters, tends to read literally, and there the novel fails. This is, of course, a fault in the novel: the novelist must inform the reader how to proceed, and failing to do that, he cannot, as Lawrence did, complain about misinterpretation. Only repeated readings show that Lawrence attempted to integrate action and speech in a supra-realistic manner; only repeated readings show the inter-relationship of parts, the paralleling of scenes and characters, the rise and fall of action in the first and second halves of the book, the rhythmic and contrapuntal interplay of the novel.

The chapter "Rabbit," for example, is meaningless, even extraneous, until its connection to the entire novel can be demonstrated, and this connection, in turn, must be figurative rather than literal. For Lawrence gives the rabbit the spunk and verve, the anti-mechanical quality, that elsewhere Birkin argues for *ad infinitum*. The rabbit is *alive*, so much so that it resists human touch and restriction, and in its anger arouses Gerald's wrath—characteristically, Gerald, who cannot tolerate opposition, not even from a rabbit. Gudrun suggests some affinity, seriously jesting that men are not rabbits, yet . . . ! And Gerald, seeing the rabbit's mystery, once again feels his own death-stroke.

In another strikingly bitter scene, the one in the Bohemian hangout, the Pompadour Café, Birkin's views, taken literally, become the butt of ridicule and outrage. Lawrence, in effect, parodies himself, in Birkin's letter, by stating his views in the most absurd abstractions: "And in the great retrogression, the reducing back of the created body of life, we get knowledge, and beyond knowledge, the phosphorescent ecstasy of acute sensation." This is language meaningless to the uninitiated and tedious to the knowledgeable. This is Birkin at his most tiring telling the Bohemians that their lives and loves are sterile, that their promiscuity denies real feeling, and that only he, Birkin, through sermon and example, can lead them out of Hell. Birkin's feelings lend themselves easily to parody when taken at their face value because they contain the arrogance and haughtiness of a pompous preacher. The chapter "In the Pompadour" illustrates what happens when Lawrence presents the bare words of his Messiah; he is informing the reader here how to accept Birkin, for by presenting the vicious Bohemians as they mock Birkin's views he makes the reader take sides. One is made to feel the way Gudrun does: that the Bohemians are obscene and that Birkin is a fool, but that foolishness is preferable to obscenity. Given the choice, one must, says Lawrence, accept Birkin.

To accept Birkin, Lawrence recognized, the reader must be ready to change his philosophy of life and love; in effect, initiate a revolution in feeling. Toward this end, Lawrence poured out a vast quantity of poems, travel books, novels, letters, and essays in the years after *The Rainbow* and *Women in Love*, but everything became merely a thinly disguised variation on the views expressed in these two novels. By the time he was thirty, Lawrence had indicated what he stood for, and his later publications came from the same frame of mind. Even his doctrinal prose works—like *Fantasia of the Unconscious* (1922), *Psychoanalysis and the Unconscious* (1921), *Reflections on the Death of a Porcupine* (1925), *and Apocalypse* (1931)—were derived, as Lawrence said, from his novels and plays. He claimed that his philosophy came out unwatched from his pen, and that his attempts to gain a satisfactory mental attitude toward himself and toward things in general made him try to abstract some definite conclusions about his experiences. He tells us: "The novels and poems are pure passionate experience. These 'pollyanalytics' are inferences made afterward, from the experience." Even the explanatory works, then, are merely a gloss on the early novels.

Lawrence's later work, both prose and poetry, was chiefly concerned with defining the unique individual, with trying to show the meaning of the regenerate life, with illustrating what true polarity between individuals means, with attacking mental consciousness, with redefining the primal unconscious as the source of creativity, with inveighing against mechanical systems and scientific theories which restrict the individual (Darwinism, Freudian psychology, modern physics), with stressing man's dynamism while exposing his spiritual sterility, with underlining the need for the dualism of light and dark, sex and spirit, body and mind—all ideas suggested or stated directly in *The Rainbow* and *Women in Love*. Already, his attitudes are fixed: animals are good, mines are bad, feeling is good when it is responsibly derived, mind is bad when it stifles emotion, nature is good, mechanical contrivances bad.

Characteristic of Lawrence's later persistence is a passage he wrote in the United States, which later became part of *Studies in Classic American Literature* (1923), begun about a year after he revised *Women in Love*. Lawrence, in "Spirit of Place," was trying to define freedom:

> Men are free when they belong to a living organic *believing* community, active in fulfilling some unfulfilled, perhaps unrealized purpose. Not when they are escaping to some wild west. . . . The true liberty will only begin when Americans discover It, and proceed possibly to fulfil It. It being the deepest *whole* self of man, the self in its wholeness, not idealistic halfness.

The remainder of Lawrence's writing life was spent in an attempt to define and illustrate *Itness*, the "whole self," to ridicule *halfness* and sterility.

The Lost Girl (1920), *Aaron's Rod* (1922), *Kangaroo* (1923), and

St. Mawr (1925) were all foreshadowings of *The Plumed Serpent* (1926), a major effort in which Lawrence tried to wed his ideas to the Mexican mythical god, Quetzalcoatl (bird-serpent), a symbol of the dualism of spirit and earth, the joining of "above and below." Don Ramón, the "hero" of *The Plumed Serpent*, attempts to activate a spiritual rebirth in Mexico through reviving the old Aztec Gods who will provide, according to him, an authentic objective correlative for religious devotion. He recognizes that socialism, democracy, labor unions, and traditional Catholicism all lack the essential spiritual wholeness necessary to vivify a sick Mexican peasantry. Only a Mexican myth which unites the bird of the air and the serpent of the ground can sustain a sufficient spiritual revival.

A great deal of *The Plumed Serpent* is given over to long scenes of incantation, involving chants, dances, ceremonies, beating drums, sermon-like disquisitions, and so on. Once again, Lawrence mixed styles, beginning with realistic scenes and then suddenly shifting to a metaphorical key in which realism is almost completely forsaken. This novel, however, is less successful than *Women in Love*, failing, unlike the latter, on both its literal and figurative planes. Don Ramón is never meaningful; his aide, General Cipriano, is too full of dark mysticism to come alive; and their goddess, the Irishwoman Kate, is more attracted by their sex than their ideas—she finally marries Cipriano out of weariness.

This particular figurative style, already suggested by *Women in Love*, is here unfortunate, for it allowed Lawrence no restrictions, and in his complete freedom he wrote expressively of what was close to his heart without trying to forge a successful medium for his ideas. In *Lady Chatterley's Lover* (1928) and *The Man Who Died* (1929), however, he kept, respectively, within a realistic and a fabulous key. *Lady Chatterley's Lover* was Lawrence's attempt to say everything about love unimpeded by any restrictions of time, place, or middle-class morality. It was to be a summation of his fictional quest for sexual polarity, and it is a curiously puritanical book, full of shy characters who seem to feel they are being wicked and yet know that they are *really* innocent. Connie and her gamekeeper, Mellors, try to become Adam and Eve in a garden unpolluted by the sins of her crippled, impotent husband. The question is, How can a man live so that his own soul will remain intact and unspoiled, private and withdrawn, in a world that allows no hermits? Conrad's Heyst, in *Victory*, had asked the same question while noting the passing of the frontier, that virgin territory into which a man might pass so as to retain his own purity. Every contact, both Conrad and Lawrence perceived, is fraught with possible pain and doom, and yet both knew that life is only possible through contact, even if it prove destructive. The later Lawrence finally reached the recognition of this sad irony, as had Conrad: that life which creates can also destroy, and that also the converse is true.

Lawrence wrote in *Lady Chatterley's Lover* that the novel genre is of vast importance if properly handled. "It can inform and lead into new places the flow of our sympathetic consciousness and it can lead our sympathy away in recoil from things gone dead. Therefore, the novel . . . can reveal the most secret places of life: for it is in the *passional* secret places of life, above all, that the tide of sensitive awareness needs to ebb and flow, cleansing and freshening." The novel, then, has a deeply moral purpose—it must reveal candidly what have hitherto been secret places, and it must do this by informing our sympathetic consciousness.

The secret places Lawrence chose to inform were those unrevealed aspects of sexual communion never before described in detail in an English novel meant for the general public. In the relationship between Connie and Mellors, Lawrence underlined their use of touch, and we see that touch is merely another word for polarity, the reaching-out of each individual self to create a relationship in which self is transformed into a perfect and absolute union with another. "Sex is only touch, the closest of all touch. And it's touch we're afraid of. . . . Especially the English have got to get into touch with one another, a bit delicate and a bit tender." This, simply stated, is Lawrence's doctrine from *Sons and Lovers,* through *The Rainbow, Women in Love,* and the present novel, to *The Man Who Died.*

Men live only by touch, and all of Lawrence's villains deny this fact. Significantly related to their inability to touch is their great business competence: so Clifford Chatterley, as he regresses into childhood desires and refuses to become a man, increasingly succeeds in business, where his inhumanity becomes his forte rather than his failing. So, too, Gerald Crich must identify with a mechanical world of order to make up for an inner deficiency. Lawrence suggested that any form of existence is preferable to vegetating with an impotent inner self incapable of being touched, and thus his persistent use of the "sensual music" of teeming animal life to emphasize aliveness: rabbits, horses, foxes, snakes, and hens. Accordingly, Connie identifies with the quickness and animation of hens, which she embraces while rejecting the deadly Clifford, and Mellors communes with a friendly Wordsworthian natural order that informs his soul and vivifies his body.

This juxtaposition of men and animals leads directly to *The Man Who Died* (1929), with its attempt to inject body into a moribund Christian myth. First called "The Escaped Cock"—the parable of the cock is a key to the phallic meaning—this brief novel, written shortly before Lawrence's death, is a fitting summation of his life's work, for it combines the core of his doctrine with one of the few institutions that could possibly incorporate it. Having written about bodily resurrection in the secular world in *Lady Chatterley's Lover*, Lawrence turned to bodily resurrection in a religious sense in *The Man Who Died*. Resurrection of the body had concerned Lawrence since *The Rainbow*, in which he wrote, prophetically of his later work: "The resurrection is to life, not to death." The Christ of *The Man Who Died* is the Christ of the resurrection who reigns, as Lawrence asserted, from Easter through the fertile later spring and summer until Annunciation, a period of richness and growth, all watched over by the Risen Christ. Concomitantly, in an essay, "The Risen Lord," Lawrence had shown his interest in the resurrected Christ who symbolizes fertility, sex, the body, Christ risen in the full flesh, who would go out to do his share in the world's work.

Lawrence felt that Christianity by stressing Christ crucified had emphasized the lesser half of the tradition; to Christ Risen belongs the positive side of Christianity, the Christ of the body as well as the spirit. In the body, in sexual conjunction, Lawrence found a religious communion in which the self is nourished and renewed, as he stressed in the phallic marriage of *Lady Chatterley's Lover*. By wedding, here, the idea of a phallic marriage—the living link between man and woman—to both the pagan myth of Isis and Osiris and the myth of Christ searching for his body, Lawrence found a perfect form for his parable.

The Man Who Died begins as a fable, and its success can, in part, be attributed to its consistency of tone—the fusion of elements all takes place on a fabulous level. The first sentence is typical of the fable or parable, with the memory of the medieval bestiaries never too distant:

> There was a peasant near Jerusalem who acquired a young gamecock, which looked a shabby little thing, but which put on brave feathers as

spring advanced, and was resplendent with arched and orange neck by the time the fig trees were letting out leaves from their endtips.

At the same time the cock was growing into "cockiness," a man "awoke from a long sleep in which he was tied up. He awoke numb and cold, inside a carved hole in the rock." The crucified Christ, unlike the cock, is full of death rather than life, too physically tired and spiritually exhausted to move. Finally, he arises and is taken in by the very peasant who owns the cock. The perky animal, in its vibrating life, in its cry of triumph, in its will to power, symbolizes everything Christ had rejected before his crucifixion and everything he is too weary to embrace now. "The doom of death was a shadow compared to the raging destiny of life, the determined surge of life." With the cock constantly before him, Christ questions his past, realizes that he has fulfilled his mission, and that now he is free: "My way is my own alone." He also realizes that "the body, too, has its little life, and beyond that, the greater life . . . now he knew that virginity is a form of greed; and that the body rises again to give and to take and to give, ungreedily."

As his wounds heal, Christ regrets his apartness from the world, his singularity in a world that requires union. As the cock is rejuvenated by each touch of the hens, so Christ hopes to meet a woman who can lure his risen body and yet leave him his aloneness. Ruing that he once preached sermons that attacked the variety of life by stressing its sameness, Christ decides to be himself; and leaving the triumphant cock amidst its harem, he goes out into the world both wanting and fearing human touch.

As Christ searches for his self (his manhood), he makes his way to the priestess of Isis, the goddess searching for the pieces of her dead Osiris. Isis in Search is paralleled to Christ in Search, Isis Bereaved to Christ Bereaved—the missing part in each is the phallic center; Isis needs to fertilize her womb, Christ to revive his ashen body; Isis is looking for the re-born man, Christ for the re-born self. Just as he had recognized the importance of the body in the cock, so here he sees the fecundity of life, first in the two slaves who have sexual conjunction under his gaze and then in Isis herself, the womb-like creature waiting to receive Osiris.

The priestess of Isis sees in Christ the lost Osiris, for just as her mistress is in search so is she, since no man, not even the golden Anthony, Lawrence pointedly remarks, has been able to stir her. On his part, Christ ponders whether he should allow himself to be touched, because touch in the past meant that of his torturers. But he also realizes that only human contact can restore him, and like many another Laurentian hero, he allows the power of touch to vivify his soul.

Restored by the oil, Christ wishes that in the past he had loved people in the flesh, that he had kissed Judas with love, and then perhaps he, Judas, would not have kissed him with death. Christ had foolishly offered the corpse of his love: "This is my body—take and eat—my corpse—," not love itself. After the lower areas of his body are rubbed with oil, Christ begins to stir and sees the priestess as a soft white rock of life—he exclaims, "On this rock, I built my life." Rejuvenated by union with her, he exalts, "I am risen"; and in this cry of triumph Lawrence brings together all the elements of the parable—the cock, the Christ, Isis-Osiris, and the phallic marriage. Through touch, he is warmed by the life-giving sun, and, in its turn, spring is fulfilled in this act of fertility.

The child that Christ plants in the womb of the priestess will be a combination of the East and West, the forerunner of a new civilization that will recognize both body and spirit—Lawrence's insistent doctrine since *Sons and Lovers*. The traditional celibacy and diffidence toward sex of the Christian Church can only be quickened, Lawrence claimed, through an alliance with the fertile East. Christian dogma of anti-sex, in Christ, Paul, Hugo of St. Victor, et al., must be altered so that body becomes part of the living flux. Sexual communication, to Lawrence, meant living marriage, vital being, and only in this way can the effeminacy of the twentieth century be replaced by purposeful individuality and alliance. Sexual conjunction was, for Lawrence, a way of gaining the warmth of the sun: "What we want is to destroy our false, inorganic connections, especially those relating to money, and re-establish the living organic connection with the cosmos, the sun and earth, with mankind and nation and family. Start with the sun and the rest will slowly, slowly happen."

The last lines of *The Man Who Died* can now be clarified: by sowing the seed of his life, Christ has united East and West in the torch of the fertile sun, and, in turn, his "flowing serpent," his phallic power, has been awakened for further creative power on another day. A resurrected Christ means a resurrected Christian Church.

A great deal of Lawrence's doctrine here seems, at first, far indeed from accepted Christian tradition, but Father Tiverton, in *D. H. Lawrence and Human Existence* (1951), claims otherwise. In matters ot sex and resurrection of the body, Tiverton suggests that Lawrence is very close to Christian doctrine once certain problems in language are overcome. Thus, Lawrence has come full circle; having rejected Christianity as dead (from *The Rainbow* through *The Plumed Serpent*), he now finds that a church founded on the "rock" of phallic marriage is possible provided that sex is finally seen as a correspondence of blood and not as the disintegrative, nervous "white sex" that concerns his critics.

At the end, Lawrence's ideas were delicate and puritanical. We realize that in his desire to make sex meaningful, as a counter to promiscuous sex or secretive masturbation, he became a conspicuous martyr to his ideal. His obsession seemed sex, and yet how pure his work is, how carefully he avoided the flowery and false sex of his popular contemporaries. In back of all of Lawrence's work is his feeling of shame at sex in its degraded form, shame that an industrialized world had to industrialize human passion as well. The following passage, from one of Lawrence's essays, is perhaps his best epitaph:

> If there is one thing I don't like it is cheap and promiscuous sex. If there is one thing I insist on it is that sex is a delicate, vulnerable, vital thing that you mustn't fool with. If there is one thing I deplore it is a heartless sex. Sex must be a real flow, a real flow of sympathy, generous and warm, and not a trick thing or a moment's excitation, or a mere bit of bullying.

D. H. *Lawrence* : SELECTED BIBLIOGRAPHY

BLACKMUR, RICHARD P. "D. H. Lawrence and Expressive Form," *The Double Agent*. New York: Arrow Editions, 1935.

CHAMBERS, JESSICA [E. T.]. *D. H. Lawrence: A Personal Record*. London: Cape, 1935.

ELLMANN, RICHARD. "Lawrence and His Demon," *New Mexico Quarterly*, xxii (Winter 1952), 385–393.

HOFFMAN, FREDERICK J. and HARRY T. MOORE. *The Achievement of D. H. Lawrence*. Norman: University of Oklahoma Press, 1953.

HOUGH, GRAHAM. *The Dark Sun: A Study of D. H. Lawrence*. London: Macmillan, 1957.

LAWRENCE, D. H. *The Letters*, ed. by Aldous Huxley. London: Heinemann, 1932.

LEAVIS, F. R. *D. H. Lawrence: Novelist*. New York: Knopf, 1956.

MOORE, HARRY T. *The Life and Works of D. H. Lawrence*. New York: Twayne, 1951.

———. *The Intelligent Heart: The Story of D. H. Lawrence*. New York: Farrar, Straus, & Young, 1954.

SCHORER, MARK. "Fiction With a Great Burden," *Kenyon Review,* xiv (Winter 1952), 162–168.

SPILKA, MARK. *The Love Ethic of D. H. Lawrence.* Bloomington: University of Indiana Press, 1955.

TIVERTON, FATHER WILLIAM [WILLIAM ROBERT JARRETT-KERR]. *D. H. Lawrence and Human Existence.* New York: Philosophical Library, 1951.

WEST, ANTHONY. *D. H. Lawrence.* London: Barker, 1950.

James Joyce xx *Life*

More than any other writer of this century, James Joyce has come to be a symbol of the artist-exile in contemporary society. For his public he shaped this image of himself with great meticulousness so that there could be no doubt of his own view of his personal and literary intent. Stephen Dedalus, a surrogate for Joyce the youthful artist and thinker, may not be Joyce in every factual detail of his experience, but he epitomizes the embittered artist-exile as straight autobiography perhaps never could. Concerned with literary theories, aesthetics, the writing of poetry, the reading of philosophy and theology, and the practice of the occult, Stephen (and Joyce) would seem to be the product of a startlingly unusual intellectual heredity and environment.

Yet Joyce's beginnings made it quite unlikely that he would develop as he did. He was born on February 2, 1882 in Dublin—a time and place most inauspicious for the flourishing of non-conformist brilliance and artistry. The recent assassination of Lord Cavendish in the Phoenix Park had brought almost martial law to Ireland. The Irish economy was sick. For a writer of eccentric style and substance, the chance to publish was very small and would remain so for many years. And the hold of the Church over the minds and activities of its people was particularly tenacious and all-embracing in late-nineteenth-century Ireland. Nor did Joyce's family background give evidence of encouraging deviation from middle-class "soundness" and practicality or of congeniality to genius. Joyce's father was, at the time of his son's birth, a garrulous and gregarious civil servant, a political appointee of the Parnell administration, more interested in his cronies and his pint than in any philosophical or literary study. Joyce's mother, though she was sensitive and, some say, artistic, had little opportunity to exert more than a passive influence on her gifted son, for raising ten children with almost no help from her husband taxed her delicate health. Nor would her distress over Joyce's deviation from religious ritual and her uneasiness over her son's reading (she suspected Ibsen of having a dangerous and unwholesome effect on her son) testify to her potential effectiveness as mentor to her unconventional offspring. The severe environmental and hereditary handicaps which Joyce had to overcome have much to do with the prodigious extent of his later personal non-conformity and literary unconventionality.

His education, too, attempted to fit him into a conservatively respectable mold. At Clongowes Wood School, which he entered in 1888, he received for almost three years probably the best elementary education available in Ireland, under the direction of Jesuit instructors. Called home permanently when his father's financial condition worsened following Parnell's repudiation and fall from power, Joyce continued his studies at the Jesuit Belvedere College in Dublin and afterward at University College, in his home city, from which he was graduated in 1902.

He was convinced by this time of two things: that he could no longer find adequate to his spiritual needs the ministration of his Church; and that his writings would not find a congenial reception or even a fair hearing in the narrow environment of Ireland. The results were a gradual withdrawal from involvement in religious obligations and a seeking to throw off the restrictions on free mental activity imposed by family, Church, and nation. Determined to be close to the center of European cultural life, Joyce suffered through a brief term as a medical student in Paris, did a two-year stint as occasional book reviewer for the newspapers, covered an auto race as a reporter, translated Hauptmann into English but was unable to sell his version to Yeats or any other dramatic impresario, and, after a brief return to Dublin for his mother's death, eloped to the continent with Nora Barnacle to spend the rest of his life in exile in Paris, Trieste, Rome, and Zurich.

From his earliest school years, Joyce excelled in the art of writing. His efforts in composition classes were praised and his earliest published work, *Et Tu, Healy!*, was privately printed by his father when the boy was only nine years old. As an undergraduate, he surprised his teachers and fellow students by publishing a major review article of Ibsen's *When We Dead Awaken* in the *Fortnightly Review*, Europe's most distinguished literary publication. His essay on Mangan and his attack on the Irish theater in "The Day of the Rabblement" are works of his teens and early twenties. *Chamber Music*, though it appeared in 1907, is the product of this early period as are the stories of *Dubliners*, mainly completed by 1905 but withheld from publication until 1914 through a series of unfortunate delays.

Joyce's literary career on the Continent was fraught with difficulties which might have overcome the resolve of a less singleminded artist. Forced to earn a living for his family by teaching English for long days, he had to relegate writing activities to the late evening and early morning hours, writing in badly heated or unheated apartments. There was, moreover, little hope that his earlier writings would appear or, if they did eventually achieve publication, would bring in any money to release him for more ambitious writing projects like the *Portrait of the Artist as a Young Man* (1916) and *Ulysses* (1922). Furthermore, his eyes, which had never been good, became steadily worse so that he suffered from headaches, nervous afflictions, and a progressively impaired eyesight. Like Milton, he was forced either to keep in his head large portions of a complicated manuscript like *Ulysses* or to depend on the secretarial help and other aid supplied by his circle of Paris friends—the Eugene Jolases, Paul Léon, and others. In addition, he had the nagging worry of broken contracts, unreliable promises from publishers, the illness of his daughter, and, most irksome, perhaps, to a writer, difficulties with censors—moral, political, bureaucratic, and spiritual. Though he was freed eventually from the necessity to work outside his writing career by the financial assistance he received from Harriet Shaw Weaver, Joyce realized almost no profit from his various publications during his lifetime. Litigation tied up most of his royalties while the difficulty of obtaining copyrights for allegedly obscene publications meant infringement by unscrupulous international pirates. The recent edition of Joyce's letters gives a clear picture of the tragic pettiness of Joyce's business correspondence over the years.

In spite of annoying distractions, a full life as husband and father, and the obligations which worldwide fame brought to Joyce, he was able, even in his blindness, to complete by 1939 his last novel, *Finnegans Wake*, which he had been publishing in sections as *Work in Progress* for more than a decade. Joyce bemoaned the fact that the book was largely ignored upon publication owing to the excitement of the new war in Europe. To him the war brought personal grief:

the fall of France, hounding by the Nazis, the death of his friend, Paul Léon, the fear of separation from his daughter, ill in an institution in France. Worry and physical ailments combined to bring about his death on January 13, 1941, in Zurich.

Joyce is in the great tradition of European men of letters—the tradition of Mann and Proust and Gide and Conrad. It is a tradition which demands, on the one hand, detachment and impersonality of the most stringent kind, while it involves, on the other, almost total identification of the artist with his material and, most often, with his protagonist. It calls upon the artist to make his life what Milton called "a true poem" and thus it demands an existence of constant self-analysis, evaluation, and rededication to individual and artistic integrity. It means exposing the writer's psyche to the view of any reader, with the inevitable misunderstandings which must occur when complex spirits attempt to communicate in their authentic voices with lesser intellects and sensibilities. In so doing, Joyce was merely following the precept of his literary heroes—Ibsen, Hauptmann, and even Cavalcanti. Like them, he paid the price for being different in the loneliness and alienation which can come even to those whom the world will not let alone.

James Joyce xx *Works*

The young artist who early blocked out the chapters of A *Portrait of the Artist as a Young Man* (in the semi-autobiographical fragment now called *Stephen Hero*) certainly did not intend that it should be followed by the gigantic sequel of *Ulysses*. Yet the two books are so closely bound together developmentally, in evolving strength of language and of symbolic structure, that they seem two volumes of the same work. One novel is peopled by many of the characters of the other. The time sequence continues almost uninterrupted from the earlier to the later book. Experiences which strike the protagonist, Stephen Dedalus, with traumatic force in A *Portrait*, like the pandying at Clongowes Wood College, return as motifs in the more mature stream of consciousness of Stephen as a man.

That the two novels can stand independently as individual works, however, is unquestionable. So long as the reader keeps in mind their deep artistic interconnection—a necessity in reading any part of the Joyce canon: poetry, essays, epiphanies, drama—he may find it advantageous to approach the novels separately. For so much has been written about Joyce's work in cross-section, as it were, that often the particular excellences and defects of one book or another have been obscured in the general approbation or disapproval.

A PORTRAIT OF THE ARTIST AS A YOUNG MAN

A *Portrait of the Artist* is, except for its final chapter, a deceptively simple novel. Intensely concerned with the significance of his titles, Joyce here, as in *Dubliners*, engages in no trickery: the title is flatly descriptive, apparently unambiguous, and not particularly helpful. The more than casual reader may discover from Joyce's friend, Frank Budgen, that the author wanted the emphasis placed on the final four words of the title, *"as a Young Man,"* so that he might be spared the accusation years later of being wholly a copy of his unenviable fictional counterpart, Stephen Dedalus. He may speculate with the model for Buck Mulligan of *Ulysses*, the late Dr. Oliver Gogarty, that the "artist" of the title meant to Joyce merely a practical joker in the Dublin slang of the period. Unless the reader agrees with Gogarty, however, that Joyce's entire subsequent literary production is an enormous legpull, a hilarious hoax, he will probably take "artist" as Joyce would have taken it—a sensitive and gifted human being who sees more deeply into reality than ordinary men and who, as a priest of the eternal imagination, is able to transmute the dross of life into the beauty of art. A catalogue of Joyce's heroes suffices to establish the context of his title: Ibsen, Hauptmann, Dante, Mangan, Shelley— men set apart from the middle-class by their vision and their craft, content to struggle in isolation and even disgrace to insure the integrity of their view, to bear their "chalice safely through a throng of foes." Though Joyce's concept of art may have leaned toward the classical, his idea of the artist is almost a stereotype of the nineteenth-century romantic idea.

The truly meaningful word in his title is, of course, *"Portrait,"* for it suggests Joyce's contribution to the modern novel—his presentation directly of the thoughts and the point of view of his protagonist as painted by the highly selective and sensitive brush of the artist. Not the first to experiment with such impressionistic recording of a character's interior monologue, Joyce was, through his title, stressing his technique as perhaps the major contribution to his novel. There may be exterior Realism of the Arnold Bennett variety in the Christmas dinner scene, or even Naturalism of the all-inclusive Zolaesque type in the interminable sermon which fills the center of the novel. But these labels of literary schools are accidental and incidental to one element: the mind of Stephen Dedalus as exposed to the reader's view by the painter who is privy to its contents.

The impressionistic portrait which emerges has delighted and frightened readers of Joyce from the beginning. The sophisticated and intelligent publisher's reader who saw the manuscript in 1916 asked for major revisions and a job of careful pruning to keep the book from falling apart in ineffectual fragments. Students in the 1950's have been known to resent the seemingly unmotivated absence of narrative continuity in the book. How old is Stephen when the novel opens? Why is no information provided concerning his activities between his resignation from Clongowes and his middle terms at Belvedere? Why must the reader wait until page one-hundred sixty-six to discover that Stephen is sixteen years old precisely? Why do the scenes of youthful love and fantasy blend so confusingly that one can scarcely distinguish Eileen from E. C., Mabel Hunter from Mercedes? Why does Joyce allow the book to end anti-climactically with random entries from a young boy's diary? Why the inordinately long sermon at Belvedere? Why the space and the important location allotted to the exposition of Stephen's aesthetic theories?

Ideally, the answer to all these questions is easy. What is significant to the reader in terms of information simply does not matter in an impressionistic work. Nor, if it is possible philosophically to separate author from transcriber, does it matter what Joyce would like his readers to know and when in the story he would like them to find out. What counts is the recording of Stephen's thoughts as they develop by an artist sensitive enough to discern the artistic pattern into which they flow and from which they will attain a "meaning" more universal than any one or any group of them might separately contain. If the reader cannot describe Mrs. Dedalus after he has finished the novel, it is not that Joyce has omitted a vital Dickensian function through oversight or lack of talent. Dickens is thinking of Dickens, of his readers, of his duty as omniscient author to tell all simply and straightforwardly. Joyce's sole concern is to present what in the external world is important to Stephen's private mental and psychological processes. If Mrs. Dedalus as a visually perceived object fails to impinge powerfully upon Stephen's consciousness, she retains throughout A *Portrait* a faintness and pallidness of outline which in traditional fiction might indicate weakness of characterization. Conversely, the painfully attenuated sermon is explained by the great significance which Stephen's psyche attaches to hearing it. The separate strands of fantasy which blend in Stephen's nervous and impressionable mind are, without explanation or apology, made by Joyce part of the faithful rendering of the young man's confused images of love and rejection.

Ideally, it has been said, all questions of narrative confusion and artistic proportion can be turned aside by insisting on the author's duty to present and interpret the thoughts of his protagonist without regard to ease of comprehension or to fictional balance. In practical terms, obviously, the answer does not come so easily. A hero whose interior monologue is uniformly dull and insipid, though it is faithfully represented by a competent author, may be a dead and useless weight for a novel to carry. Moreover, an extreme imbalance in the mind of a protagonist may result in a pseudo-fictional case study, not in a narrative of universal validity. Further, in *A Portrait*, for instance, there is really no Stephen Dedalus with whose monologue Joyce is familiar. There is only an author and the fictional creation for which he alone is responsible. There is still need, consequently, to discuss the question of proper proportion and of the limits of comprehension.

As with all Joyce's work, the structural planning of *A Portrait* is most meticulous. The five chapters into which the story is divided follow the traditional pattern of chronological development: 1, babyhood and pre-adolescence; 2, early adolescence, high school, romantic fantasies, and introduction to sex; 3, the sermon on hell and heaven, and Stephen's confession; 4, mortification of the flesh, rejection of a career as a Jesuit, and the decision to be an artist; 5, college life, repudiation of family, country, and religion preparatory to assuming the obligations of a "priest of the eternal imagination." Certainly there can be no argument with the simple, direct chronological progression. The problem arises elsewhere—in the conveying of the story pattern to the reader.

Much as Proust introduces his *Remembrance of Things Past* with an all-inclusive "Overture" in which all threads of his giant narrative are discernible, Joyce enunciates his themes in the first two pages of *A Portrait*. Cryptically, with extreme economy, and in the language suitable to the child Stephen, he begins with birth and motherhood in the story of the moocow. That this apparently irrelevant tale is related to the Betty Byrne there mentioned, and that both anticipate the parallel of Cranly as John the Baptist and Stephen Dedalus as a Christ-figure has been established by a recent critical study. The attraction of music and rhythm for the embryo artist is immediately asserted too by the snatches of song and rime that dot the first two pages. Present also is the theme of violent and parliamentary nationalism in the "brush with the maroon velvet back . . . for Michael Davitt and the brush with the green velvet back . . . for Parnell." Finally, Joyce introduces the theme of sexual repression and guilt in the "Eileen" paragraph, followed by the theme of punishment by society [his mother and his nurse] for ambiguous sins. The morbid concluding verse of the opening section, deliberately confusing the

Promethean torture for rebellious artists with Joyce's own painful eye ailment, marks the first appearance of the swelling "apologise" theme in the novel.

Joyce's desire to establish so early and so prominently the motifs by which his story will be told shows the importance to him of a structural framework more compelling than that afforded by a loose, unsurprising, and undistinguished plot. If Stephen's interior monologue, apparently rambling and even aimless as unchannelled thought associations often are, is to carry forward the substance of the novel, then somehow this monologue must be given a hardness and a vigor which it might in actuality not possess. For this purpose Joyce employs the motif. Thoughts seldom occur to Stephen only once. Rather the frequency with which a concept reappears at key points shows the importance to the protagonist of a particular set of associations and helps Joyce keep his readers oriented while concealing his own hands and feet.

Like Eliot, Joyce can suggest an entire mythic framework simply by his choice of a name. By calling his hero Stephen Dedalus (a variant of Joyce's own youthful pseudonym) the author insures identification for his artist with St. Stephen, a martyr stoned by the citizenry though he was guilty of no crime; and with the Daedalus-Icarus myth. Daedalus, the maker of wings, the creator of beautiful structures, is an artist in his own right. Imprisoned in the labyrinth of his own making on Crete, he uses his artistry to escape from that island with his son. Sensing the strong mythic ties which bound the Greek to the Irish artist, Joyce sees himself—and through him Stephen—as both father and son, the soaring creator and the child who plunges to earth through disobedience. In *Ulysses* he will develop the Icarus motif in more detail.

The theme of flight and of birds who fly may serve as a fair example of Joyce's employment of motif as a structural device. To reinforce the motif, the author peoples his novel with characters who bear bird names: Cranly, Heron, Daedalus, the hawklike man. The instrument of punishment in the first section of the book becomes significantly the eagles who will pluck out Stephen's eyes. The two signs which confirm for the protagonist his appropriate role in life—the defiance of authority, the attitude of *"non serviam,"* in order to bring beauty and a higher civilization to men—are the hawklike man and the girl on the beach whose "bosom was as a bird's, soft and slight, slight and soft as the breast of some dark-plumaged dove." Later, Stephen sees his own girl friend as a bird:

> And if he had judged her harshly? If her life were a simple rosary of hours, her life simple and strange as a bird's life, gay in the morning, restless all day, tired at sundown? Her heart simple and wilful as a bird's heart?

Following this reverie, the youth is conscious of the presence of birds: "A bird twittered, two birds, three. The bell and the bird ceased. . . ." That there is a mystic and symbolical element in many of these references becomes clear later:

> Why was he gazing upwards from the steps of the porch, hearing their [the birds'] shrill twofold cry, watching their flight? For an augury of good or evil? A phrase of Cornelius Agrippa flew through his mind and then there flew hither and thither shapeless thoughts from Swedenborg on the correspondence of birds to things of the intellect and of how the creatures of the air have their knowledge and know their times and seasons because they, unlike man, are in the order of their life and have not perverted that order by reason.

Stephen's thoughts go on to use the birds as a philosophical focus in somewhat the same way as Keats used his nightingale. Throughout time men have watched birds circling: therefore the birds serve as a link of past to present. Augurs in the classical past had foretold the future by means of birds; hence, these creatures are in a sense prophets, or at least the instruments of prophets. Moreover, just as Keats accepts unquestioningly the immortal singing strength of his bird— perhaps a symbol of the eternal beauty of the poet's song—so does Joyce by implication ally himself as artist and intellectual with these winged creatures.

Nowhere does Joyce make his kinship with birds clearer than in his conversation with the unspoiled nationalist, Davin:

> When the soul of a man is born in this country there are nets flung at it to hold it back from flight. You talk to me of nationality, language, religion. I shall try to fly by those nets.

Like the birds, Stephen will be a singer. Like them, too, he will fly, following the lead of the hawklike man of a former age. Like them (and Joyce supplies the hint of his indebtedness to Swedenborg), he wishes to be associated with heavenly intellect. Swedenborg puts it this way:

> What correspondence is is not known at the present day. . . . This was not so with the ancient people. To them the knowledge of correspondences was the chief of knowledges. By means of it they acquired

intelligence and wisdom; and by means of it those who were of the church had communication with heaven; for the knowledge of correspondences is angelic knowledge. . . .

He continues:

. . . at the present day no one can know the spiritual things in heaven to which the natural things in the world correspond except from heaven. . . . But the nature of the correspondence of spiritual things with natural I shall be glad to illustrate . . . birds correspond, according to their species, to the intellectual things of the natural mind or the spiritual mind.

Perhaps like Baudelaire, Joyce saw himself at this early point in his literary career as the instrument by which men would be raised above the mundane and, through reading of the profane Word, placed in communication with true knowledge. If so, the bird-girl on the beach would be a most potent sign that his protagonist was on the right track.

Possibly less important to the casual reader of A *Portrait* than the symbolic meaning of this motif, or any motif, is simply its material presence in the novel. For these reiterations of key concepts, gestures, names, songs, and the rest, are clues which the reader can follow as he explores the labyrinth of Stephen's mind, keeping a grasp on the threads which will lead to the exit. So conscious is Joyce of his role as trailblazer in an uncharted country that he will intrude the motif even when the story line does not require its presence. On the Clongowes playing field, the ball which the boys use is referred to as a "greasy leather orb [which] flew like a heavy bird through the grey light." And near the end of the novel, as Stephen and Cranly leave the college, "the bird call from Siegfried whistled softly followed them. . . ." In *Ulysses*, Joyce would develop the motif to a highly complicated, almost statistically employed, science. In A *Portrait* it is more loosely and suggestively introduced.

Motif or otherwise, every word in the novel has as its aim the unambiguous revelation of Stephen Dedalus as a fully-realized human being and literary protagonist. It is ironic, therefore, that the issue most hotly debated by critics today is Joyce's attitude toward Stephen and, indeed, his relationship to the character he created. For many years after the appearance of the novel, Joyce was equated by most critics with Stephen ("Stephen-Joyce" is a frequent designation in works on this writer), to such a degree that the author himself tried, in conversation with Frank Budgen, to dissociate himself from his own character. To be identified as Stephen was no unmixed blessing. It meant bearing the stigma of priggishness, conceit, arrogance, holier-than-thou-unholiness, disobedience to God, country, and mother, ineffectuality in love, a brilliant though largely unproductive aestheticism, and an aversion to physical cleanliness. To Budgen, Joyce commented that in writing *A Portrait* the author had not let the young protagonist off easily.

More recently, some critics have called into question the approved version of Stephen's relation to his creator. They prefer to take Stephen as an ironic figure, detached from the author and presented with comic intent as almost a mockery of the rebellious hero in a commercial society—the kind of anti-hero which has become the stock in trade of Kingsley Amis. Those who incline to this view are fond of quoting from a scene at the end of the third chapter. Stephen, on the verge of hysteria after listening to the frightful sermon during retreat, has confessed his sins. He returns to his home and Joyce reports on his state of newly-acquired serenity:

> He sat by the fire in the kitchen, not daring to speak for happiness. Till that moment he had not known how beautiful and peaceful life could be. The green square of paper pinned round the lamp cast down a tender shade. On the dresser was a plate of sausages and white pudding and on the shelf there were eggs. They would be for the breakfast in the morning after the communion in the college chapel. White pudding and eggs and sausages and cups of tea. How simple and beautiful was life after all! And life lay all before him.

Unquestionably, the tone of the paragraph is capable of ambiguous interpretation. The boy must have suffered an overwhelming shock to equate "white pudding and eggs and sausages and cups of tea" with the beauty of life. The crowning line, "And life lay all before him," conjures up an eternal feast of eggs and sausages as the ultimate reward for those who, like Stephen, are saved by confession.

Yet it is quite possible to take the paragraph as the straight and serious musings of an adolescent, to whom spiritual well-being and a hearty appetite are integrally connected. After all, Stephen had vomited shortly before his confession from the physical upset which his spiritual condition had evoked. Further, a knowledge of Joyce's earlier fiction, in which Stephen, or a Stephen-like narrator, plays a part, offers little encouragement to the advocates of the detached-mockery school. The first three stories in Joyce's *Dubliners* collection are told in the first person by a young boy who possesses all the characteristics of Stephen and of young Joyce. At least two of these, when they were published earlier in magazine form, were signed "Stephen Daedalus," as if to identify the "I" of the narration and to connect Joyce with his later autobiographical hero. These stories, almost too serious and too intensely personal—as the later stories in the volume, concerning other people, are not—seem conclusively to establish the kinship between the author and his fictional self.

But a more likely source of verification is the fragmentary first draft of *A Portrait* itself. Published in the forties under the title of *Stephen Hero*, it contains in greatly expanded form, what in the final version would be chapter five. Polemical in style, realistic in narrative treatment, and lacking the suggestive symbolism of the later distillation, it brings one closer to the mind and heart of its author, even though he calls himself Stephen Daedalus. From this version perhaps the most telling charge that can be adduced against the author is a lack of detachment and of the perspective which is necessary for mockery and humor. Of course, Joyce may have changed during the ten years or so which intervened between the one draft and the other; it is true that *A Portrait* is a more balanced book than its manuscript predecessor, and differently styled. The burden of proof for detaching Stephen from Joyce, except as the author may have altered objective events in his life for artistic effect, is, however, on the recent critics.

Whether Stephen is or is not a facsimile of Joyce, he is surely as fully realized a small boy as had been conceived in literature up to the present century. A typical paragraph from young Stephen's stream of consciousness shows the reason:

> It would be nice to lie on the hearthrug before the fire, leaning his head upon his hands, and think on those sentences. He shivered as if he had cold slimy water next his skin. That was mean of Wells to shoulder him into the square ditch because he would not swop his little snuffbox for Wells's seasoned hacking chestnut, the conqueror of forty. How cold and slimy the water had been! A fellow had once seen a big rat jump into the scum. Mother was sitting at the fire with Dante waiting for Brigid to bring in the tea. She had her feet on the fender and her jewelly slippers were so hot and they had such a lovely warm smell! Dante knew a lot of things. . . . Father Arnall knew more than Dante because he was a priest but both his father and Uncle Charles said that Dante was a clever woman and a wellread woman. And when Dante made that noise after dinner and then put up her hand to her mouth: that was heartburn.

The importance of physical sensation to the child is immediately obvious from this passage as from almost every page of the first chapter. Seeking to approximate the mind of a child, Joyce has endeavored to reduce the outside world for Stephen to a series of impingements on the senses. "Nice" people are recalled in terms of pleasant physical sensations—a warm fire, tea, the smell of heated slippers, and even the sound of a wholesome belch. On the other hand, his tormentor Wells is associated always with coldness, sliminess, and dirty water into which a rat may jump. The passage shows the homesick schoolboy alternating thoughts of his miserable existence as a boarder with memories of a happier life at home. By the swiftness with which Joyce forces Stephen's mind to jump from point to point, the author obviously seeks to approximate the restless vagaries of the young stream as well as the short span of attention to any one train of thought which most children display. In addition, Joyce departs from logical order in presenting the stream of consciousness, because the interior monologue is by its very nature as often illogical as logical. So, for instance, he reverses what would normally be the expected order of these sentences: "He shivered as if he had cold slimy water next his skin. That was mean of Wells to shoulder him into the square ditch. . . ." Though the reader is able easily to follow the turn of the young mind, having to disentangle and reverse the order encourages a feeling of participation in Stephen's experience which reading "logical" expository prose does not provide.

Other qualities of this paragraph, chosen almost at random, also merit attention. A highly sophisticated European writer with a firm grasp of prose style, Joyce is faced, in *A Portrait*, with the problem of talking and thinking in the idiom and the pattern of a naive eight-year-old. That he could do this in his own life is attested to by his grandson, Stephen Joyce, who marvels at the ease with which the elderly intellectual was able to establish rapport with a child. That he can do it successfully in fiction is clear from the first chapter of the novel. It will be noted that, except for the last sentence of the paragraph reproduced above, all the sentences fall into the subject-verb-object category. The deliberate monotony of rhythm which such an arrangement provides goes far toward approximating juvenile speech and thought. To heighten the impression of a youthful mind at work, Joyce reduces the language of his paragraph to words of one or two syllables, except for the proper names like "Mozambique." Then, further, in his choice of specific words to carry the narrative, he selects those which, though they fall short of "baby talk," will epitomize the intellectual and emotional level of his youngster. To lie near the fire would be "nice"; Wells is "mean." It is not enough for the boy to think of Wells's hacking chestnut: he must fall into the jargon of the boys and refer to it here and elsewhere as "the conqueror of forty." A boy is "a fellow" and a pleasant odor is "lovely." Finally, the psychological background of the paragraph is interesting in its depiction of the child's mind as a temporary repository of false values and jumbled levels of meaningfulness. Dante's great knowledge boils down to a few elements of basic geography. The mere taking of holy orders by a man places him for Stephen above all laymen in intelligence. And Dante is in one long breath categorized as a well-read woman and one who makes a noise resulting from heartburn.

The first chapter stresses the physical elements of life. In fact, earth, air, fire, and water are very much in evidence as muted motifs. Just as Stephen is in the Class of Elements at school, he is at the chronological age when physical sensations and real, material things are alone meaningful. Significantly, even God and his heaven are viewed in these terms:

What was after the universe? Nothing. But was there anything round the universe to show where it stopped before the nothing place began? It could not be a wall but there could be a thin thin line there all round everything. . . . God was God's name just as his name was Stephen. Dieu was the French for God and that was God's name too; and when anyone prayed to God and said Dieu then God knew at once it was a French person that was praying. . . .

From such childish musings, childishly expressed, Joyce advances deliberately in A Portrait, making his prose mature as his protagonist develops physically and intellectually. So skillfully does he accomplish his purpose that it is possible to reconstruct Stephen's age and mental level by arranging unidentified samples of prose from the novel. Without attempting to do that here, it may be worth while to compare with the paragraph just quoted a section on religion taken from the final chapter:

He smiled as he thought of the god's image, for it made him think of a bottle-nosed judge in a wig, putting commas into a document which he held at arm's length and he knew that he would not have remembered the god's name but that it was like an Irish oath. It was folly. But was it for this folly that he was about to leave for ever the house of prayer and prudence into which he had been born and the order of life out of which he had come?

The tone has changed too obviously to require comment. The frame of reference is adult. The rhythm of the sentences is irregular, far from monotonous, and decisively mature. In the final four lines, indeed, the cadence resembles that of psalms in the Old Testament. Joyce's hero has grown up and, with him, his stream of consciousness.

As Chester Anderson has pointed out in detail, *A Portrait* is a much more complicated book symbolically than would at first appear. If Cranly, whose head Stephen concentrates on perceiving to the exclusion of his body, is indeed "the precursor," as Joyce identifies him near the end of the final chapter, then Stephen must be Christ. In this role it is easy to see the relevance of his martyrdom, his assumption of the first priesthood of art, his defiance of the authorities of this world, and the essential sadness of his separation from humanity during the course of *A Portrait*. Recognition of Stephen's part as a deity leads to logical explanations for many troubling passages in the book. The hero's decision to go wading in the sea becomes an urge to baptism to prepare him for his duties as priest in the final chapter. There he takes communion, says mass, has his neck washed by his mother, listens to a mad nun invoke "Jesus!" and delivers a sermon to Lynch—the long exposition of aesthetic theory which parallels Father Arnall's sermon on hell and heaven earlier in the story. In a very important study, Mr. Anderson goes on to elucidate most of the mysteries of Joyce's final chapter by reference to the Biblical parallels on which the author is drawing to give more than autobiographical texture to his novel. Thus, the consumptive little man whom Stephen meets becomes a type of Christ after crucifixion: ". . . an ugly little man who has taken into his body the sins of the world . . . a crooked ugly body for which neither God nor man have pity." Thus Davin, the eager-hearted, simple peasant lad, is Adam, who tells a story of temptation by a country woman. And even the crucifixion is present as Stephen and Lynch end their walk:

> As they approach the library, the sky is appropriately "veiled" and it begins to rain. Emma stands silently among her companions . . . and Stephen watches her with "conscious bitterness." . . . She is specifically identified with the Virgin by the medical students' otherwise pointless talk of obstetrics, which the dying Stephen hears ". . . as if from a distance in interrupted pulsations." . . . As she prepares to go away with her companions, Stephen considers forgiving her.

This seminal study of *A Portrait*, tremendously valuable for its detailed contributions to textual analysis of the novel, is not at all surprising for the light which it throws on Joyce's methods of creating fiction. Perhaps in order to gain a fuller understanding of the complexity of Joyce's early work, the student should reverse the normal order of study and go first to *Finnegans Wake*, then to *Ulysses*, and finally to the manageable, traditional novels and short stories. For, from first to last, Joyce's Talmudic turn of mind compelled him to submit even the simplest plot to the complicated tracery of analogy, parallelism, symbolism, allegory, mythic paraphernalia, anagrammatization, counterpoint—any legitimate device which would serve to comment on the simple narrative substructure. Though readers have now come to expect this method of operation in his large works, they still find it hard to acknowledge its presence in ostensibly delicate stories. A look at *Ulysses* will confirm Joyce's predilection for the structurally complicated work of art.

ULYSSES

The history of *Ulysses* is full of paradoxes. One of the weightiest of modern novels, it was first planned as a short story to be called "Mr. Hunter in Dublin." Though unquestionably the most controversial novel of our times for at least a quarter-century, it was almost impossible to acquire in English-speaking countries for much of that time owing to laws forbidding importation of obscene matter. The man who wrote it was disturbed by the mildest vulgarity in the speech of those who knew him; yet his name has, through misunderstanding of *Ulysses*, become for many synonymous with filth. What Joyce hoped would be received as a great comic work has instead been regarded as the fictional equivalent of T. S. Eliot's lugubrious *Waste Land*. In spite of the fact that Joyce labored prodigiously to give the acme of form to the novel—weighing with precision each episode, each motif, each word, and often considering for hours the exact position in sentences of words he already had decided to use—*Ulysses* for decades had to face charges of formlessness, linguistic anarchy, and lack of artistic polish. It is the only major work of fiction to present Dublin with literary integrity and dramatic intensity, but it has alienated Joyce from his countrymen while endearing him to most expatriates. Even Shaw, recognizing the stark truth of the picture, was at the same time repelled by it. Almost medieval in its thoroughness, classical in its sources and restrictive self-discipline, it has been wildly attacked and applauded as the Revolution of the Word and the novel of the future. A symbolist work in spirit, the ultimate expansion of literary Naturalism in the degree of detail which it utilizes, it has found a home in no school.

What is *Ulysses* about? A writer of fiction tries to formulate his view of reality in the make-believe world he creates. He may seek to escape from his age in time or from his locality geographically if he finds the world as he knows it too painful or hopeless to bear. But his very act of rejection in a way is revelatory of the relationship between himself and his world. Nor can he escape from his responsibility by wandering far in time or space or fantasy. His novels must have people, conflict, background, commitment or detachment, judgment or the refusal to judge which is in itself a judgment. A writer's vision of real life is, therefore, implicit in his handling of the world he creates whether that world be the one outside his window, or in Tripoli, or in dream. Hawthorne, setting *The Scarlet Letter* in an early New England background, fools no reader into thinking that he is dealing with matters of purely historical or local interest. Nor does Samuel Butler intend that his audience shall settle for Erewhon as a quaint land of fancy unrelated to this world. Even Lewis Carroll's Wonderland makes abundantly clear its author's problems in Victorian England.

Since the naturalist outpouring of the 1880's in France, England, and the United States, it has become fashionable—a point of pride, maybe—for writers to deal directly with the issues of their age and environment, though the truly great have ignored the fashion at will. Zola set the pace; George Moore trotted doggedly behind; and the voluminous realists who followed them established a trend. To capture the sweep of history in depicting the shifting fortunes of a familiar protagonist, a family, a clan, became the problem—admirably solved by Thomas Mann in works like *Buddenbrooks*, Arnold Bennett in *The Old Wives' Tale*, and even Galsworthy in his *Forsyte Saga*. Three or four generations play their parts on the fictional stage while the author standing in the wings more or less unobtrusively directs the rise or fall of the dynasty.

Ulysses looks at Joyce's own world but the other way round. Disdaining a crystal ball and a telescope in favor of a high-powered microscope, the author restricts himself, in his almost eight-hundred page novel, to the events of one day (June 16, 1904) in one small city (Dublin). All time and all space he reduces to the eighteen-hour span during which his characters go about the process of living in the few miles of area allotted to Dublin on this sphere. The concentration in space and time—almost painful in its searching intensity—allows Joyce the latitude which his fellow Dubliner, Swift, enjoyed in writing of the voyage to Lilliput.

Very little in Dublin escapes detailed naturalistic presentation in *Ulysses*. The accuracy of Joyce's memory (for he wrote the entire novel while in exile abroad) is verifiable through Baedekers of the period and in the admiring assent of grudging Dubliners. As the lava of Vesuvius preserved in tableau the citizens of Pompeii, so Joyce's pen captures the life of the Irish capital at the selected moment. The hotels, the pubs, the stores, the cemeteries, the churches, the brothels, the restaurants, the hospitals, the newspaper offices, the beaches, the parks, the homes, the bridges, the theaters, and especially the streets suddenly come alive with the scores of people who carry forward the action of the book. In their few hours of fictional life, in the few miles which constitute their stage, they make their entrances and exits, they meet and separate, love and hate, plot and worry, act and interact as though unconcerned with the smallness of their contribution to the advance of this planet.

Concerned, as Flaubert was, with the middle-class, the artisan, salesman, professional group, the white-collar worker, Joyce gives no more than a passing mention to the truly ignorant, depressed slum dwellers and to the representatives of high society. The closest the reader comes to the lieutenant general or to an M.P. is a glimpse from the sidewalks of the viceregal procession, or a respectful greeting on the street from a fawning constituent. If *Ulysses* fails, indeed, to be the epic of modern Ireland, perhaps it owes its failure to overemphasis, certainly deliberate, on one socio-economic group to the virtual exclusion of the rest. Much of the unrelieved ugliness and drabness which critics of the novel have found there results from the author's single-minded concentration on the Philistia of Ireland. A Joycean who knew of Dublin only through *Ulysses* was recently surprised, when he visited Joyce's city, to find that it afforded truly attractive vistas and noble sights to the receptive tourist. Joyce often affirmed in private his belief that Dublin was a beautiful city, but he carefully expunged any trace of this attitude from his restricted canvas in all his fiction, notably in *Ulysses*. The novel is much less an all-inclusive guidebook to Dublin than a relatively narrow point of view about the place.

Yet within the limits he sets himself, Joyce pursues mercilessly each detail which goes into making the life of June 16, 1904. Believing with Virginia Woolf that life is not a series of gig-lamps, symmetrically arranged, he hurls detail after detail into the naturalist hopper in the hope that from the chaos of minutiae which impinges on the consciousness of modern man at every moment of existence would emerge a meaningful pattern for artistic exposition. It has never been determined how serious Joyce was in *Ulysses* in offering the profusion of minute details which slows the pace and tires the patience of many readers. If the precedent of the sermon in A *Portrait* holds—and there is no reason to believe otherwise—the stretching of Naturalism to the breaking point is essential to the "all or nothing at all" technique which he had determined to follow in order to render verbally the overwhelming pettiness and stifling cloggedness of the contemporary waste land. His magnifying-glass technique results in such passages as this:

> What did the first drawer unlocked contain?
> A Vere Foster's handwriting copybook, property of Milly (Millicent) Bloom, certain pages of which bore diagram drawings marked *Papli*, which showed a large globular head with 5 hairs erect, 2 eyes in profile, the trunk full front with 3 large buttons, 1 triangular foot: 2 fading photographs of queen Alexandra of England and of Maud Branscombe, actress and professional beauty: a Yuletide card, bearing on it a pictorial representation of a parasitic plant, the legend *Mizpah*, the date Xmas 1892, the name of the senders, from Mr and Mrs M. Comerford, the versicle: *May this Yuletide bring to thee, Joy and peace and welcome glee:* a butt of red partly liquefied sealing wax obtained from the stores department of Messrs Hely's, Ltd., 89, 90 and 91 Dame street: a box containing the remainder of a gross of gilt "J" pennibs, obtained from the same department of the same firm: and old sandglass which rolled containing sand which rolled: a sealed prophecy (never unsealed) written by Leopold Bloom in 1886 concerning the consequences of the passing into law of William Ewart Gladstone's Home Rule bill of 1886 (never passed into law): a bazaar ticket No 2004, of S. Kevin's Charity Fair, price 6d. 100 prizes. . . .

The passage has been quoted for less than half of its actual length.

In this frightening world of Dublin on this typical day, Joyce follows in the main the activities of three people: Stephen Dedalus, Leopold Bloom, and Molly Bloom. It is in depicting their reactions to their disintegrating world that the author hopes to make clear his own position. He requires, consequently, protagonists who shall be completely realized—people whose every thought and emotion is potentially communicable to the audience. For accomplishing this purpose, Joyce's experiment with stream of consciousness in A Portrait proved the ideal preparation. In Ulysses, the increased complications of its employment are great. Joyce needed no special training in psychology to know that no two people have identical thought patterns, speech rhythms, or habits of emotional response. Women, so the cliché goes, are different from men. An intellectual and a non-intellectual sensualist display widely divergent thought patterns. Young men and old men may differ sharply in the quality of their response and in their patterns of cerebration. Religious and racial differences may affect the way people think and feel: certainly they are likely to influence the verbal representation of thought and feeling. Joyce is therefore faced with the task of representing three distinctively separate interior monologues tailored to the peculiar specifications of his main characters. Though the details of Joyce's technique in working out these streams are intricate and fascinating, their full study would require another book.

In depicting Stephen Dedalus, Joyce had a headstart in A Portrait. As that book ended, the hero was leaving Dublin for the mainland of Europe, where he hoped to develop himself as an artist. Ulysses opens just a few months later with Stephen back in Ireland, called home at the death of his mother which has occurred shortly before the opening scene of the novel. Stephen is still the arrogant intellectual of the earlier fiction, but more bitter at the turn of events which has broken his flight—like Icarus's—and landed him wounded back in his island prison. He has failed as a medical student in Paris. He has not conquered the literary world, even of Dublin. His poverty pinches and his alienation from his father hurts. His refusal to adopt piety at the behest of his suffering mother has added remorse to his psychological makeup, but it is still an unfamiliar quality for Stephen, one which he scarcely knows how to handle. All in all, however, he is much the same young man who set out to forge "the uncreated conscience of my race." The interior monologue in which he expresses himself, therefore, is basically unchanged from the earlier novel: a bit sharper, perhaps; and the bitterness provides a cutting humor absent from the self-analysis of the former college student. Stephen still lives in and for his books: his monologue is a crisp medley of allusions to philosophy, literature, history, myth, current affairs, and religion. As he muses on the beach at Sandymount in the "Proteus" episode, though he exists as an animal being, his stream emphasizes, in content and linguistic form, the primacy in him of the mind. Hence the tightness and heavy texture of such passages as this one:

> Ineluctable modality of the visible: at least that if no more, thought through my eyes. Signatures of all things I am here to read, seaspawn and seawrack, the nearing tide, that rusty boot. Snotgreen, bluesilver, rust: coloured signs. Limits of the diaphane. But he adds: in bodies. Then he was aware of them bodies before of them coloured. How? By knocking his sconce against them, sure. Go easy. Bald he was and a millionaire, *maestro di color che sanno*. Limit of the diaphane in. Why in? Diaphane, adiaphane. If you can put your five fingers through it, it is a gate, if not a door. Shut your eyes and see.

In *Ulysses*, Stephen is relegated to a role of secondary importance to make way for Joyce's supreme tragi-comical creation, Leopold Bloom, whose every unwillingness to dominate dominates the novel. Poldy, as he is called by his wife Molly, is in almost every way ordinary and average. At thirty-eight, he is neither young nor old. Born a Jew, he has tasted Protestantism before becoming a Catholic in order to satisfy his wife's practical requirements. No fool, he is certainly no intellect: his principal interest is practical science, which he is constantly muddling by foolish judgments. A failure at many businesses, he is, on June 16, 1904, a mediocre canvasser for advertisements on the staff of a Dublin newspaper, but his lack of aggressive salesmanship suggests an early end to this career.

Timidity is the key to understanding this anti-heroic hero. Normally sensitive to sexual attraction, he is too backward to enjoy feminine charms except in fantasy or at secondhand. His wife refuses to fill her normal role since the death in infancy of their only son, Rudy. Bloom is consequently forced to derive what satisfaction he can from correspondence with a flirtatious secretary or from staring at the exposed undergarments coyly displayed by lame Gerty MacDowell. Though he knows that his promiscuous wife will be entertaining Blazes Boylan at four o'clock on the day of the novel, his timidity prevents him from interfering with Molly's latest beau and, in fact, from returning to his own home until after the jaunty operatic manager is no longer present.

Bloom's Jewishness, his minority status, provides much of the motivation for his actions. An exile and an alien in the Dublin of Michael Cusack—The Citizen—his whole life is an accommodation to his role as underdog. Snubbed by Lawyer Menton, suspected by Buck Mulligan, cuckolded by almost every member of the cast of *Ulysses*, attacked physically by The Citizen, perturbed by the anti-semitic songs of Stephen Dedalus, Bloom seeks to find his level by a variety of stratagems: by a broadminded anti-semitism directed against his own race; by ignoring provocations; and by standing up, as he does in Barney Kiernan's pub, for the rights of his own people. So used to personal misfortune is he that he has developed the very rare quality of humanity. He may be maligned for stinginess and insidious shrewdness by the hangers-on of Dublin pubs, but he is the first to champion causes which arouse sentimental adherence. He contributes to the fund for Dignam's family when Paddy dies, he lends Joe Hynes a few shillings and refrains from asking for their return, he buys food for the ungrateful gulls, he watches over Stephen at Bella Cohen's brothel, he visits Mrs. Purefoy during her confinement at the Mater Misericordia Hospital, and he reacts sympathetically and tactfully to Molly's affair with Boylan. A member of a race which has been persecuted through the ages and which, as Bloom tells The Citizen, is still under fire at this very moment, he has deep within him a desire to alleviate the suffering of his fellow creatures.

But Bloom is devil as well as angel. Devoted to Molly by habit, he cannot resist the female form even in museum nudes and pays a visit to such an institution on the day in question to look into female anatomy. His spirit may be willing to abstain from the sweets of sin, but his flesh is weak: Martha Clifford, his paramour by correspondence, is as far as he can travel toward promiscuity. Branded a cuckold by all who know him, he wears his horns with resignation and "equanimity." In fact, he caters to his chronically unfaithful spouse even as he ticks off her infidelities in his mind.

For Bloom's stream of consciousness, Joyce requires a much more uncertain, human, wandering though predictable monologue than for Stephen. Bloom, wavering between action and inaction, heroism and cowardice, intelligence and stupidity, good taste and vulgarity, effeminacy and potent sexuality, shrewd commercial individualism and altruistic collectivism, is best represented by a nervous, shifting, "human" stream, for he is at dead center as a human being. This passage from the "Lestrygonians" episode is as typical as any:

> Her stockings are loose over her ankles. I detest that: so tasteless. Those literary ethereal people they are all. Dreamy, cloudy, symbolistic Esthetes they are. I wouldn't be surprised if it was that kind of food you see produces the like waves of the brain the poetical. For example one of those policemen sweating Irish stew into their shirts; you couldn't

squeeze a line of poetry out of him. Don't know what poetry is even. Must be in a certain mood.

> *The dreamy cloudy gull*
> *Waves o'er the waters dull.*

He crossed at Nassau street corner and stood before the window of Yeates and Son, pricing the field glasses. Or will I drop into old Harris's and have a chat with young Sinclair? Well-mannered fellow. Probably at his lunch. Must get those old glasses of mine set right. Goerz lenses, six guineas. Germans making their way everywhere. Sell on easy terms to capture trade. Undercutting. Might chance on a pair in the railway lost property office. Astonishing the things people leave behind them in trains and cloak rooms. What do they be thinking about? Women too. Incredible. . . .

As more than one critic has pointed out, if Stephen represents the primacy of the intellect, and Bloom the more or less unsuccessful fusion of mind and body, then Molly epitomizes without question the Flesh, proud and uninhibited. She is under observation in *Ulysses* from eight o'clock in the morning until after midnight that evening; yet she is never seen except in a reclining position in her bedroom. Unintelligent and unalert, most of her remarks to others take the form of animal-like noises of satisfaction or dissatisfaction. She has much in common with the cat in the "Calypso" episode in the quality of her oral responses. Attempts to educate her elicit a bored "O, rocks." Though she can read, her tastes run to the *Sweets of Sin*, which Bloom buys for her at the booksellers. The long "Penelope" episode which ends the novel—Molly's uninterrupted, torrential interior monologue—is almost entirely concerned with the sensual element in a woman's life: her conquests, her physical attractions, her sensations when aroused, and her misgivings concerning her future as a woman. The list of her lovers includes most of the able-bodied Dubliners mentioned during the course of the novel, indicating that her role is as unambiguous to the characters in the book as to the audience.

The psychologist C. G. Jung has expressed amazement at the depth of understanding which Joyce displays in *Ulysses* of the thoughts and desires of a woman. For the author the problem was perhaps not so much one of comprehension—understanding women is not a science nor can it be taught—as of inventing the techniques which would give verbal form to Molly's unintellectual stream. The Flesh, in this episode, had to be made Word. Joyce's solution is startlingly appropriate though it has come to be taken for granted in the generation since it was first published. If a woman—or, at least, the Female principle—might be represented in Jungian psychology as a body of water (in *Finnegans Wake*, Anna Livia Plurabelle, the sparkling wife of Earwicker, is actually the river Liffey, as it flows through Dublin), then a smooth-flowing verbal stream, poured out with spontaneity and almost without interruption, might most effectively simulate the essence of Molly's being. Moreover, Molly's special type of femininity fits easily into the scheme. Lacking mind, missing the hardness and angularity which logic, reason, and judgment add to the total personality, Molly substitutes physical softness. Her amply-flowing curves are matched by the flimsiness and lack of definite structure of her thought processes. To approximate this liquid flow of emotional sensuosity, Joyce surrenders almost all punctuation. The long monologue is an overwhelming continual outpouring. For the eye to attempt to separate the word groups into sentences is like trying to pick up a handful of water. Yet failure to do so hardly matters. The essence of Molly's soliloquy rightly lies outside the logical or the syntactical in the deeper realm of emotion and sensation. These qualities are successfully rendered by the images which flow through the episode, their meaning clear though their precise grammatical relationships may cause the unemotional scholar to ponder. A sample will suffice:

frseeeeeeeefronnnng train somewhere whistling the strength those engines have in them like big giants and the water rolling all over and out of them all sides like the end of Loves old sweet sonnnng the poor men that have to be out all the night from their wives and families in those roasting engines stifling it was today Im glad I burned the half of those old Freemans and Photo bits leaving things like that lying around hes getting very careless and threw the rest of them up in the W C Ill get him to cut them tomorrow for me instead of having them there for the next year to get a few pence for them have him asking wheres last Januarys paper and all those old overcoats I bundled out of the hall making the place hotter than it is the rain was lovely just after my beauty sleep I thought it was going to get like Gibraltar my goodness the heat there. . . .

Thus the novel is divided into three unequal sections: three short episodes devoted to the interior monologue of Stephen Dedalus; the major part of the book given over to the stream of Leopold Bloom; and the final episode devoted to Molly's soliloquy. Hedged in on the one side by excess of mind/spirit and on the other by excess of body/flesh, Bloom, always in the middle, displays weak attributes of both.

Now the significance of the novel begins to emerge. Bloom is a contemporary Everyman in a world in which even the hero is a compromise. Though he protests that his roots are in Ireland, he does not really feel at home here. He is a temporary tenant in his own apartment, and only an occasional occupant of the marital bed. A seller of space in daily newspapers, he is denied all but ephemeral and unsubstantial satisfaction for his labor. And if Bloom's past is undistinguished, his future is indeed black. He has no son to carry on his name and give permanence to his existence—nor any hope of having a son with his wife. A wanderer through the streets of Dublin on June 16, 1904, when he finally comes "home" to number seven Eccles Street after a long day's journey, he cannot enter with Stephen Dedalus because he has forgotten the key, even though preoccupation with crossed keys and Keyes and related allusions has disturbed him from the morning on.

Nor are Stephen's meetings with Bloom during the day accidental or random in the plan of the novel. If Bloom has lost a son through death, Stephen has lost a father through repudiation on his part of any spiritual kinship with Simon Dedalus. He has nothing but scorn for the drunken, sentimental braggart who shuffles through *Ulysses* making life unbearable for his children. Like Bloom, Stephen has left the home of his father; like Bloom, also, he has no key, for Mulligan has taken it in the first episode of the novel. Stephen knows that he can't go home again. Joyce thus unfolds the spectacle of a father wandering the city in search of a son—a future, a meaning of life that will ease the pain of existing; and of a son seeking release from torment of conscience. Stephen had called on Daedalus, "old father, old artificer," to stand him "now and ever in good stead," but in the few intervening years the hawk-like man had not fully responded.

Both Bloom and Stephen feel voids in their lives—Joyce implies that this is the plight of all sensitive men in modern society—and both grope haltingly toward fulfilment through the other. But Stephen, who has been thinking and talking about fathers all day, is not yet ready to respond, except condescendingly, to Bloom's offer of communion, while Bloom, more than eager to be fatherly, finds himself at a loss for the practical amenities in conversing with the cold, intellectual young man. If Joyce intends in bringing together the two men—father and son—to dramatize the wide chasm that divides man from higher spiritual authority, he succeeds in the final inconclusive session of Bloom and Stephen. Both men are embarrassed by the silences as much as by the petty conversation which illuminates their sharp differences.

To emphasize the universality of his story, as well as to provide the chaos of naturalistic detail with a firm underpinning, Joyce conceived the idea of paralleling the episodes of *Ulysses* unobtrusively with their original counterparts in Homer's *Odyssey*. He worked out the symbolic approximations scrupulously and in great detail; yet only the title of his novel, a last minute concession to reader comprehension, suggests the seriousness of his effort at literary borrowing. In fact, when his own chart of epic parallels found its way into the hands of his American publisher who wanted to reproduce it in the novel as a guide to readers, Joyce was furious merely at the suggestion. He even refused to give titles to his eighteen episodes, perhaps further to conceal his mythical substructure.

The mythical base serves as more than simply a convenient structural device. If Bloom, Stephen, and Molly are contemporary protagonists, their special attributes stand out in clear relief when matched with those of their Homeric forebears. Bloom may be wily and shrewd like Odysseus, but he has not distinguished himself in war, nor does he return in triumph to Eccles Street to kill Molly's (Penelope's) suitors and claim his unfaithful wife. Nor can Stephen qualify as the loving son, Telemachus, who sustains his aged father in battle, for he rejects or ignores Bloom's overtures of friendship and paternity with singular selfishness. Thus the modern world is revealed as unheroic, trivial, petty, unsatisfying. Heroic wanderers have become advertising canvassers and faithful heroines adulterers. The world appears to be heading for extinction, with Eliot's appropriate "whimper." The powerful nobles of Homer have given way to lame Gerty MacDowell as Nausicaa and anti-semitic Mr. Deasy as Nestor. The existence of the Homeric equivalent alone acts powerfully as a commentary on Joyce's own civilization.

But Joyce's mind, full of the symbolism of Dante and Catholic writing, nurtured on mediaeval correspondences, did not stop at one set of analogies. Each episode bears a heavy (and perhaps unfortunate) weight of subsidiary equivalents. Each has its own distinguishing color, its separate rhetorical technique, its relation to a part of the human body, its identifying structure in Dublin, and other paraphernalia.

Though Joyce concentrates mainly on the *Odyssey* for his mythical undertones, he does not neglect the riches of Biblical analogy. The reader may trace the progress of Stephen as Christ, for he is implicitly so identified in *A Portrait of the Artist*. Ironically, now it is the boorish and insensitive Buck Mulligan, substituting for Cranly, who represents John the Baptist and, in the role of precursor, opens the novel by introducing Stephen. As usual in Joyce's writing, the author avoids mechanical allegory. Allusions to Stephen's Christ-like attributes are here and there discernible, but there is no attempt to turn the young man into the Biblical figure or to have him follow rigidly the chronological regimen of the gospels. Quite the contrary, only vague hints, presented and withdrawn, impinge upon the reader's consciousness to suggest Joyce's fleeting intent. As A. M. Klein has shown, for instance, close reading of the first episode of *Ulysses* reveals Stephen as Christ: he is an "impossible person," he is referred to as "love," he takes part in a black mass perpetrated by Mulligan, and he is placed in opposition to Haines, who appears in this episode as the devil.

To complicate matters, Joyce often shifts his ground, first drawing a parallel between Stephen and Christ, for instance, and then, as in the "Cyclops" episode, between Mr. Bloom and Christ. Though slow to be roused to anger, when Bloom finally snaps back at his tormenters in Barney Kiernan's, it is with devastating force:

> —Mendelssohn was a jew and Karl Marx and Mercadante and Spinoza. And the Saviour was a jew and his father was a jew. Your God.
> —He had no father, says Martin. That'll do now. Drive ahead.
> —Whose God? says the citizen.
> —Well, his uncle was a jew, says he. Your God was a jew. Christ was a jew like me.

Later, in an important passage of the "Circe" episode, all the principal participants in the action are related to Christ. A further complication in working out definite analogical relationships is the still undetermined biographical connection between Bloom and Stephen. At times they seem to be facets of one compound-protagonist who embraces universal features of each. Joyce himself in the "Ithaca" episode blends the two into a Blephen-Stoom combination. Critics investigating the factual details which the novel provides in order to determine the extent to which the picture of Stephen is autobiographically true of Joyce have been surprised to discover that many dates in the career of Bloom are significant in Joyce's own life as well. Informed opinion is coming more and more to hold that Bloom-

Stephen, as one entity, closely approximates the mixed character of its creator. And the recently acquired documents of the Cornell University Joyce Collection tend to support the hypothesis.

The variety of structures which give firmness and balance to *Ulysses* is bewildering. Attempts have been made to show that in addition to the Homeric and the Biblical backdrops, Joyce has provided a Viconian mythical structure almost as complex as his use of Vico in *Finnegans Wake*. Others have shown the influence on his novel of the anti-clerical blasphemies of Leo Taxil. The extent of his literary allusions is awesome: his use of the Oscar Wilde affair, of the Hamlet theme, and of the writings of the Church Fathers. More diffuse than T. S. Eliot's employment of historical and literary allusions, Joyce's use of them attains much the same end: a view of a contemporary wasteland against a rich backdrop of man's achievements.

Ulysses is perhaps the one English novel about which it is almost impossible to generalize. Each of its eighteen episodes differs from the rest not only in content but often in style, in language, in mood, in intent, and in tempo. It is difficult to find any relationship between the fragile, melodious "Sirens" episode and the heavy catechism of "Ithaca"; between the deeply intellectual "Proteus" section and the wild nightmare of the "Circe" drama. It seems best, therefore, with this novel alone, to devote special attention to a characterization of each episode separately.

I. TELEMACHUS — 8 A.M. — MARTELLO TOWER

The first three episodes of the book deal with Stephen Dedalus, who is living with Buck Mulligan in a Martello Tower on the sea shore. The protagonist of *A Portrait* is haunted by guilty visions of his dead mother, for he feels that he has failed to make her last days happy. His austere sadness is balanced by the flippant banter of Mulligan and the slow politeness of the visiting Englishman, Haines.

Stephen's stream of consciousness recalls past experiences: school days, Mulligan's offensive remarks on his mother's death, his mother's appearance, snatches of poetry which now take on personal significance. Most of the themes of *Ulysses* are introduced in this episode: the father-son theme ("The Father and the Son idea. The Son striving to be atoned with the Father."); the Hamlet theme ("Elsinore that beetles o'er his base into the sea"); Irish nationalism; Irish art ("the cracked lookingglass of a servant"); the motif of the key; the theme of the usurper and pretender (Mulligan); the Christ motif ("I'm the queerest young fellow"); and the thread of anti-Catholic blasphemy.

A. M. Klein has shown convincingly that this first episode of *Ulysses* is deliberately arranged as a black mass with Mulligan as celebrator of the proscribed rites. A close examination of the episode leaves no doubt that Joyce is describing a perverted religious ritual:

> Stately, plump Buck Mulligan came from the stairhead, bearing a bowl of lather on which a mirror and a razor lay crossed. A yellow dressing-gown, ungirdled, was sustained gently behind him by the mild morning air. He held the bowl aloft and intoned:
> —*Introibo ad altare Dei.*

Mulligan thereupon introduces Stephen to the reader, as John the Baptist-Cranly had in A *Portrait* prepared the way for Christ-Stephen. As the episode proceeds, the name of the deity is pronounced backwards, Mulligan does a frenzied dance, the participants perform many gestures meaningful only in terms of the ceremony in progress, and Stephen even undergoes several temptations at the hands of Haines, whom Klein identifies as Satan. The importance of these identifications at the outset cannot be overstressed.

In the first episode, Joyce looks backward to the mother whom Stephen would like to forget—or at least to remember without the frightening accompaniment of visions from the grave and a deep "Agenbite of inwit." She becomes the sea, the "mighty mother," rendered in microcosm as the bowl of shaving lather which Stephen sees also as his mother's bowl of green bile, constantly beside her during her last days. But the episode also looks forward to paternity— to the father whom Stephen has not yet found. Thus, the tower is an appropriate symbol and locale for the events of the "Telemachus" section.

II. NESTOR—10 A.M.—MR. DEASY'S SCHOOL

This episode shows Stephen as a bored but sensitive teacher of history in an elementary school near Dublin. The keynote of the episode is frustration, with references to Pyrrhic victories and the defining of a pier as a "disappointed bridge." Stephen is repelled by, yet envies, the frank knowing wholesomeness of his middle-class pupils, unreasoning creatures who are not divorced, as he is, from the main stream of human life. Only the misfit, weak-eyed Sargent draws his pity and his special attention, for he reminds Stephen of his own appearance at the same age.

The influence of history ("a nightmare from which I am trying to awake") is considered. The episode repeats the Hamlet theme, extends the Miltonic motif of death by water ("Lycidas"), and introduces several important new threads: a discussion of the Jews by Mr. Deasy sets the tone for the later anti-semitic tormenting of Bloom. And by his letter to a newspaper on the cure of foot and mouth disease among Irish cattle, Deasy hints at the degeneration of Irish stock and the sterility of life in Ireland. The motif of the horse-race which will involve many of the main characters during the day is likewise introduced by Deasy's remarks to Stephen. These references are fortuitous in another sense too, for Deasy must carry the Homeric characteristics of Nestor, to whom Telemachus comes for advice and information in the search for his father, and Nestor is known for his prowess with horses and for his sacrifice of fine animals.

This episode and the first are, by comparison with the others, relatively discursive and uncomplicated. The general technique here is informal dialogue on ostensibly simple topics, ordinarily easier to follow than extended interior monologue unbroken by the interruption of a listener and without the prop of interpretation by another character in the novel. The difficulty comes in recognizing allusions carelessly introduced and in evaluating the weight which they bear in supporting Joyce's own plot. The lines from "Lycidas" are no more than establishers of mood unless the reader knows that Edward King was to have been a clergyman; or that he was drowned in passage between Ireland and England; or that Milton draws an analogy between the devoted student, now dead, and a spirit of the water, and Christ as a walker of the waves. The relationship to water of Christ, Lycidas, Stephen, and possibly Joyce, once established, says more as interpretation of the episode than many of the speeches made by Haines or Mulligan.

It is important to Joyce that these opening episodes be more public and penetrable than some which follow. The reader must bridge the gap from A Portrait to Ulysses. He must become familiar with the milieu which produces the cry of "non serviam" and the hopelessness of Stephen's search for acceptance on his own terms. The Stephen-Christ and Mulligan-John the Baptist relationship must be established and the ironic lack of rapport clarified. In short, Joyce must make the struggle to penetrate Stephen's mind worthwhile or lose his audience.

III. PROTEUS—11 A.M.—SANDYMOUNT STRAND

The most difficult of the episodes comprising the "Telemachia," this section is almost exclusively Stephen's thick-textured interior monologue. As he walks along the beach alone, his mind filled with undigested bits of literature, history, philosophy, and sundry arcana, the play of his intellect whips the discrete items into something resembling a pragmatic system by which a lonely young man may exist, even if he cannot be happy. As his mind grapples with illusion and reality, with philosophical systems and their refutation, the principal themes of the novel emerge once more, this time examined almost academically by an inverted Jesuit.

History becomes linked navelcords forming a telephone wire which can communicate with the Garden of Eden. Thoughts of birth reintroduce the Father-Son motif on a personal level and then on the theological. Theology implies heresy, so heretics find a place in Stephen's thoughts. Mystics and madmen are recalled, Stephen's spiritual brothers—Joachim Abbas, Swift, Pico della Mirandola. Religious rituals and sexual analogies run through Stephen's mind—and sardonic comments on the literature he has not yet produced. Student days in Paris, his unspectacular, sad return to see his dying mother, his isolation in a land of pretenders and usurpers recall on the one hand his physical weakness and cowardice, on the other, pretenders of the past and present. As the episode ends, he writes a poem, cries out in his loneliness, shows himself bound to physical needs by urination, and considers a drowned man. As noon approaches he takes on the characteristics of a suffering Christ once again in a few significant lines:

> Come. I thirst. Clouding over. No black clouds anywhere, are there? Thunderstorm. Allbright he falls, proud lightning of the intellect, *Lucifer, dico, qui nescit occasum.*

For a moment Christ and the devil coalesce.

The Homeric analogies of the "Proteus" episode are particularly important to Joyce's choice of language in this section. Telemachus and Menelaus seek the whereabouts of Odysseus from Proteus, the

Old Man of the Sea. But they are warned that he will seek to evade them by changing into many animal forms, and that they must hold fast till he yields. Taking his cue from this, Joyce makes the "Proteus" episode the chapter of change. The dog on the beach seems many animals, the tides alter the waterline, sands shift, sun becomes clouded over, people are not what they seem. Mulligan and Haines may smile, but they are pretenders beneath it. Leo Taxil, a slippery anti-clerical blasphemer, whose career included many shifts from piety to blasphemy, gets his share of attention. In addition, changes in Irish history are catalogued. Finally, language and syntax change. Stephen can turn adverb into verb: "I am almosting it."

IV. CALYPSO — 8 A.M. —
BLOOM'S HOME AT #7 ECCLES STREET

Because Leopold Bloom is introduced to the reader in this episode, Joyce provides no passages of significant difficulty, preferring to wait until the new interior monologue has become familiar. From the start Bloom's interest in and enjoyment of food are stressed in contrast to Stephen's predilection for the intellectual. Both Bloom's trip to the privy and his interlude in the butcher shop are included with the same artistic motivation. The few excursions into serious thought in which Bloom does indulge lead nowhere, are at best pseudo-scientific, and suggest a juvenile *Popular Mechanics*. His thoughts on politics are ridden with slogans and contain no original ideas. Bloom's talisman, his potato, makes its appearance. His latchkey is revealed as missing. His frustrated sexuality, now that Molly ignores her husband, is shown by the vagaries of his mind as he watches a woman shopper or thinks of his correspondence with Martha Clifford. His searching for a home, or a homeland, receives dramatic embellishment through the introduction of the Agendath Netaim plan to sell shares in a lush garden spot to be reclaimed from the desert of the Holy Land.

On the debit side, there is Molly. Unlike the nymph Calypso in the *Odyssey*, she has little interest in the man whom she holds captive in her domain. Bloom is a messenger whose orders come from the vicinity of Molly's bed—delivered in a sleepy, almost wordless manner by an abstracted wife. The impending visit of Molly's operatic manager and newest lover, Blazes Boylan, is heralded by mention of the "La ci darem" aria, the Don Giovanni theme.

Before the end of the episode, Joyce has fairly launched his attempt to portray his protagonist as completely as linguistic devices will permit.

V. THE LOTUS-EATERS — 10 A.M. — THE BATH

This episode, which culminates with Bloom's bath, continues the interior monologue and the mood of the "Calypso" section. Because this episode first relates Bloom to his neighbors in Dublin, the section contains many of the characters of the short stories in *Dubliners*. M'Coy, probably an early sketch for Bloom himself, meets his illustrious successor. Tom Kernan is recalled. Bob Doran, now married to Polly Mooney and miserable in his cuckolded state, staggers through on a bender.

Additional themes are introduced or reiterated: Hamlet, fathers and sons, Don Giovanni, Martha, the sardonic comment on the ritual and the business acumen of the Catholic Church. Finally, Bloom buys the soap which he will carry about throughout the day and, lying in his bath, contemplates the instrument of fatherhood. Stephen has earlier avoided the water. Bloom has sought it. If water carries its usual symbolic associations, this places languid Bloom in the stream of life while eliminating Stephen, who is afraid to save a man from drowning, from the common fate.

VI. HADES — 11 A.M. — GLASNEVIN CEMETERY

One of the most popular episodes in the novel, Hades is a hilarious spoof in spite of its gloomy locale and its occasional moments of high symbolic seriousness. It is Joyce's first opportunity to allow ordinary Dubliners free rein in conversation. In the carriage on the way to Paddy Dignam's funeral, Martin Cunningham, Mr. Power, Simon Dedalus and Bloom discuss life with the platitudinous wisdom which death often encourages.

For Bloom, the ride is less restful and pleasant than for his companions. He is aware of his social inferiority and enters the carriage last. He moves Simon Dedalus to profanity by pointing out Stephen, walking by on the sidewalk, the first crossing of paths for Bloom and Stephen on June 16, 1904. He is forced to bear the pain of hearing suicides denounced by Mr. Power, who is unaware that Bloom's father had taken his own life. He is forced to hear anti-semitic remarks in which he joins to gain social approval. And finally, he is made conscious by the others of Boylan's proximity and of his relationship to Molly.

Bloom's reflections on death and funeral customs show the practical turn of his mind: burial down a chute; burial of the corpse standing up to increase available cemetery space; inclusion of a telephone in every coffin in the event that the "corpse" revives. Yet his inventive mind is subject to the superstitions of ignorant citizens:

> Air of the place maybe. Looks full of bad gas. Must be an infernal lot of bad gas round the place. Butchers for instance: they get like raw beefsteaks Who was telling me? Mervyn Brown. Down in the vaults of saint Werburgh's lovely old organ hundred and fifty they have to bore a hole in the coffins sometimes to let out the bad gas and burn it. Out it rushes: blue. One whiff of that and you're a goner.

When his superstitious gaze discovers that Paddy's mourners number thirteen, humor gives way to serious Ibsenesque symbolism. The "chap in the macintosh" becomes the personification of death (assuming Gregers Werle's role in "The Wild Duck" and Mr. Browne's in "The Dead").

The "Hades" episode is particularly easy to follow in its Homeric analogies. On the way to the region of the underworld, the mourners cross the requisite bodies of water. The ceremony of death is presided over by an animal-like priest, muzzled, toadlike, resembling a puppy: Cerberus. Red-faced Elpenor is paralleled by apoplectic Paddy Dignam. For the uninitiated, "Hades" represents a suitable starting point in the reading of *Ulysses*.

VII. A E O L U S — N O O N — T H E   N E W S P A P E R   O F F I C E

The structure of this episode is obviously controlled by the newspaper headlines which separate it into small fragments of narrative. That this should be so is explained first by the format of a newspaper itself, snippets of information introduced by bold heads; and then by the Homeric association with Aeolus, the keeper of the winds. The technique of the chapter requires gustiness, hot air, windiness provided by the headlines as separators and dissipators of continuity. To the Dublin newspaper headquarters are drawn both Stephen and Bloom, one to arrange for publication of Deasy's missive, the other to work out details of a contract for an advertisement which the House of Keyes wishes to insert. Attracted also to this modern home of the winds are several windbags whose rhetorical bombast still thrills impressionable Dubliners—Simon Dedalus, Professor MacHugh, Ned Lambert and J. J. O'Molloy.

As usual, Bloom is on the receiving end of abuse. His walk imitated by newsboys, his request for the Keyes advertisement brutally rejected by the editor, he is clearly the retreating, self-effacing, timid exile who slips rather than marches through the pages of the novel. The garrulous cronies advance his homeland theme by introducing the theme of Moses and the Promised Land, while Stephen Dedalus— in his epiphany of the spinsterish virgins spitting plum pits from their high perch down on Dublin below—reinforces the motif of Bloom's quest and his own by entitling his anecdote "A *Pisgah Sight of Palestine*." But the meeting and homecoming of father and son are not yet in order. Bloom and Stephen, though in the same building simultaneously, do not meet in this episode.

VIII. LESTRYGONIANS—1 P.M.—THE LUNCH

Homeric parallels seem less essential in this section than in any other. It is actually unnecessary that Bloom should be repelled at lunchtime by the eating habits of fellow Dubliners just so that an analogy may be drawn between the cannibalistic episodes of Homer and Joyce's text. Yet the episode—Homer apart—has its narrative significance.

Bloom over and over again establishes his love for his fellow creatures. He buys food for the ungrateful gulls and feeds them. He shows compassion for Mina Purefoy in her difficult confinement though he hardly knows the woman. And he sympathizes with Mrs. Breen, whose husband is frantic at the receipt of a mysterious postcard bearing the cryptic message: "U.P." Though Bloom can feel little love for men in the mass as they tear at their food in a luncheonette, he is the most loving character in the novel when it comes to individual living things. In this spirit, for instance, he guides the blind stripling across the street, impelled simply by charity.

IX. SCYLLA AND CHARYBDIS—
2 P.M.—THE LIBRARY

Steering a painfully cramped course between the philosophy of Plato, on the one hand, and of Aristotle, on the other, Stephen in this episode expounds at length on fatherhood and sonhood before the bookish lights of Dublin—librarians, literati, and the mocker Mulligan. Developing his theme by reference to the Hamlet story, he postulates biographically that the Ghost represents Shakespeare, Hamlet is Hamnet Shakespeare, the son of the bard, and that Gertrude, the guilty queen is a rough approximation of Anne Hathaway. Proceeding in this manner, he accuses Anne of seducing the youthful Shakespeare, a traumatic experience for Will, he feels, forcing him into a marriage from which he shortly escaped to London and the theater; and of subsequent seductions of Shakespeare's brothers, Richard and Edmund, and of final reconciliation with her husband through the common love of a granddaughter. After the elaborate explanation, Stephen promptly says "no" when asked if he believes his own theory.

The motif is important not only because it states clearly Stephen's belief that fatherhood is a spiritual matter, not merely a physical affair of merging chromosomes, but also because Shakespeare takes on attributes of Stephen and Bloom: the artist, the God of Creation, the father, the cuckolded husband, the youth whose future is jeopardized by usurping mockers. It is meaningful too that Bloom's path crosses that of Stephen in this episode as business takes the wandering Jew to the library to consult newspaper files.

The language of the episode is even more daring and experimental than comparable prose in the other episodes. And rightfully so, for Joyce is here seeking to approximate the freedom and excitement of Elizabethan word play. Unusual words (like "nookshotten") abound. Puns are common, as when Stephen thinks of his debt to George Russell, the "A.E." of Irish verse ("A.E.I.O.U."). Literary allusions are thicker than usual ("Art thou there, truepenny?" and "As for living, our servants can do that for us.")

Allusions to Joyce's contemporaries are naturally introduced: John Eglinton, Padraic Colum, George Roberts, Edward Martyn, George Moore, Synge, and the rest. But the climax of the episode is Mulligan's flippant warning to Stephen that Bloom, the "ancient mariner," has designs on Stephen, a warning which the artist resents as he does Mulligan's whole manner throughout the day. That young Dedalus has been frustrated in the cool and amused reception of his Hamlet theory by people he considers his inferiors does not improve his disposition to enjoy barbed frivolity.

X. THE WANDERING ROCKS — 3 P.M. — THE STREETS

This episode is formed of eighteen vignettes of Dublin life. It comes approximately in the middle of the volume and acts as a recapitulation of the material thus far presented and a preview of things to come. As *Mrs. Dalloway* is held together by Virginia Woolf's device of skywriting, visible simultaneously above London to all of the principal characters and calling forth from each typical responses, so Joyce adopts an analogous device in the "Wandering Rocks." The representative of spiritual authority, Father Conmee, wanders through Dublin streets to begin the section; William Humble and his Lady, ranking English officials, parade through the streets in their carriage to bring it to a close. In between, ordinary Dubliners go about their business in the middle of the afternoon. Conmee is properly respectful to an M.P., properly clerical to a man and woman in love. Corny Kelleher spies for The Castle. Molly bestirs herself to throw a coin to a wounded veteran. Boylan buys flowers, Lenehan and M'Coy discuss Molly's charms and Bloom's insensitivity. Bloom buys *Sweets of Sin* for his wife. Stephen's sister, Dilly, seeking romance in vain, acquires a French grammar. And the blind stripling curses a passerby.

By stopping the clock at three in the afternoon and focusing the camera quickly at a selection of characters from the novel, Joyce helps his reader to remember that *Ulysses* hopes to put all time "in a notshall," that the lives of Stephen and the Leopold Blooms are in reality the lives of all people at all times.

XI. THE SIRENS — 4 P.M. — THE ORMOND HOTEL BAR

Joyce's simultaneous love of vocal music and interest in the "Revolution of the Word" as a desirable end in literature combine to formulate the "Sirens" episode. Planned in the form of a musical composition, it contains a fugal opening which enunciates the themes to be developed in the main body of the piece. Thus, the first line of the overture, "Bronze by gold heard the hoofirons, steelyringing," is developed later as "Bronze by gold, Miss Douce's head by Miss Kennedy's head, over the crossblind of the Ormond bar heard the viceregal hoofs go by, ringing steel." Similarly, another mysterious introductory pattern, "Chips, picking chips off rocky thumbnail, chips," becomes intelligible later as "Into their bar strolled Mr. Dedalus. Chips, picking chips off one of his rocky thumbnails. Chips. He strolled." If most of these fragmentary motifs need later elaboration before they are comprehensible to the intellect, in the overture they must obviously depend for effect on their musical, tonal qualities. In this respect, Joyce may have attempted the impossible, for scraps of words, ostensible nonsense syllables, however euphonious, can hardly carry the weight of a novel for more than a page.

When the author leaves the introduction for the main body of the work, his artistry is more clearly apparent. Since "The Sirens" is the musical episode linguistically, he brings together in it as many of his vocal motifs as the narrative will bear. The time is four o'clock—the appointed trysting hour for Boylan, the operatic manager, and his client, the soprano Molly Bloom. In its pages, one of the barmaid sirens sings lines from "Floradora." References to opera and operetta abound. Molly is "Daughter of the Regiment" and "My Irish Molly, O." The talk is of singers, Jenny Lind and others. The Don Giovanni motif comes into play once more. Bloom composes a letter to Martha Clifford as the bar cronies sing the significant refrain of "Martha." Bloom even analyzes the lyrics in a meaningful commentary:

> Thou lost one. All songs on that theme. Yet more Bloom stretched his string. Cruel it seems. Let people get fond of each other: lure them on. Then tear asunder. . . . Gone. They sing. Forgotten. I too. And one day she with. Leave her. . . .

Having steeped himself in sentiment induced by the words of popular songs, the wandering Jew considers once more his own circumstances:

> I too, last my race. Milly young student. Well, my fault perhaps. No son. Rudy. Too late now. Or if not? If not? If still?
> He bore no hate.
> Hate. Love. Those are names. Rudy. Soon I am old.

And in a trance of self-pity the modern Odysseus, his ears effectively sealed, escapes the charms of the Ormond barmaids:

By rose, by satiny bosom, by the fondling hand, by slops, by empties, by popped corks, greeting in going, past eyes and maidenhair, bronze and faint gold in deepseashadow, went Bloom, soft Bloom, I feel so lonely Bloom.

XII. CYCLOPS — 5 P.M. — BARNEY KIERNAN'S PUB

Though much of this episode contains deliberate empty bombast, it is a crucial section of the book for the light it sheds on Bloom's character and his stated association with the figure of Christ. Narrated by a Dublin cornerboy, nameless as Odysseus is nameless to Polyphemus, the episode parallels rather closely Homer's story of the one-eyed giant and the escape of Odysseus from his toils. Because much is made of the great size of the Cyclops as compared to the puny dimensions of Odysseus and his hapless crew, Joyce is able to experiment linguistically with a technique which he calls gigantism. Alternating the informal, slangy narration by a low-class Dubliner, the breezy dialogue of the barflies, and the anxious mouthings of Bloom, on the one hand, with passages of formal catalogues, official guest-lists, wordy scientific jargon, on the other, Joyce is able to create the effect of two worlds simultaneously. The ultranationalist Citizen, imposing in size and manner, recalls Finn MacCool and the giants of the ancient Irish past. Next to him, mere contemporary adult males shrink to proper miniscule size.

But Bloom, though in prudent flight, cuts The Citizen down to size, as does his Homeric counterpart. He has wandered into Barney Kiernan's looking for Martin Cunningham on an errand of charity. Surrounded by men who are actively or passively hostile, he at first keeps silent under provocation. The Citizen rails at "foreigners" who impoverish Ireland. Bloom argues timidly that an Irish navy would be as firm in discipline as the British. Gaining confidence, though losing his usual ability to articulate smoothly, he stands up for his own Irishness:

—What is your nation if I may ask, says the citizen.
—Ireland, says Bloom. I was born here. Ireland.

But all these essays are minor triumphs compared with his sharp insistence on asserting his Jewishness in what to The Citizen must be the most offensive manner:

—Mendelssohn was a jew and Karl Marx and Mercadante and Spinoza. And the Saviour was a jew and his father was a jew. Your God.
—He had no father, says Martin. That'll do now. Drive ahead.
—Whose God? says the citizen.
Well, his uncle was a jew, says he. Your God was a jew. Christ was a jew like me.
Gob, the citizen made a plunge back into the shop.
—By Jesus, says he, I'll brain that bloody jewman for using the holy name. By Jesus, I'll crucify him so I will.

An announcement of such purport to the novel is properly anticipated by the blasphemous conversation at Kiernan's which suggests a direct relationship between the Holy Family and Bloom's menage. The Citizen, earlier in the episode, begins the discussion of Bloom with broad sarcasm:

—That's the new Messiah for Ireland. . . .
Well, they're still waiting for their redeemer, says Martin. For that matter so are we.
—Yes, says J.J., and every male that's born they think it may be their Messiah. And every jew is in a tall state of excitement, I believe, till he knows if he's a father or a mother.
—Expecting every moment will be his next, says Lenehan.
—O, by God, says Ned, you should have seen Bloom before that son of his that died was born. . . .
—Do you call that a man? says the citizen.
—I wonder did he ever put it out of sight, says Joe.
—Well, there were two children born anyhow, says Jack Power.
—And who does he suspect? says the citizen.

When the reader compares these gibes with comparable blasphemies which Leo Taxil directs against Joseph and Mary, the full importance of this chapter becomes evident.

XIII. NAUSICAA — THE ROCKS — 8 P.M.

Paralleling the discovery by the princess Nausicaa and her maidens of Odysseus, who swims ashore naked to find himself befriended in a strange country, Joyce's episode places Bloom on the rocky beach near the counterpart of Nausicaa, a crippled girl named Gerty MacDowell, out for a day of picnicking with her girl friends and several tots for whom they act as baby-sitters. To approximate the emptiness of Gerty's mind—the shallowness of her romantic ideals—Joyce adopts the prose style of a *True Confessions* magazine, replete with clichés and extravagant heroics. For interminable pages Joyce pursues his stylistic *tour de force*, perhaps unnecessarily. The Gerty MacDowell episode ends appropriately with a display of exhibitionism by the lame girl to the accompaniment of a fireworks display, clearly sexual in analogy, which excites Bloom and leads him into the interior monologue that concludes the section.

In Bloom's stream the romantic idealism is submerged, and the stark facts of sexual attraction stressed. Matter-of-factly Leopold considers the wages of virginity ("Virgins go mad in the end I suppose"); the menstrual cycle ("Depends on the time they were born"); girls in convent schools; prostitutes; and other plain matters of sexual life.

The chapter anticipates Joyce's use of Vico's cycles in the *Wake* as Bloom muses on the returning seasons: "The year returns. History repeats itself. Ye crags and peaks I'm with you once again. Life, love, voyage round your own little world. And now?" He goes on: "All that old hill has seen. Names change: that's all. . . ." This train of thought leads finally to his conclusion: "So it returns. Think you're escaping and run into yourself. Longest way round is the shortest way home."

XIV. OXEN OF THE SUN — 10 P.M. — THE LYING-IN HOSPITAL

This difficult and much discussed episode revolves around the birth of a child to Mrs. Purefoy, allowing Joyce to play at length with what he calls the embryonic development of language. The episode proceeds from a rough approximation of Anglo-Saxon alliterative language through the style of mediaeval romance and travel literature, then to the Arthurian style of Malory, and on through writers like Pepys, Defoe, Carlyle, Dickens, and others. It culminates in a breakdown of language—a combination of pidgin English, revival meeting jargon, and assorted outlandish patois. There is little doubt that *Ulysses* would have been quite as effective without the series of extended parodies in which the substantive content of Joyce's epic is largely engulfed, though the parodies, generally ingenious and excellent, are worth attention outside of their role in telling the story.

Many important narrative threads emerge from the dense prose of this section. Bloom has gone to the hospital out of pity for the expectant mother. Stephen is there expecting a carouse with the wild medical students who are his only "friends." In a scene reminiscent of a Last Supper, Stephen and Bloom share the same table with the rowdy medicals. The talk, centering about pregnancy, immaculate conception, and fertility (to parallel Homer's interest in the subject in the *Odyssey*), turns to birth control and children, a topic which fills Bloom with sadness, for he is without an heir. Stephen, as Christ, offers communion. In the midst of the conversation, the baby is born. Its presence in the world allows Joyce to expand further on the motif of fathers and sons, from the divergent points of view of Stephen and Bloom.

The group of young students rushes off to Burke's with Stephen in the lead and Bloom following to keep an eye on his adopted son. The stage is set for the scene in the brothel.

XV. CIRCE — 12 MIDNIGHT —
BELLA COHEN'S BROTHEL

Succinct description of the events of this episode is extremely difficult because the effect of this almost two hundred page-long section is incommensurately more powerful than the sum of its separate parts. By midnight of June 16, 1904, the two male protagonists, Bloom and Stephen, are weary, almost done in by their day of frustrated wandering. Their thoughts are wild, fantastic, alive. Taking advantage of these considerations, Joyce stages in the "Circe" episode an hallucinatory expressionist drama in which fleeting thoughts are objectified and projected as personages on a stage. Trivial fears and lifelong ambitions are realized. Bloom takes form as Lord Mayor of Dublin for a moment, as a roué, and as a prisoner at the bar. Soap can talk, dead people (Stephen's and Bloom's mothers, for instance) come to life in a nervous nightmare world of all too real imagination.

Because its center is the brothel, the episode is named for Circe, a practitioner of magic who turned men into swine. This is precisely the business of the "Madame" of the house of prostitution, Bella Cohen, so that the Homeric associations are honored.

"Circe" is a crucial episode for Bloom and Stephen. Both are subjected in it to physical and emotional pressures under which the human personality might easily disintegrate, but they manage not only to escape but to advance as human beings. Stephen is able finally to dispel the influence of his dead mother as he has not been successful in doing as the book opens. This accomplished, he can turn to communion with the father. Bloom, in the latter role, emerges from the nightmare of the brothel to experience a vision of his dead Rudy, deliberately sentimentalized in a totally uncongenial environment.

All themes come to a climax in "Circe." The mysterious soap and potato perform their magic functions. Stephen, formerly the hydrophobe, chants in Latin of the water. Bloom's charity to gulls, dogs, and women is recapitulated. The persecution of the Jews—and of all humanity through Bloom-Christ—is given extensive treatment. Bloom is hounded as a cuckold, a lecher, an exile, a vulgarian, and, in various hallucinations, as a man who enjoys suffering. And the black mass celebrated by Mulligan in "Telemachus" is here explicitly performed at midnight.

The episode serves also to widen the reader's conception of Bloom as a fully developed character by projecting him in imagination into situations in which he makes known his views on subjects which ordinarily would not enter his interior monologue. So, for instance, as alderman Bloom, he can exclaim:

> These flying Dutchmen or lying Dutchmen, as they recline in their upholstered poop, casting dice, what reck they? Machines is their cry, their chimera, their panacea. Laboursaving apparatuses, supplanters, bugbears, manufactured monsters for mutual murder. . . . The poor man starves while they are grassing their royal mountain stags. . . . But their reign is rover for rever and ever and ev . . .

or later:

> I stand for the reform of municipal morals and the plain ten commandments. New worlds for old. Union of all, jew, moslem and gentile. Three acres and a cow for all children of nature. . . . Electric dishscrubbers. Tuberculosis, lunacy, war and mendicancy must now cease. . . .

Symbolically, the episode is most noteworthy, perhaps for the elaborate identification of Bloom with Shakespeare (the creator) and God. Stephen puts it this way:

> What went forth to the ends of the world to traverse not itself. God, the sun, Shakespeare, a commercial traveller, having itself traversed in reality itself, becomes that self. Wait a moment. Wait a second. Damn that fellow's noise in the street. Self which it itself was ineluctably preconditioned to become. *Ecco!*

This identification having been made, it is but one step to the idea that there is a bit of Bloom in all of us—and the consequent extension to "Florry Christ, Stephen Christ, Zoe Christ, Bloom Christ.

Kitty Christ, Lynch Christ" and A. J. Christ Dowie. Thus, from the nadir of spirituality, a Dublin brothel, emerges a message of Love and Humanity whose form is the vision of Rudy.

XVI. EUMAEUS — 1 A.M. — THE CABMAN'S SHELTER

Before returning to his palace at Ithaca, Odysseus takes refuge in the hut of a loyal and ancient servant who does not recognize his master after the passage of so many years. So Bloom stops with Stephen at a place of refuge before returning to Eccles Street and Molly. The place is an all-night diner which serves questionable food to questionable customers. Presided over by a man who is supposed to have had a hand in the murders perpetrated by the Invincibles gang, it is hardly a hospitable stopping-off place. But Bloom and especially Stephen are done in, exhausted by the day's wandering and the excitement of the night. Desperation leads Bloom to the shelter, and a desire to minister to Stephen's need for rest, food, and sobriety.

Again Joyce matches the prose to the mood of the protagonists. Tired, wandering heroes call for tired, wandering prose, weary syntax, and monstrously involved paragraphing. The first two sentences will do for an illustration:

Preparatory to anything else Mr Bloom brushed off the greater bulk of the shavings and handed Stephen the hat and ashplant and bucked him up generally in orthodox Samaritan fashion, which he very badly needed. His (Stephen's) mind was not exactly what you would call wandering but a bit unsteady and on his expressed desire for some beverage to drink Mr Bloom, in view of the hour it was and there being no pumps of Vartry water available for their ablutions, let alone drinking purposes, hit upon an expedient by suggesting, off the reel, the propriety of the cabman's shelter, as it was called, hardly a stonesthrow away near Butt Bridge, where they might hit upon some drinkables in the shape of a milk and soda or a mineral.

Yet the episode has its share of excitement in spite of the language in which it is couched. Bloom's solicitude for Stephen is touchingly significant: ". . . where . . . will you sleep yourself? . . . why did you leave your father's house?" Bloom urges Stephen to eat solid food, "a roll of some description," but when the coffee and bun arrive Stephen says simply, "Couldn't," thus refusing more than Bloom's hospitality. And though the young artist manages a sip of the "offending beverage," on the next page, the mood is one of rejection. Yet Stephen, in his bleary-eyed way, knows what he is doing —understands the implications of his action, for a few pages further on, he mumbles, "*Christus* or Bloom his name is."

That Bloom has taken Stephen to his heart is clear from several details of the episode. He reveals to his spiritual son the details of his encounter with The Citizen in Barney Kiernan's—a tale reserved for special ears. And he shows Stephen a photograph of Molly in her prime. Finally, he invites Stephen to spend the night at the Bloom apartment. All these evidences of special favor, however, are insufficient to bridge the gap which Stephen feels.

> . . . he passed his left arm in Stephen's right and led him on accordingly.
>
> —Yes, Stephen said uncertainly, because he thought he felt a strange kind of flesh of a different man approach him, sinewless and wobbly and all that.

More from lethargy than from assent, Stephen allows himself to be led by Bloom to Eccles Street.

XVII. ITHACA — 2 A.M. — THE HOUSE OF BLOOM

The extended question-answer method of this episode has been attributed to several possible artistic motives: on the Homeric level, Odysseus asks and answers many questions preparatory to reinstating himself in his palace. Or, as a parody on the objective, pseudo-scientific method of Zola and the naturalists, Joyce may be spoofing a technique which he himself uses to good effect in many places. Finally, the method of church catechism as a device cannot be ignored since Joyce had made it a trademark in *A Portrait* and was to use it later even in *Finnegans Wake*.

Whatever the reasons for the choice of impersonal scientific language used to propound and answer questions, the result is a rich store of information regarding the life of Leopold Bloom, past and present. If he is to be the most fully developed character in fiction, the reader must know more of his background than any ordinary stream of consciousness can logically supply. The "Ithaca" chapter gives Joyce a chance to intrude, as author, to fill in informational gaps. In addition, the episode is of dramatic importance—an importance deliberately played down by the dull matter-of-factness of the prose in which it is couched—for it marks the final (imperfect) communion between symbolic father and son. In it the irony of Joyce's Biblical and Homeric structures superimposed on Dublin's Bloom and Stephen becomes clear. The two men are unlike in almost all important characteristics, similar in a few minor ways that hardly count.

The symbolic content of the episode is evident from the start, when Bloom finds himself without the key to his own home and is forced to leap the fence, fall, and then rise again to admit Stephen. Bloom is shown leading Stephen, pointing the way with a candle, heating water ("Bloom, waterlover," admired its "universality: its democratic equality."), and then offering his guest "Epp's mass product, the creature cocoa." Significantly, Stephen drinks it and thus communion is at least ritually attained, though Stephen rejects an invitation to stay the night. This whole motif has been explicitly analyzed by William York Tindall (see Bibliography).

The final section of the chapter, with Bloom telling the day's doings to his wife, prepares the way for the stream of Molly Bloom in the final episode.

XVIII. PENELOPE — 2:45 A.M. — THE BED

Probably the most notorious of the episodes of *Ulysses*, "Penelope," is the uninterrupted interior monologue of Molly Bloom—a forty-odd page outpouring of the feminine heart, almost unbroken by punctuation. In it the speaker puts expertly the woman's point of view on love, sex, marriage, and related topics.

It is as foolish to summarize Molly's remarks as to offer a jar of water to one who wishes to see the Pacific Ocean. Yet the final outpouring does add to the reader's knowledge of Bloom's marital life in many ways. For the first time it is apparent that, beneath Molly's irritation with Poldy, there lies something approaching affection— almost love. Her concern with Bloom's whereabouts, apprehension lest he take up with prostitutes, shows her real interest. Her main complaint is that her husband is not "natural," occupying himself, as he does, with women's underclothing and with perverse demands on his wife's sexual nature.

As she reviews her parade of former lovers, Molly offers a vivid picture of herself as the embodiment of the feminine principle. She lives to love, to be loved, to be attractive to the senses, and to respond to the sensuous demands of others. Penelope in the *Odyssey* seeks to keep her unwelcome suitors at arm's length; Molly opens her arms to all of them except her bumbling spouse. Though Molly may be accused of unthinking hedonism, gold digging, and worse crimes, the indictment must always be softened by the thought that she *knows* (in D. H. Lawrence's sense of the word) not what she does. She acts from instinct, perhaps the one trustworthy element left in the Dublin of 1904, for Joyce ends the novel on her reiterated note of affirmation: "Yes."

James Joyce : SELECTED BIBLIOGRAPHY

BUDGEN, FRANK. *James Joyce and the Making of 'Ulysses.'* New York: Harrison Smith and Robert Haas, Inc., 1934.

CAMPBELL, JOSEPH and HENRY MORTON ROBINSON. *A Skeleton Key to 'Finnegans Wake.'* New York: Harcourt, Brace and Company, 1944.

COLUM, MARY and PADRAIC. *Our Friend James Joyce.* New York: Doubleday Company, 1958.

GILBERT, STUART. *James Joyce's 'Ulysses.'* London: Faber and Faber, Ltd., 1930; New York: Alfred A. Knopf, 1931.

GIVENS, SEON. *James Joyce: Two Decades of Criticism.* New York: Vanguard Press, 1944.

GLASHEEN, ADALINE. *A Census of 'Finnegans Wake': An Index of the Characters and Their Roles.* Evanston, Illinois: Northwestern University Press, 1956.

GORMAN, HERBERT. *James Joyce.* New York: Rinehart and Company, 1939.

HANLEY, MILES L. and OTHERS. *Word-Index to James Joyce's 'Ulysses.'* Madison: University of Wisconsin Press, 1937.

HUTCHINS, PATRICIA. *James Joyce's Dublin.* London: The Grey Walls Press, Ltd., 1950.

——. *James Joyce's World.* London: Methuen, 1957.

JOYCE, JAMES. *Epiphanies,* edited by O. A. Silverman. Buffalo: University of Buffalo, 1956.

——. *Letters of James Joyce,* edited by Stuart Gilbert. New York: The Viking Press, 1957.

——. *Stephen Hero,* edited by Theodore Spencer. Norfolk, Conn.: New Directions, 1944.

JOYCE, STANISLAUS. *My Brother's Keeper: James Joyce's Early Years.* New York: The Viking Press, 1958.

KAIN, RICHARD M. *Fabulous Voyager: James Joyce's 'Ulysses.'* Chicago: University of Chicago Press, 1947.

KENNER, HUGH. *Dublin's Joyce.* Bloomington: Indiana University Press, 1956.

LEVIN, HARRY. *James Joyce: A Critical Introduction.* Norfolk, Conn.: New Directions, 1941.

MAGALANER, MARVIN and RICHARD M. KAIN. *Joyce: The Man, the Work, the Reputation.* New York: New York University Press, 1956.

MAGALANER, MARVIN, editor. *A James Joyce Miscellany.* New York: The James Joyce Society, 1957.

————, editor. *A James Joyce Miscellany: Second Series.* Carbondale, Illinois: Southern Illinois University Press, 1959.

————. *Time of Apprenticeship: The Fiction of Young James Joyce.* New York and London: Abelard-Schuman Ltd., 1960.

NOON, WILLIAM T. *Joyce and Aquinas.* New Haven: Yale University Press, 1957.

SCHUTTE, WILLIAM M. *Joyce and Shakespeare: A Study in the Meaning of 'Ulysses.'* New Haven: Yale University Press, 1957.

SLOCUM, JOHN J. and HERBERT CAHOON. *A Bibliography of James Joyce: 1882–1941.* New Haven: Yale University Press, 1953.

STRONG, L. A. G. *The Sacred River: An Approach to James Joyce.* New York: Pellegrini and Cudahy, 1951.

SULLIVAN, KEVIN. *Joyce among the Jesuits.* New York: Columbia University Press, 1958.

TINDALL, WILLIAM YORK. *James Joyce: His Way of Interpreting the Modern World.* New York: Charles Scribner's Sons, 1950.

————. *A Reader's Guide to James Joyce.* New York: The Noonday Press, 1959.

USSHER, ARLAND. *Three Great Irishmen: Shaw, Yeats, Joyce.* New York: Devin-Adair Company, 1953.

WILSON, EDMUND. *Axel's Castle: A Study in the Imaginative Literature of 1870–1930.* New York: Charles Scribner's Sons, 1931.

Aldous Huxley xx Life

The ancestral background of Aldous Huxley, who was born in England on July 26, 1894, contains several famous figures from the nineteenth century whose influence extends into many of his books. Brother of Julian Huxley, the well-known scientist, he is the son of Leonard Huxley, editor and writer, and of Julia Arnold, Matthew Arnold's niece and sister of Mrs. Humphrey Ward, the Victorian novelist. Further, Thomas Henry Huxley, Darwin's stalwart supporter, was his grandfather and Dr. Thomas Arnold, the most famous schoolmaster of the century, his great-grandfather. From childhood, obviously, Huxley was destined for a life of achievement and culture, and in his early years moved among the great of the English literary and artistic world.

A prodigious reader, Huxley found his education tragically cut short at Eton because of failing eyesight, an affliction which finally he partially cured himself through exercises. After three years of poor sight that left him nearly blind, Huxley went to Balliol College, Oxford, where he made a brilliant record in English literature. In his early twenties, he began to publish poetry, and his first volume, in 1916, contains mannerisms more characteristic of nineteenth-century French poetry than of his English predecessors, revealing particularly the styles of Rimbaud and Laforgue, two strong influences also on Huxley's contemporary, T. S. Eliot.

Always a prolific writer, Huxley had published eight volumes of poetry, short stories, and novels by the time he was thirty; and his international reputation was made. By this time, now married, he started his frequent journeys into both familiar and remote areas, from Europe to India, travels that would finally land him permanently in Los Angeles, California. While temporarily settled in Italy in the 1920's, he met D. H. Lawrence and began a friendship that ended only with Lawrence's death in 1930. Since then, Huxley has turned out a continuous stream of novels, stories, and essays, whose contents chronicle his ever-growing and changing interests. His novels include: *Crome Yellow* (1921), *Antic Hay* (1923), *Those Barren Leaves* (1925), *Point Counter Point* (1928), *Brave New World* (1932), *Eyeless in Gaza* (1936), *After Many a Summer Dies the Swan* (1939), *Time Must Have a Stop* (1944), *Ape and Essence* (1948), and *The Genius and the Goddess* (1955).

His novels, however, are less than half of his total publications. In addition to his music, art, and drama criticism, book reviews, intro-ductions, and sundry articles on diverse topics, there are several vol-umes of essays and belles lettres, which include: *On the Margin* (1923), *Along the Road* (1925), *Essays New and Old* (1926), *Jesting Pilate* (1926), *Proper Studies* (1927), *Do What You Will* (1929), *Vulgarity in Literature* (1930), *Music at Night* (1931), *The Olive Tree* (1936), *Ends and Means* (1937), *The Art of Seeing* (1942), *The Perennial Philosophy* (1945), *Science, Liberty, and Peace* (1946), *Themes and Variations* (1950), *The Devils of Loudun* (1952), *The Doors of Perception* (1954), and *Tomorrow and Tomor-row and Tomorrow* (1956). Huxley has also published five volumes of short stories: *Limbo* (1920), *Mortal Coils* (1922), *Little Mexican* (1924), *Two or Three Graces* (1926), and *Brief Candles* (1930); a biography (*Grey Eminence*, 1940); a travel book (*Beyond the Mexique Bay*, 1934); several volumes of poetry; and four plays.

Huxley's versatility has enabled him to probe into nearly every aspect of the modern era; and his novels and essays read like an intel-lectual tour of man's endeavors to lift himself from selfishness into self-effacement, from materialism into mysticism. More moralist and sermonizer than fictionist, Huxley seems himself to have tried every new idea for size before committing it to paper. In each area of expe-rience, he has sought some justification for an absolute, if, at times, even the absolute denial of absolutes, but usually some kind of divine reality which would give meaning to an otherwise inane existence. As one critic has written, "The tale his books tell is a twentieth-century Pilgrim's Progress, in which Darwin, Freud, and their colleagues patrol the frontier between the realm of ape men and the free state of God-men. . . . He echoes our frustrations, articulates our dilemmas, chronicles our struggle with the Janus-headed monster that has Time on one face and Ego on the other."

Huxley, without attaining the heights of great literature, has attempted to reveal the underlying discontent of the twentieth century, and in so doing has demonstrated a range greater than that of any other novelist of his time.

Aldous Huxley xx *Works*

Aldous Huxley's reputation was made in the decade or so following the First World War, in which his disillusionment, reflected in his playful but bitter humor and in his mordant portrayal of human futility, fitted an era that reduced positive values to witty ironies. Huxley's freedom from traditional values, his license in discussing world-weary practitioners of sex, and his detached, ironical manner gave him stature as a sophisticate with a wry awareness of the world's corruption. Ideas, rather than carefully drawn characters or dramatic situations, were the stuff of his novels. From *Crome Yellow* through *Antic Hay* and *Point Counter Point* in the twenties to *Eyeless in Gaza* and *After Many a Summer Dies the Swan* in the thirties, he presented character types who signified certain topical ideas. When these ideas came together, however, they created a dialectic more of conflicting philosophies than of living people. In such terms, Huxley's novels rarely attain the status of "literature"; closer to tracts or fictional essays, they have been called, among other things, "novels of ideas." Therefore, to apply literary standards to Huxley's fiction is often futile, for his characters, situations, and dramatic conflicts simply fail to sustain the work as a whole. Unlike Conrad and Lawrence, who wove ideas into their characters and thus gained density, Huxley handles his characters as puppets who speak, write, or think their ideas, without ever *being*. His narratives, accordingly, even when he experimented with various techniques, as in *Point Counter Point* and *Eyeless in Gaza*, remain only thin threads tenuously holding together the several parts.

However, after we recognize Huxley's novelistic shortcomings—several of which will be apparent when his novels are discussed—there still remains his value as a spokesman for the twentieth century. For of contemporary novelists, Huxley, perhaps more than any other, has run the range of modern ideas and has involved himself in every possible intellectual stance while attempting to find cures for society's malaise. The ills of the modern world, so consciously dissected by every major novelist, when complemented by Huxley's own disgust with life, create an inferno-like atmosphere of frustration and meaninglessness unique in the contemporary English novel. Apparently, the key to Huxley's interpretation of the twists and turns of the twentieth century is *disgust*—disgust for life, for people as individuals, even for ideas, which themselves, he recognizes, must eventually fail. Disgust, not love, pity, or compassion, is central to *Crome Yellow, Antic Hay, Point Counter Point, Brave New World,* and *Eyeless in Gaza*; disgust describes his female figures, his intellectuals, and his sensualists.

Huxley's typical people, as one critic remarked, are either specimens, statistics, or demonstrations of something; and perhaps this inert characterization is inevitable once we recognize Huxley's assumptions. If, for a moment, we return to a novelist of one hundred years ago, Jane Austen, for example, we see that each of her characters took the general moralitiy of the day for granted; their departure from a certain expected norm allowed Jane Austen her freedom of movement, but the norm was ever in view, solid and never-changing. When we come to Huxley, it is obvious that the departure is now meaningless, for the norm itself is without meaning. Nothing can be taken for granted, nothing assumed in behavior, ideas, or morality. The only test for an idea, in Huxley, is its ability to work, to be accepted as it clashes with the world around it. Once all norms are questioned and scrutinized objectively, Huxley's disgust is not unreasonable; it is, in its way, similar to Axel Heyst's and Martin Decoud's world-weariness, and to D. H. Lawrence's repulsion by modern industrialism. Since Huxley's range of interest is broader than either Conrad's or Lawrence's, his disdain can fall upon a wider area; and, further, since he supports few positive values, at least in his early novels, his personal scorn seems all the more forceful.

Once this is noted, one sees that the real dramatic worth of Huxley's fiction lies in the conflict of ideas, in the relationship between character and idea, or in the tensions of varying historical forces. In several of Huxley's novels, the idea, not the character who holds it, is the center of dramatic interest. As illustration, *Eyeless in Gaza,* which is substantially closer to a sermon or a morality than a novel, depends for much of its effectiveness on the *ideas* Anthony Beavis embraces, not on whether his conversion itself is plausible. Similarly, in *Antic Hay*, Gumbril Senior is the only positive element in the book because he offers the only positive ideas, not because he might be a particularly effective character. In *Point Counter Point*, the same can be said of Mark Rampion, whose positive nature is summed up less by his person than by his beliefs. With ideas as bases for his novels, Huxley could alternately be cynical, grim, witty, cruel, or brilliant, but not warm, compassionate, or understanding.

CROME YELLOW

In *Crome Yellow*, Huxley's short first novel, several of the major themes, characters, and attitudes that would later be developed more fully appear, although only sketchily. The basic situation is the familiar one in which the author brings together at a house party a number of dissimilar people. Denis, the young and self-conscious poet, is a kind of untried Philip Quarles, the self-conscious novelist of *Point Counter Point*. Scogan, the mechanistic realist, recurs later in various guises, as Quarles again and Anthony Beavis, for example. Barbecue-Smith, the merchant of platitudes with his pipeline to infinity, becomes Burlap of *Point Counter Point*. Anne, the seductress who wants to live fully, is a less destructive version of Myra Viveash (*Antic Hay*), Lucy Tantamount (*PCP*), and Mary Amberley (*Eyeless in Gaza*). Henry Wimbush, the historiographer of the past of Crome, the Wimbush country place, is in his isolation from the world the same type as Lord Edward Tantamount (*PCP*), who would rather study newts than people, and Shearwater (*Antic Hay*), who peddles and sweats while his wife moves from one responsive embrace to another.

Of them all, Denis and Scogan are the most important, for in the former's dilettantism Huxley foreshadows several of his later aesthetes, the demonstration of whose inadequacy becomes part of his indictment of the mind; and in Scogan, whose Victorian positivistic ideas destroy all art, feeling, indeed all life, Huxley was already attacking the false belief that makes science an end in itself, not a means. As the grandson of Thomas Henry Huxley, the great Darwinist, Aldous Huxley understandably was upset by the perversion of science, used as a destructive force by men like Scogan who reduce all life to fact; and, as well, he mistrusted the Denis type for its irresponsibility, self-satisfaction, and selfishness. Later, the pilgrimage of several of Huxley's major positive characters would be away from this type of self-indulgence to a realization of a social self, climaxed by Anthony Beavis's commitment, despite possible personal danger, to affirmative action at the end of *Eyeless in Gaza.*

Crome Yellow, however, while directly reflecting a sophisticated intellectual atmosphere in the years after the Great War, also exposes each character as he evades reality; everyone, says Huxley, is really dishonest, emotionally sterile, and unable to come to terms with the world. When a human response is needed, it is voided by vacuous talk or by an evasion, or else by a retreat to the past. Every character is exposed as a fraud; sincerity is an outworn phrase, and vapid sophistication the ideal of the younger generation. Denis's world, as befitting a young *fin de siècle* romantic, concerns only his own states of feeling, where he experiences discontent and frustration; his is a world that remains, to the end, confused and out of control. This is truly a novel without a hero.

Appearing in 1921, shortly before *The Waste Land,* Huxley's novel is cut from the same material as Eliot's poem. In fact, the Huxley of the early 1920's and the Eliot of the same years were, intellectually and emotionally, not far apart, although in time they diverged. Both were appalled by the chaos of the post-war years, and both looked for order and pattern. Eliot by the late twenties was ready to give himself up to outside order in the form of the Anglican Church, while Huxley only a few years later was to find inward order by turning to a kind of transcendental mysticism, the spiritual insight that gives meaning to Anthony Beavis's life in the 1930's when he was approximately the same age as Huxley himself. This dissatisfaction with the inane present takes many forms in *Crome Yellow,* particularly in Scogan's voice from a Victorian past, in the historical researches of Henry Wimbush, and in Denis's outdated romanticism. Scogan's rationality, as noted above, disallows imagination and speculation; having tasted life, nature, and the arts and found them all wanting, he is completely disillusioned and finds solace only in reason. He turns his disdain upon every aspect of the present world and posits a scientifically-controlled future, whose success Huxley was to develop at greater length in *Brave New World.*

In Henry Wimbush's detailed studies of the Lapith family, Huxley touched on several themes, the chief of which is the apparent order of the past when contrasted with the chaos of the present. Wimbush, like Gumbril Senior of *Antic Hay*, finds fulfillment only in the recreation of historical times. His study of Sir Hercules and his gross son, a parable for our times, shows the futility of sensitivity and good feeling in the face of barbaric manners and physical cruelty. The artistic sensibility of the dwarfish Sir Hercules is swept aside by the brute strength of Ferdinando, for sensitivity, Huxley implies here and elsewhere, immediately puts one at a physical disadvantage in a crass world. Wimbush's studies throw every nuance of Crome's past into perspective, even to the plumbing which Sir Ferdinando installed. It is these details that enable the historian to escape a present world which defies categorization and ordering. Present day Crome, with Denis as its sensitive spirit, Barbecue-Smith as its religious prophet, and Scogan as its jaded intellectual, is clearly insufficient as a basis for life; yet, Huxley suggests ironically, so is the past.

The material on the Lapith family reveals several of Huxley's preoccupations: among them, the emphasis upon and disgust with the natural functions—thus Sir Ferdinando places privies near the top of the house for spiritual reasons; similarly, food itself is disdained because it eventually must be eliminated—thus the secret orgies of eating by the three Lapith sisters; further, the recurring juxtaposition of the grotesque with the sensitive—thus the bloody death of Sir Hercules. The repetition of these attitudes in *Crome Yellow* and later, particularly in *Eyeless in Gaza* when a dog falling from a passing airplane splashes two nude lovers on a roof with blood and pieces of flesh, shows Huxley's closeness to Jonathan Swift, both of whom see innocence as something to be sullied and reality as the direct opposite of the ideal. An English critic, David Daiches, has, in fact, drawn a close parallel between the two writers, remarking that both have a sentimental picture of the world that could not be justified by what sharp observation revealed in reality. With the predisposition of a romantic, Huxley, like Swift, could only be repelled by the real. This marked distinction between what he expects to exist and what actually does exist becomes the basis of his early satires and later the reason for his advocacy of personal salvation through identification with one's Atman, a point out of time and thus not subject to the laws of the world.

This distinction between the ideal and the real in *Crome Yellow* is perhaps best seen in the exchange between the idealistic Denis and the realistic Scogan (in Chapter 20): " 'One suffers so much,' " says Denis, " 'from the fact that beautiful words don't always mean what they ought to mean.' " He then mentions the word *carminative*, which he had, since childhood, associated with physical self-satisfaction, with a nobler, more spiritual glow than wine evokes. He had imagined the word to have affinities with song (*carmen*), with carnival and carnation, with the idea of flesh, "rose-coloured and warm," with interior ripeness. Denis suggests that the poetic connotations of the word were endless; so that he wrote a line that went: "And passion carminative as wine," in which he compared the effects of love with those of wine, Eros with Bacchus; but then he realized that he had never looked up the word in a dictionary, that he had always taken it for granted as one of the world's verbal marvels, evocative and suggestive. Checking the word, which he had come to love, in an English-German dictionary, he finds: carminative—*windtreibend*. The word he had associated with the passions of love itself means "expelling wind from the alimentary canal, relieving colic, griping." After Denis's discourse, Scogan, unperturbed as ever by the young poet's sophisticated disillusionment, remarks, " 'A mental carminative . . . that's what you need.' "

ANTIC HAY

When we come to *Antic Hay*, all the previous attitudes are expanded and given further life. Here, each belief is satirized and the only positive character, Gumbril Senior, is devoted to the past, to recreating London along the design of Sir Christopher Wren after the great fire of 1666. Except for Gumbril, and he lives more in the seventeenth than twentieth century, the novel parades characters each of whom stands for a value no longer viable, whether it be love, art, social reform, religious belief, or tradition. Myra Viveash makes a mockery of the feelings between Gumbril Junior and Emily; Lypiatt is a bad artist with the pretentious vision of a Messiah; Gumbril Junior, a former schoolteacher, "creates" pneumatic trousers for sedentary people; Shearwater is a scientist whose senseless laboratory work closes his mind to all but his experiments; Mercaptan is a parasitical dilettante who retreats from all contact with real life; Rosie Shearwater is out for fun and lives vicariously by having casual affairs; and so on. Each side is played off against the other, each person against the other; the result is a wasteland of spirit in which even the temporary relief to be obtained from physical sensations is vitiated by boredom and despair. Typical of the entire cast, Mrs. Viveash, that modern love goddess, looks out upon a world that has only one meaning: ". . . time kills everything, kills desire, kills sorrow, kills in the end the mind that feels them; wrinkles and softens the body while it still lives, rots it like a medlar, kills it too at last."

Antic Hay, published in 1923, along with Joyce's *Ulysses* (1922) and the novels of Lawrence, drew the final curtain on Victorian morality. Huxley's aim clearly was both to shock and to satirize. With everyone and everything going wrong, Huxley catalogued mercilessly futility in its several aspects. In this world, he assumes, only the false survive for another round of absurdity; the sincere are either crushed or reduced to clowns.

The play within the novel (Chapter 16), a mock reproduction of the *Hamlet* interior play, creates in small the attitudes that the novel represents in large—the play, in fact, becomes an evident symbol of Huxley's attitude in this and all his early novels. Mrs. Viveash's complete boredom at the scene is significant, for the play of course mirrors her own existence, which she recognizes as intolerable. In the play, the chief character, called the Monster, although sensitive, is frail and impotent; despite bandy legs and shredded lungs, he harbors thoughts of virility, of Spartan youths wrestling naked, of hard breasts and flat bellies. The girl he admires is wholesome and desirable, though crass and mindless; she and her boy friend, "a snub-nosed lubber with curly hair and a face like a groom's," mock the Monster, who then turns to a whore for comfort. But she humiliates him by demanding cash on the line in exchange for love. He pays. In the final scene, the Monster has deteriorated even further, now syphilitic as well as consumptive; caged in an asylum, he has visions of the infinite. He defies the world, and while trying to get beyond humanity through a manhole placed on the entrance to society, he topples, head foremost, to the floor and dies. His body is removed to the dissecting floor as the curtain falls.

Huxley's intention is apparent. The Monster, like the characters in the novel, is only half alive, and by denying the human part of him, he must, as Lawrence also claimed, destroy himself. Intellect, Huxley suggests, cannot be enough, just as sensation in itself must fail. This point Huxley makes apparent in Philip Quarles's remarks in *Point Counter Point,* in the savage satire on science in *Brave New World,* in Anthony Beavis's quest in *Eyeless in Gaza,* in Propter's naturalism in *After Many a Summer Dies the Swan*. Man, like the Monster, is weak and diseased, is, really, a Monster. In the background, the constant refrain in the jazz bar is "What's he to Hecuba?"; Hamlet's line, in its modern setting, is answered, "Nothing"—these people have no responsibility either to others or to themselves. Unlike Hamlet, who examined his conscience, they search for further sensations. Unlike Hamlet who plotted revenge in his father's name, they plan further diversion. Unlike Hamlet, who was tortured by his realization of human sordidness, they revel in their despair.

Trapped in his own hell, while partaking of black masses in the jazz bar and following the anti-Virgin, Myra Viveash, Gumbril Junior, a modern jaded Hamlet, asks, " 'Am I the physiologue's keeper? . . . He's with his glands and his hormones, I suppose. Not to mention his wife.' " And Coleman, the diabolist who is high priest at the black mass, answers, " 'Where the hormones, there moan I.' " After the Monster crashes to his death, the party retires to Gumbril's room to pass the rest of the evening where the new Hamlet relates, in mocking style, his innocent affair with Ophelia-Emily, the only person in the book to have shown love and warmth.

The novel, like the play within it, proceeds through a series of contrasts, involving a conflict of both situations and characters. The above scene, for example, in Gumbril's room ironically contrasts with an earlier scene there in which Gumbril and Emily come together in a moment of unsullied affection and feeling. Similarly, an earlier scene (Chapter 5) involving an ironic contrast occurs outside a coffee stall when Mrs. Viveash's party becomes involved with a carter, whose life-and-death struggle to retain his horse is played off against a discussion between Shearwater and Mercaptan about kidneys and their functions. Nevertheless, despite these carefully placed ironies, the novel proceeds more through the interactions of diverse characters than diverse scenes. In the contrast of ideas, attitudes, and desires, Huxley was able to demonstrate his wit and comment paradoxically on a world that fell short, both morally and actually, of what he expected. In this sense, *Antic Hay*, like all of Huxley's novels, is a dialectic of ideas.

Perhaps the central contrast of the novel occurs between Gumbril Junior as an ordinary man and as a complete man, once outfitted with a beard. In Gumbril's beaver, Huxley is using a mock-heroic device to create a contemporary hero. The beaver gives Gumbril courage, virility, completion—without it he is like everyone else; with it he can, like the heroes of old, seduce and conquer. From a mild and melancholy ex-school teacher, he is transformed into a jovial Henry the Eighth, "into a massive Rabelaisian man, broad and powerful and exuberant with vitality and hair." With a padded-out American coat covered by his broad toga, a massive Malacca cane, and of course the beard, he is confident that his appearance as complete man will belie the average person underneath. Appearance, Gumbril recognizes, is more important than substance, and the novel derives from there.

Mercaptan (whose name pointedly signifies a chemical compound containing sulfur) proceeds entirely on appearance—from his white satin couch to his effeminate tastes and witty epigrams based on esoteric allusions to decadent literature. He feels, he says, no shame in being civilized, though civilization in his terms destroys life and feeling. His culture denies the natural and apotheosizes the artificial, the seeming rather than the being. Accordingly, the soul of Crébillon Fils, signifying the artificial, is his ideal. He glorifies the middle way "between stink and asepsis," although his ideals lean more to the latter. His desire for small comforts is so great that Gumbril thinks him a prospective customer for pneumatic trousers, but Mercaptan disdainfully rejects them as too Wellsian, too Utopian.

With Mercaptan as a typical purveyor of contemporary taste, Lypiatt, the pseudo-artist, becomes rough grist for his refined mill. Lypiatt bursts with life, sincerity, industry, but his paintings are vapid pastiches and his prose works unbroken platitudes. Beneath this human volcano lurks a humdrum mind and a trite talent; and this, Mercaptan recognizes. Lypiatt's art, despite its fierceness and integrity, is closer to vermouth posters than to real art. Neither Lypiatt nor Mercaptan has any sense of reality; the latter offers carefully phrased artificialities while the former can only bare his soul. Huxley reminds us that brilliant articulation is not quite art and sincerity no index to genius, or even talent.

If, says Huxley, industry and application are all that are needed for great achievement, then Shearwater would be a first rate scientist rather than a laboratory statistician. If beauty really existed, then Rosie would find satisfaction in more than the sensual and the artificial. If God really existed, then Coleman's diabolism and sensuality could be countered by tenderness and understanding. If education were effective, then Gumbril Junior would not have turned from teaching to designing pneumatic trousers. If there were justice in the world, then Porteous Senior's lot would not be the burden of a wastrel son. If there were love in the world, then Emily would not have to go through life convinced that all men are potential rapists.

By contrasting Gumbril's feelings toward Emily with his lingering passion for Mrs. Viveash, Huxley makes his most mordant (although obvious) comment on modern love. Myra Viveash stands for the traditional seductress, the beautiful lady who, since Venus, has tempted serious men into her bower and then unmanned them. Mrs. Viveash's demands are relatively simple—her infinite boredom requires infinite entertainment. Once in love and her lover having been destroyed by the war, she makes her mission to neutralize all men. Fascinating, irresistibly charming, her eyes and voice hold death for all she seduces. Like Hemingway's Lady Brett, a symbol of modern lost woman, she contrasts with Emily, whose chastity and fear of sexual contact mark her as a pitiful remnant of the Victorian maiden. Having had an unfortunate sexual experience when young, she turns to Gumbril as someone apparently different and idealizes their relationship. She is all feeling, all sensitivity, all fond hope, the innocent alternative to Mrs. Viveash. In rejecting Emily, Gumbril realizes that he has forsaken his only possible salvation; the way to Mrs. Viveash is the way toward death.

In the differences between Emily and Mrs. Viveash, the values of the nineteenth and twentieth centuries distinctly clash; and as part of this contrast is the everpresent clash between the older people in the novel and the younger: betwen Gumbril Senior, full of integrity and good deeds, and his son, anxious to capitalize on bourgeois desires for comfort; between Porteous Senior, an impecunious and upright scholar, and his decadent son, throwing away the family funds in senseless debauchery. In these conflicts, Huxley's satire dissects a world whose false values preclude every form of decency, and he submits this condition as man's fate. Not for more than a decade was he to offer an alternative.

In a statement of despair that parallels Hemingway's "Our nada who art in nada. . . ." in "A Clean Well-Lighted Place," Huxley, the better classicist, offers his version of "Nil" as the Negro chorus chants, " 'What's he to Hecuba?,' " the recurring chant that mocks man's irresponsibility. Huxley writes:

> Nil, omnipresent nil, world-soul, spiritual informer of all matter. Nil in the shape of a black-breeched moon-basined Toreador. Nil, the man with the greyhound's nose. Nil, as four blackamoors. Nil in the form of

a divine tune. Nil, the faces, the faces one ought to know by sight, reflected in the mirrors of the hall. Nil this Gumbril whose arm is round
one's waist, whose feet step in and out among one's own. Nothing at all.

In the end, there is truly nothing. For Shearwater pedaling fiercely
while enclosed in a· coffin-like box is a real symbol for our times.
Manufacturing quarts of perspiration from his own body and yet
going nowhere, Shearwater undertakes his meaningless journey to
escape from Mrs. Viveash and from all life, a journey of complete
futility. When he leaves the box, he will be just where he started, a
mock-scientist too childish to control himself. And this, Huxley suggests, is the problem the twentieth century must face.

POINT COUNTER POINT

In *Those Barren Leaves*, published two years later, one of the characters, Calamy, a disillusioned hedonist, tries to meet the problem of
futility. Recognizing that his daily round of pleasure-seeking is a life
without meaning, he seeks "spirit" somewhere beyond the pale of
ordinary human experience, and departs at the end of the novel to
try renunciation in a mountain retreat. Calamy's motivation, however, is only murkily suggested, and his quest seems more spiritually
expedient than dramatically cogent. As if acknowledging the insufficiency of Calamy's search in the form it takes, for his next novel,
Point Counter Point (1928), Huxley returned to the world of *Antic
Hay*. In this, his first mature novel, Huxley broadened his range and
increased his depth while still retaining his early theme: the inability
of an age without values to come to terms with the forces that will
eventually destroy it.

Point Counter Point is Huxley's first attempt to write a "modern
novel": that is, one in which form approximates idea, and technique
and content would exist only in each other's terms. In this novel, unlike the others, the modernity is not obtained solely through the
interplay of "modern ideas" but also through several devices which
theoretically would enable the author to attain what he called the
"musicalization of fiction."

By this musical development (elaborated in Chapter 22, in Philip
Quarles's notebook), Huxley rejected Mallarmé's ideas on literature as
music, having in mind more the application of a musical development to the structure of the novel than the use of musical prose. As

the composer in the classical sonata form alternates from one mood to another, while stating his theme, developing it, and then re-stating it when it seems to have disappeared, so the novelist, Huxley says, can work with abrupt transitions, rapid shifts, contrapuntal characters and plots. This musical effect can be gained through the alternation of themes, through the repetition of motifs, through dissimilar people involved in the same problem, or, contrariwise, similar people confronted with dissimilar problems. Here, the variations are inexhaustible, and the thematic development complex: thus, the title, *Point Counter Point*, with its reference to a fugue-like structure of polyphonic themes developed contrapuntally.

Undoubtedly, Huxley was aware of Joyce's experiment with similar techniques in *Ulysses*, which appeared episodically for several years before its publication in 1922. Huxley also knew Gide's *The Counterfeiters*, which was probably the strongest single influence upon the form of *Point Counter Point*. Both Huxley and Gide were concerned with creating a pure novel; that is, one stripped of inessentials, in which the reader's imagination is relied upon to do the work that the traditional novelist had always done. "The novelist," says Gide, "does not as a rule rely sufficiently on the reader's imagination." "The character of each personage," Huxley writes, "must be implied, as far as possible, in the ideas of which he is the mouthpiece." To try to attain a type of reality which interpenetrates every layer of the novel, Gide and Huxley introduced a novelist into the novel, who is himself writing a novel that is related in theory to the larger one. Huxley, following Gide, realized that a synthesis suitable for long fiction could be achieved only through form, and that in writing a novel he wanted the form that would best show how to write a novel. Philip Quarles's notebook, although much less successful than Edouard's intermittent comment in Gide's novel, creates a sense of continuity that is essential to the theme of *Point Counter Point*. Like Gide, Huxley did not allow his central narrator the omniscience of the novelist, but chose instead, through omnipresent manipulation of Quarles and the other characters, to destroy the realism of the fictional events. Thus, the point of view is always continuous, even though the characters seem to have superficial freedom of movement.

Quarles, in planning his novel, speculates on putting a second novelist inside the novel of the first, and a third inside the novel of the second, and so on to infinity, like Chinese boxes. "At about the tenth remove you might have a novelist telling your story in algebraic symbols or in terms of variations in blood pressure, pulse, secretion of ductless glands, and reaction times." This method would lead to an endless number of possible variations, like Beethoven's Diabelli variations, whose several inter-relationships would allow comment on the whole range of thought and feeling beyond the particular moment. Similarly, Gide's Edouard tried to extend the limits of the novel by removing it as far as possible from everyday reality. The problem, he realized, is between the general and the particular—to be general, yet particular, is the ideal. The general, in art as in life, is more important, but it can exist, paradoxically, only because of particulars. Commenting on this in another context, Huxley attacked the assumption that a man's particular function in society gives him his place, whereby, he claims, only the whole man (general man) should prevail. Through generalization, the novel, like man himself, will be removed from the hindering explicitness of reality.

Put another way, the novelist's struggle is between what reality offers him and what he desires to make of it, between the facts presented by reality and the ideal reality. One starts, both Quarles and Edouard realize, with an idea and not with a fact. The subject of their inner novelists' books will be concerned with the rivalry between the real world and the representation of it which they make to themselves, between the world of appearances and the ideas the novelist tries to impose upon it. This novel of great diversity will accommodate all currents of thought, all traces of sensibility, every suggestion and intimation of human feeling. It will contain every possible variation and modulation, every inter-relationship. It will be Joyce's *Finnegans Wake*!

Despite their seeming agreement, however, Huxley and Gide do diverge in practice. *The Counterfeiters* does approximate the latter's doctrine by which the novel is to run free without contours, and the novelist is to let it flow where it will. Gide's relationship to reality in the novel permitted each point to be a starting as well as a termination. The novel has no ending, as theoretically it should not, for the idea continues to generate itself. This form is evidently what Huxley desired, but *Point Counter Point* falls considerably short. Philip Quarles's notebook, unlike Edouard's, is, in fact, almost irrelevant to the novel as Huxley develops it. The form of Huxley's novel, with all its fierce insistence on modernity, is not particularly enhanced by his techniques—it still remains "real" in the pejorative sense.

As illustration, a novel supposedly based on musical counterpoint, would, *prima facie*, need a type of character development that would be, if not musical, at least capable of variation and flexible in movement. Yet none of Huxley's characters, including Quarles himself, *moves*; none modulates, varies, develops, or changes in any way. The character as we meet him is the character as we leave him; unfailingly, the situations are simply grafted onto the characters, whose reactions are then tabulated and noted before new situations are set up for the still *unchanged* character. Consequently, the novel breaks down into separate episodes. Even if we grant that Huxley is working more with ideas than characters and situations, we must admit that not even the situations effect any basic changes in his people. The counterpointing of characters on one hand and of ideas on the other is a static affair —they counterpoint, as it were, without any sense of inner growth.

Huxley's so-called musical theme as indicated in the title is misleading, then, for the music is merely imposed upon the novel and talked about, but not integrated with it. With ideas that rarely develop and characters who rarely vary, the counterpointing becomes the traditional contrast of scenes and characters in which irony is evoked because of pointed juxtapositions. Thus, Chapter 11 is full of scenic shifts—from Lucy Tantamount and some friends who are talking about Beatrice in ludicrous terms to Beatrice herself as the virgin of purity about to be seduced by Burlap, back to Lucy, the anti-virgin, then to Lord Edward and his pseudo-scientific speculations with Illidge, then back and forth to Lucy and the Rampions, with interstices of passages on Lord Edward, Bidlake, Polly Logan, and so on. The result is not musical, but, rather, a narrative that proceeds with complete literary logic, causing in the reader none of the sense of inner discovery that ordinarily occurs when two genres are made to overlap.

Nevertheless, if *Point Counter Point* is not the technical achievement that Huxley intended, it still remains an engaging document in which characters, each standing for certain ideas, are witty and even, on occasion, brilliant. Huxley is a master of polemical dialogue—the forte of the essayist—which examines a wide range of contemporary and historical attitudes. Further, he intensified the polemical nature of the novel by presenting, only thinly masked, characters based on prominent figures within the English literary world. Mark Rampion, for example, is obviously a sympathetic portrait of D. H. Lawrence, and his courtship of Mary Rampion parallels Lawrence's of Frieda von Richthofen. Burlap is a vitriolic recreation of Middleton Murry, the well-known critic, essayist, and editor, of whose intellectual clashes with Lawrence Huxley was well aware, intimate as he was with the latter. Beatrice in her relationship with Burlap is a slightly disguised Katherine Mansfield, the short story writer, whose connection with Murry seemed to many outsiders to partake of the contemptible qualities Huxley suggests. Quarles himself is evidently a spokesman for Huxley; for the ideas the former expresses here reappear under Huxley's name in later essays and novels. Spandrell, the diabolist, is perhaps modeled on a Baudelaire-like figure, a type of composite character whose mother fixation makes him debase himself in abnormal behavior. Like Baudelaire in his attitude toward his mother's second marriage, Spandrell explains his revenge on all women as the result of his mother's attachment to a military man, a well-meaning but limited general (Baudelaire's mother had married General Aupick). In addition to these literary figures, Everard Webley, the little dictator, was becoming a familiar type in the twenties, an Oswald Mosley character, who with his green-shirted legions was trying to indoctrinate an indifferent England with Mussolini's ideas. Illidge, the Communist, is the only one really excited by Webley, and this conflict between Communists and Fascists is also Huxley's attempt at direct historical veracity. On the other side of the spectrum, the old painter, John Bidlake, is probably a composite picture of people Huxley had met in English country houses or London town houses, the successful artist of notorious reputation now at the end of a life full of triumphs. Lord Edward Tantamount seems to be Huxley's personal creation, an extension of Shearwater in *Antic Hay*, the scientist who fumbles through life. Lucy Tantamount is also a Huxley original, first encountered in Mrs. Viveash and then repeated in Mary Amberley of *Eyeless in Gaza*, and later to become a healthier Lenina in *Brave New World*. She, as a female diabolist, parallels Spandrell, although her perversities are more venial than mortal.

The chief motif of the novel—how the individual should live in a world that presents a multiplicity of not so superficial temptations— is worked out in the interchanges between Philip Quarles and Mark Rampion. The latter is a type who will recur frequently in Huxley's later fiction, transformed into the noble Savage of *Brave New World*, into Miller of *Eyeless in Gaza* (a combination of the Savage and Jesus Christ), into Propter of *After Many a Summer*, and so on. To counter Quarles's intellectualization and studied dissections, Rampion offers what Lawrence had himself called "blood consciousness." In both Christianity and science, the two main forces of our time, Rampion, like Lawrence before him, finds barbarism, in the former a barbarism of the soul, in the latter of the intellect. He, instead, identifies with the poet and painter William Blake, whose harmonization of reason, feeling, and instinct is congenial to his own desire for balance. Blake, who could reconcile all forces and attain uniqueness, was, he says, "the last civilized man."

When Burlap agrees that man must have a heart, Rampion neutralizes the former's sickly sentimentality by adding, "Not to mention bowels and skin and bones and flesh." He then proceeds to attack nearly every vested interest in society—the scientists, spiritualists, moralists, technicians, the literary and political uplifters, all of whom do not have the sense to see that man must live as a man, "not as a monster of conscious braininess and soulfulness." Rampion's paintings, again like Lawrence's, embody in conception and content his belief in a maleness and femaleness whose spirit will eventually prevail over society's artificial barriers. One painting in particular shows how man himself must create the light that illuminates nature: that man, not God, gives meaning to nature. The scene contains the naked bodies of a man and woman embracing against a background of rocks and tree trunks. The area with the bodies contains a recess of light that extends up the precipice of crags and onto the foliage, the light seeming to create an entire world of flora and fauna built into plane after plane of green landscape, all framed by a background of the sea and a sky full of huge clouds. The painting is an obvious symbol of Rampion's deification of man's sensations and feelings. To deny these qualities, he claims, is self-destructive, whether in the interest of being less than man or more than man. The scientist and moralist he condemns for reducing man's spirit, while St. Francis he ridicules for trying to be a god, "for trying to blow himself up into a Jesus and only succeeding in turning himself into the nasty smelly fragments of a real human being." Then, with fierce rancor, he turns on Quarles and claims that his intellectuality has " 'killed just as much of yourselves as the Christian maniacs.' "

Quarles's answer can be only equivocal, for he realizes that he lacks the very qualities that give force to Rampion, and this lack prevents his writing the type of novel he wants to create. Earlier in *Point Counter Point*, his wife had remarked, " 'Ah, if you were a little less of an overman, Phil . . . what good novels you'd write.' " He had to agree with her, for Huxley claims he was intelligent enough to know his own defects. Nevertheless, his intelligence continued to probe all reality through a microscope and left nothing to spirit. Every thought and feeling had to be analyzed into its parts and categorized before being filed away. Every detail had to be related, generalized, thrown into a vast pit of knowledge in which each item has some connection with the other. Nothing could be left to exist for itself, with a life of its own, casting its own light over the landscape. Had Quarles conceived Rampion's painting, the light would have come from the landscape and been thrown over the couple, searching out details of their form so as to interpret their behavior intellectually.

This inability to accept the particular, this obsession with relations and connections, is the inability of the intellectual, Rampion claims, to accept life, a failure to honor flesh and blood for themselves. As an overman, Quarles cannot come to terms with simplicities: "In art," Huxley writes, "there are simplicities more difficult than the most serried complications. He could manage the complications as well as anyone. But when it came to the simplicities, he lacked the talent—that talent which is of the heart, no less than the head, of the feelings, the sympathies, the intuitions, no less than of the analytical understanding. The heart, the heart, he said to himself." Quarles-Huxley, recognizing the deficiency, decides that "The Search for Truth" may perhaps be just an amusement rather than the highest of human tasks, more a substitute for genuine living than a noble pursuit. Quarles-Huxley perceives that the art of integral living is much more difficult than Truth-searching, that it requires a mind of strength and a will of heroic proportions. With this hard-won realization, Huxley was foreshadowing his own conversion to Eastern mysticism with its emphasis on the self-knowledge necessary to integrated living, and as well suggesting the tensions that would reappear regularly in his later novels.

The path which Quarles will follow is a type of quest that will remove him from his purgatory of doubt. However, if Quarles is in purgatory, most of the other characters are living in a kind of hell. From Antic Hay through Eyeless in Gaza and much of his later fiction, Huxley followed an inferno-purgatorio-paradiso motif, climaxed by the final scene in Eyeless in Gaza; there, after his conversion to human responsibility, Anthony Beavis, in a burst of light somewhat comparable to the blinding illumination in the Paradiso where Dante has a glimpse of the Virgin, sees truth and finds unity and peace. But this passage from inferno to paradise was a long one for Huxley both in life and art. In *Antic Hay*, there are no intimations of an immortal heaven, only a melancholic existence in a mortal hell. The jazz bar, with its " 'What's he to Hecuba?,' " is Dante's Inferno, Eliot's sterile waste land, and Conrad's darkest Congo. In *Point Counter Point*, the diabolist Spandrell oversees a black mass in which his devilish intonations are realized in the practice of nearly every character. Lucy, Walter, Illidge, the Tantamounts, old Bidlake, Webley, Quarles Junior and Senior, all except Rampion, follow an existence which has no meaning or direction. Placed in various circles of hell according to their sins of pride, gluttony, vanity, jealousy, lying, et al., they live out their days, like J. Alfred Prufrock, with warmed-over memories while fighting the ravages of time and the inroads of dissatisfaction. Each is useless or, having been once useful, is now past his prime. Each activity is an escape, merely an excuse for life, and throws the characters deeper into his personal hell.

Quarles admires Rampion because he knows how to live; yet old Bidlake also knew how to live, but now old and tumorous, he must eat infant's food. This typical irony enters into the creation of each character. The arrogant Webley, for example, on his way to a personal conquest, is killed by Spandrell and Illidge, the latter of whom, Huxley sadly suggests, had turned to Communism as a means of terrorizing the aristocracy which he yearns to enter. Spandrell himself, unable to gain any pleasure from life, neither normal nor abnormal, turns to music and commits suicide literally at his moment of ecstasy. Somewhat like Dostoevsky's Stavrogin, in his insane rejection of a world of pretense and farcical niceties, Spandrell has the soul of a mad poet, but, immobilized by personal conflicts, he can reach heaven only through Beethoven's last quartets. In the celestial melody of the *heilige Dankgesang* (literally, "holy thanks song") of Beethoven's A-Minor Quartet, Spandrell seeks a replacement for the life which never measured up to his ideal. The spiritual profundities of Beethoven's melodies, interwoven with ever-changing harmonies, are, for Spandrell, the only possible manifestation of soul. Characteristically, Rampion, while impressed by the Quartet, can only mock Spandrell for turning to spirit instead of body and for worshiping a eunuch who was ashamed of embodying his ideal. Beautiful, Rampion admits, but not earthy, not warm with life; instead, a spiritual cancer of abstractions. Yet, ironically, Spandrell is impressed precisely because the Quartet takes him away from life, away from a material cancer, and into a temporary heaven which makes ecstasy possible, if only of this limited kind. At this moment, he seeks death.

Among negative characters, Burlap is perhaps the most reprehensible. The others are at least caught by passions they cannot control, but Burlap is conscious of his acts, and, unlike many of the others, he harms society while advancing his own interests. His Christ-like manner belies his rapaciousness; his saintly statements, both public and private, thinly disguise an underlying perversion of life; and his hypocrisy dissembles a mentality that exceeds Spandrell's at its most corrupt. Seducer of the innocent in mind and body, Burlap, Huxley claims, is the modern popularizer who panders to the near-educated and pseudo-sophisticated. He tries to approximate Quarles in mind and Rampion in spirit, but both see through him for the charlatan he is. In Huxley's hell, Burlap is the spiritual medium whose religious advice embodies a Christianity reduced to hypocrisy and cant. His Beatrice—an ironic reference to Dante's virgin—is patiently seduced, and so the irony comes full turn; for in *The Divine Comedy*, Dante is seduced into goodness by his image of Beatrice, while in the modern setting, Beatrice is seduced by false appearances into the bed and bathtub of a sham Messiah. "Of such," Huxley comments, "is the kingdom of Heaven."

Among these characters either bored, hypocritical, jealous, or diminished because of bodily deterioration, only Rampion is positive, and even he sounds the note of a Messiah rather than a man. His voice is that of an idea and not a person. His doctrine, while workable for him, could not, evidently, suffice for all men. And yet Huxley offers his advice as the only hope in a world that has gotten out of hand intellectually and spiritually. Realizing with Rampion that the present world has been exhausted, at least temporarily, Huxley turned to a nightmarish future and projected onto it, in *Brave New World*, his prophecy of another version of hell, this one scientific in nature.

BRAVE NEW WORLD

In an essay published more than a decade after *Brave New World* (1932), "What Can the Scientist Do?," Huxley tried to outline the role of the scientist in the modern world. His definition took the form of a plea for science to work only for peace, and for the scientist to take his own Hippocratic oath in which he would swear to work for the good of mankind against any destructive forces. In a world in which nationalism forces destructive wars, the scientist can no longer follow nationalistic lines, but must respond selflessly to the interests of the world. Since the future, says Huxley, is in the hands of the scientist, he must assume responsibility if the world is to survive.

This essay not only reveals Huxley's concern about the future but also demonstrates his idealism in regard to science. As the grandson of Thomas H. Huxley, the great nineteenth-century scientist, Aldous Huxley naturally had high hopes for science as a liberating force. And as the great-grandson of Dr. Arnold, Matthew Arnold's father and the renowned master of Rugby, Huxley came to the world's problems with the precepts of a stern morality. If one combines the disillusionment of the moralist with the belief in the freeing power of science now frustrated by pettiness and expediency, the result can be either tragic or comic, or, more likely, tragi-comic.

In *Brave New World*, Huxley wrote his most Swiftian of satires, giving the same plausibility to absurdity that Swift conveyed in the demonic logic of *A Modest Proposal*. The logical satire of *Brave New World* derives from Huxley's concern with modern science that, once a means, has now become an end in itself. If this development continues, Huxley assumes, then the perfection of science is equivalent to the perfection of the world, and therefore life in *Brave New World*, controlled scientifically as it is at every point, is life at its highest development. For satiric purposes, Huxley assumes this is so; his society is by and large one that accepts the new world as a perfect one and eliminates or exiles the few rebels from its utopia.

In its frightening use of science to imprison man's spirit, Huxley's novel complements George Orwell's 1984, published some twenty years later. Both novels, of which Huxley's is dramatically the more mordant, are concerned with states of totalitarianism. Both foresee a future in which human rebellion can be scientifically controlled and eliminated, in which spirit is replaced by fact or pseudo-fact, in which all aspects of beauty are made subservient to antisepsis and sensual exhaustion. In Huxley's novel, Miranda's cry from *The Tempest:* " 'O wonder! / How many goodly creatures are there here! / How beauteous mankind is! O brave new world, / That has such people in't!' "—her cry of exaltation becomes, ironically, the Savage's own outcry of wonder at Lenina and her brave new world, a world whose denial of human values will eventually drive him not to happiness but to suicide. Miranda's cry of innocence is transformed, through Huxley's irony, first into one of delight and then into the plaint of a tortured individual.

The centralization of society, Huxley and Orwell assumed, can be effectively brought about only by scientific advances. Science tightens lines of communication and permits control in areas that hitherto the individual had considered inviolate. Thus, in *Brave New World*, babies are created in laboratories, conditioned en masse according to the needs of society, and then rerouted to different occupations without any appeal to individual will or desire. The control begins in the laboratory, and the individual follows a pre-determined course of behavior in which regular checks preclude rebellion. Under the circumstances, the individual will not even think of defiance; he accepts the given order and considers anyone who differs to be abnormal or deficient. The indoctrination and conditioning are complete. Science has perfected a world which cannot be upset, for it is self-perpetuating —people live only because of science, and for them to deny their maker is tantamount to denying their own existence. Henry Ford has replaced God; free love, marriage; test tubes, pregnancy. Literature has been abolished, history rewritten or forbidden to be discussed; *soma* pills are swallowed to prevent even temporary depression, *feelies* enjoyed to maintain excitement. In every instance, natural impulses have been discouraged, until they atrophy and become extinct. As science takes over, man becomes obsolete.

The only way Huxley could give both absolute and relative meaning to his new world was through the introduction of a non-conformist—specifically, an outsider from the world of the twentieth century. In the Savage, he uses for ironic purposes a type of traditional device—the introduction of a person into a completely foreign environment, an Eskimo into London, an ape-boy into civilization, a savage into high society. Consequently, there is the immediate conflict between what the Savage expects and what he finds, between *his* assumptions and those of the society in which he finds himself. Huxley's Savage, however—and here he differs from those other intruders —can make a choice; he can accept God, poetry, real danger, freedom, goodness, and sin, accept, in short, "the right to be unhappy," as Mustapha Mond remarks; or he can relieve all anxieties by approving the new world. If the former, he would then have the "right to grow old and ugly and impotent; the right to have syphilis and cancer; the right to have too little to eat; the right to be lousy; the right to live in constant apprehension of what may happen tomorrow; the right to catch typhoid; the right to be tortured by unspeakable pains of every kind." After a silence, the Savage answers, " 'I claim them all,' " and by choosing life ironically selects the path to self-destruction.

Obviously, the Savage's decision is similar in essentials to Mark Rampion's in *Point Counter Point,* and foreshadows Miller's in *Eyeless in Gaza.* His quest for life, his ideals of purity and integrity, his acceptance of a natural existence—all these were part of Rampion's Blakean doctrine. In his rejection of a mechanistic and consciously determined world, he reacts with disdain, as did Rampion to a London society that was unable to feel or to "connect." His *savageness* is his naturalness, what would *seem* savage to the pseudo-civilized. The life he is asked to accept is a prison in which the flesh can exist only at the expense of the spirit. His bloody self-flagellation is his way of trying to redeem the spirit, to take onto himself the sins of a world that no longer seems brave or goodly or beauteous. His sensual feelings for Lenina—which he believes to be unpure—have to be overcome, and this he does by beatings and hard work. Although at times the Savage's sense of sin seems more Calvinistic than the text requires, and his feelings about hard work closer to the Protestant ethic than to his basic needs, nevertheless he seeks wholeness in a society that enforces group reactions and mocks individual dignity.

In his quest for wholeness, for those qualities missing in any centralized utopia, whether scientific or economic, Huxley, unlike several of his Victorian predecessors who turned to medievalism for comfort, looked to ways of reforming the individual rather than society. Change the individual and you change society, he replied to the Marxist claim of first society and then the individual. In the mid-1930's, Huxley steadily turned from material reform to a type of spiritual revival in which the ideal is the non-attached man. This man, as he developed him in *Ends and Means* (1937), would be uncommitted to fame, love, position, power, even to art and intelligence. Disinterested, although positive, he might be a believer in Hinduism, Buddhism, Stoicism, in the Gospel of Jesus before, Huxley says, Christianity made it into *realpolitik.* The non-attached man puts an end to pain not only in himself but also to such pain as he may inflict on others. He becomes the happy as well as good man. This man, obviously, must be educated in a free society which is cognizant of individual needs as opposed to a totalitarian society which educates the masses to obey. For this reason, it is necessary, Huxley adds, that an academic education prepare one for life and provide a moral and liberal frame of reference for the future integration of self.

EYELESS IN GAZA

These ideas work themselves out fictionally in *Eyeless in Gaza*, published the previous year. The problem that Anthony Beavis faces prior to his conversion is Huxley's main preoccupation: "Query: how to combine belief that the world is to a great extent illusory with belief that it is none the less essential to improve the illusion? How to be simultaneously dispassionate and not indifferent, serene like an old man and active like a young one?" How, in short, is the skeptic to believe in himself? To find an answer is the substance of Beavis's quest. Starting as he does in the inferno-like world of *Antic Hay* and *Point Counter Point*, he finally triumphs, like the blinded Samson in Gaza, by calling on his inner powers; and unlike the tormented Savage, he escapes his temporal prison "in the state of pure, disinterested consciousness."

Eyeless in Gaza is perhaps more interesting as a signpost in Huxley's development of ideas than intrinsically as a literary achievement. Once again, the essayist predominates over the novelist, even though Huxley tried to cast the novel in an oblique form through frequent and abrupt time shifts. Thus, the first chapter begins on August 30, 1933, the second on April 4, 1934, the third on August 30, 1933, the fourth on November 6, 1902, the fifth on December 8, 1926, and so on back and forth. The shifts, however, seem artificial and, being rarely integrated with the content, have little to do with the actual development of the novel. If the crux of *Eyeless in Gaza* is Beavis's realization of a further dimension of meaning in the world, then the involved narrative seems an affectation. Huxley probably intended irony through the temporal juxtaposition of Anthony Beavis at the present with Beavis in the past: the "world-weary Beavis" with "troubled Beavis," the "doubter Beavis" with "penance-seeking Beavis" or "converted Beavis"; but a direct narrative might have been less misleading and more dramatically effective. Since the shifts throw the novel off its pace without compensating by providing new meanings through arrangement, one sees little justification for Huxley's roundabout method.

The skeptic Beavis, who accepts a sordid world without ever thinking to reform it or himself, is a hedonist whose values, Huxley claims, are typical of a scientific age: no central core of belief and no real sense of love—he confuses lust with love. He is, in addition, self-centered and cruel. Finding release in sadism and having no regard for others, Beavis can love Helen, whom he had hitherto toyed with, only at the moment she crouches helplessly, semi-hysterical and covered with blood from a shattered dog carcass. Only then can he give of himself: "Pity stirred within him and then an almost violent movement of love for this hurt and suffering woman, this *person*, yes, this person whom he had ignored, deliberately, as though she had no existence in the context of pleasure." Rebuffed by Helen, who leaves him, Beavis reviews the past—old family snapshots, his mother, Mary Amberley, Brian in the chalk-pit, and, cast over all, the dog, whose ludicrous fall has become a personal symbol to him and whose blood has bathed him in doubts and fears. Beavis begins to inquire into the bases of his life.

Huxley, by 1936, had come to question the wisdom of Lawrence's pronouncements. The latter, he felt, had been too satisfied with the animal purpose—the "cock, crowing, fighting, mating—anonymously; and man anonymous like the cock. Better such mindless anonymity, he had insisted, than the squalid relationships of human beings advanced halfway to consciousness, still only partially civilized." Lawrence, however, Huxley insisted, had never looked through a microscope, had never analyzed the crawling things under the lens. He was therefore willing to accept the raw material at its base value and had argued against working it up beyond a certain point. Man himself should operate at this level, and here, Huxley points out, Lawrence failed to see that man *is* different and can have an existence beyond the animal. Man has thought, thought not as an end, only as a means, as life itself is only a means, not an end.

With this realization, Anthony Beavis's perspective begins to change. In a discussion with Mark Staithes, his former schoolboy companion claims that freedom can be enjoyed only if the "you" is there to enjoy it. And the "you" is there only if one overcomes resolutely the obstacles that stand in the way of freedom. Beavis, conversely, foreshadows the direction he will later take by asking how there can be freedom as long as the "you" persists. He claims that the "you" requires responsibility and consistency, that it disallows the real freedom in which the self can attain realization solely by losing itself.

It is, however, through Mark Staithes that Beavis starts on the path to selflessness. Staithes, the leader at school, the admired athlete, the fully accomplished person, turns up as a man with a saintly purpose, a businessman who rejects the world in favor of ideals. The contemplation of an expedient world makes him wear a spiritual hair shirt; in his involvement in a senseless Latin American revolution, he does penance for former arrogance and selfishness. He attempts to conquer through sheer will, to dominate through the application of a persisting self. With Staithes as an example, Beavis also does penance, but his quest is for detachment from man, not involvement. He has looked through the microscope and found that time, in the form of age and death, is treacherous; for it forces selfness, which to Beavis is now equivalent to sin. Therefore, it is obvious that he must withdraw from time through complete detachment from self, from the world, from other people, finally even from God. One must become, as it were, a pure non-attached spirit identified with a world of apparent nothingness.

Huxley, thus, has turned the "Nil-nothingness" of *Antic Hay* into a positive doctrine in which while one still recognizes the void, he does not try to gain anything from it. Although the void continues to surround Beavis, now he can find peace through the imaginary cones of unity which touch and then expand in the heaving darkness and light below and above. The touching of the tips of the cones affords a unity; the hero, hitherto floating aimlessly in the void, looking vainly for something to believe in, now finds identification with the universe in a mystic revelation of selflessness. Like Yeats, Huxley finds unity in cones, the locus of whose circumference is everywhere, bringing light from darkness and peace and calm from frenzy. Then, in an intense burst of light, "the source and substance of all truth," the mystic Beavis sees the unity of subjective truth, as Dante had once seen the unity of God in the *Paradiso*.

If the nothingness of Huxley's previous novels has been rejected and then re-used to positive advantage, also Rampion's doctrines in *Point Counter Point* have been turned inside out to suit a new point of view. Rampion's arguments were at one time an answer to the void; but the dissatisfied Huxley, while accepting tentatively Rampion's depreciation of the intellect, unnatural man, and education in some of its aspects, has turned his argument inward, away from the body where Rampion intended it, into the areas where the "non-self" flows, and uses the argument, now reversed, to justify escape from the world's reality into a far greater one. In brief, he has transformed Rampion's *mystique* of the body into one of the spirit, in which *both* body and intellect are irrelevant. Rampion's concept of the involvement with one's self becomes, in its contrary, one's involvement with his non-self.

Because Huxley is a novelist and not an essayist, the question immediately arises whether Beavis's conversion is dramatically effective, or whether it is motivated solely by doctrinaire convictions without regard for its "rightness" or inevitability within a given structure. To make it convincing, Huxley suggests that the background from which Beavis is attempting to escape is filled with horror. His relationship, for example, with Mary Amberley, tinged by the ravages of time and dissolution, has become a grotesque mockery of a once sincere passion. His further relationship with her daughter, Helen, is likewise unsatisfactory, for here Beavis finds it impossible to give of himself until he suddenly feels something akin to pity and compassion on the blood-splattered roof. His relationship with his father, like the familial relationship in several Huxley novels, borders on the ludicrous. John Beavis, an academic hangover from the nineteenth century and more concerned with the origins of words than with life, lives in a world which rarely overlaps that of his son. With his mother dead, his stepmother a completely foreign spirit, and his father immersed in philological puns, Beavis has only himself to consider.

From his vantage point of hedonism, Beavis, whose ideas of chastity contrast so completely with Brian Foxe's, can mock the seriousness and integrity of his friend's practices. In seducing Joan, Brian's fiancée, Beavis becomes the Iago who, ironically, drives Othello to suicide. In every aspect of his connection with the Foxes, he has been a traitor; yet, he could claim that circumstances made his conquest of Joan possible and led to Brian's suicide. Mrs. Foxe, in her possessiveness, had unmanned her son. Joan herself is normal in her desires, and, once repelled by an unnatural Brian, turns to a not unwilling Beavis. In each case, there was an apparent explanation. Behind it all, however, lies the meaningless bet with Mary Amberley, the bet in which human lives are treated like pawns to be moved at will by a stronger force. At this point, Beavis recognizes the need to control himself, before destruction becomes a habit: "Some way, Anthony was thinking, of getting beyond the books, beyond the perfumed and resilient flesh of women, beyond fear and sloth, beyond the painful but secretly flattering vision of the world as menagerie and asylum."

From here to Dr. Miller is not far. His message, a combination of the noble Savage with Jesus Christ, is particularly appealing to Beavis now at the nadir of his fortunes. Miller, a wandering Scots jungle doctor, diagnoses Beavis's sallow skin as a physical manifestation of chronic intestinal poisoning, which, in turn, is linked to a negative way of thinking. Clean out the system, flush the mind, and health will follow, Miller suggests. He offers to help Beavis to do both. " 'I,' " he says, " 'eat like a Buddhist, because I find it keeps me well and happy; and the result is that I think like a Buddhist—and, thinking like a Buddhist, I'm confirmed in my determination to eat like one.' " In his infinite wisdom, he counsels Beavis to get beyond "this piddling, twopenny-halfpenny personality . . . with all its wretched little virtues and vices, all its silly cravings and silly pretensions." Following Miller's advice, Beavis rejects personal desire and identifies with the cones of unity which bring peace.

The whole of Beavis's conversion would seem, then, to derive from an attempt to eschew sordid reality, an escape, as one critic put it, "from the conditions of human life rather than some way of positively transforming these conditions." Unlike those who have actively sought inner truth, Beavis has, as it were, retreated into it for lack of anywhere else to go. Rejecting reality, he has a go at mysticism. If attachment has brought little satisfaction, perhaps detachment will afford happiness. Attempting to evade his father's burrow-like existence, he communes with large forces that because he can never understand them can never restrict him. Having been limited by society's pleasures, he attempts the metasensory joys of a supra-society. It becomes apparent that none of the conflicts and suffering implicit in a real conversion can be found in Beavis. At best, one could claim shock, but the effectiveness of even shock has not been dramatized in the narrative. Too much of Beavis's conversion is simply intellectualized, not made fictionally true. Huxley's failing here, as Philip Quarles had noted earlier, is an inability to turn doctrine into fiction and to make it *seem* possible. Beavis's newly-found spirituality is catalogued and filed, associated with additional experiences, related to other fragments of information, as if it were an experience like reading a book or hearing a symphony. At one point, Beavis himself comments unknowingly on the shallowness of his new faith:

Reflect that we all have our Poonas [Poona, a city in India]. Bolt-holes from unpleasant reality. The danger, as Miller is always insisting, of meditation becoming such a bolt-hole. Quietism can be mere self-indulgence. Charismata like masturbations. Masturbations, however, that are dignified, by the amateur mystics who practice them, with all the sacred names of religion and philosophy. "The contemplative life." It can be made a kind of high-brow substitute for Marlene Dietrich: a subject for erotic musings in the twilight.

The course of Huxley's work after *Eyeless in Gaza* has not substantially changed. His interests in his early work are those in his work of the 1940's and 1950's. Through several additional novels it has become increasingly clear that Huxley's inability to develop characters and situations and his failure to dramatize his ideas in fictional terms have diminished his stature as a serious novelist, even though his ideas, while not profound or wholly original, are sufficient for work of greater literary quality than he has given us. His importance, perhaps, lies more in his range than his depth; more in his realization of problems than his ability to solve them satisfactorily; more in his insight into man's timeless questions than his competence to supply new answers. What one critic wrote of Huxley's early career as a fiction writer is perhaps true of the whole: "When human life is seen as intrinsically meaningless and evil, then the work of the novelist, whose task is to present a picture of that life in terms of its significance and value, is deprived of all justification. Art and life must be thrown overboard together."

Aldous Huxley : SELECTED BIBLIOGRAPHY

ATKINS, JOHN. *Aldous Huxley: A Literary Study*. London: Calder, 1956.

DAICHES, DAVID. "Aldous Huxley," *The Novel and the Modern World*. Chicago: University of Chicago Press, 1939.

HENDERSON, ALEXANDER. *Aldous Huxley*. London: Chatto & Windus, 1935.

HOFFMAN, FREDERICK J. "Aldous Huxley and the Novel of Ideas," *Forms of Modern Fiction*, ed. William Van O'Connor. Minneapolis: University of Minneapolis Press, 1948.

ROLO, CHARLES, ed. *The World of Aldous Huxley*. New York: Harper & Bros., 1947.

SAVAGE, D. S. "Aldous Huxley and the Dissociation of Personality," *Critiques and Essays on Modern Fiction, 1920–1951*, selected by John D. Aldridge. New York: Ronald Press, 1952.

Index